T0319705

Market Development in China

ADVANCES IN CHINESE ECONOMIC STUDIES

Series Editor: Yanrui Wu, *Associate Professor in Economics, University of Western Australia, Australia*

The Chinese economy has been transformed dramatically in recent years. With its rapid economic growth and accession to the World Trade Organisation, China is emerging as an economic superpower. China's development experience provides valuable lessons to many countries in transition.

Advances in Chinese Economic Studies aims, as a series, to publish the best work on the Chinese economy by economists and other researchers throughout the world. It is intended to serve a wide readership including academics, students, business economists and other practitioners.

Titles in the series include:

Market Development in China

Spillovers, Growth and Inequality

Edited by

Belton M. Fleisher,
The Ohio State University, USA

Haizheng Li
Georgia Institute of Technology, USA and Hunan University, China

Shunfeng Song
University of Nevada, Reno, USA

ADVANCES IN CHINESE ECONOMIC STUDIES

Edward Elgar
Cheltenham, UK • Northampton, MA, USA

Published by
Edward Elgar Publishing Limited
Glensanda House
Montpellier Parade
Cheltenham
Glos GL50 1UA
UK

Edward Elgar Publishing, Inc.
William Pratt House
9 Dewey Court
Northampton
Massachusetts 01060
USA

A catalogue record for this book is available from the British Library

Library of Congress Cataloguing in Publication Data

Market development in China : spillovers, growth, and inequality / edited by Belton M. Fleisher, Haizheng Li, and Shunfeng Song.
    p. cm. – (Advances in Chinese economic studies series)
  Selected papers originally presented at the conference of the Chinese Economists Society, held 31 July to 1 August 2004 at the Georgia Institute of Technology.
  Includes bibliographical references and index.
  1. China–Economic policy. 2. China–Economic conditions. 3. Income distribution–China. I. Fleisher, Belton M. II. Li, Haizheng. III. Song, Shunfeng. IV. Chinese Economists Society. Conference (2004 : Georgia Institute of Technology)
  HC427.95.M374 2007
  330.951–dc22
                                      2006102453
ISBN 978 1 84542 851 8

Printed and bound in Great Britain by MPG Books Ltd, Bodmin, Cornwall

Contents

Contributors

Qun Bao received his Ph.D. degree in Economics from the School of Economics and Trade, Hunan University in 2004. His major research interests include the effects of foreign direct investment on the host country's economy and the relationship between environmental change and economic development. He is currently an Assistant Professor at Nankai University.

Zhihong Chen is currently an Assistant Professor at the University of International Business and Economics in Beijing. She got her Ph.D. degree in economics at Boston College, under the supervision of Arthur Lewbel, Jushan Bai, Peter Ireland and Zhijie Xiao. Her research interests are econometrics, applied economics and the Chinese economy.

Belton M. Fleisher received his Ph.D. degree in economics from Stanford University. He was Assistant Professor at the University of Chicago 1961–65 and joined the Ohio State University economics faculty in 1965, where he is currently professor. In 1989 and 1990 he taught economics at the Renmin (People's) University of China in Beijing. Professor Fleisher has authored and coauthored numerous articles in professional journals including *American Economic Review*, *Journal of Political Economy*, and the *Review of Economics and Statistics*, *Journal of Comparative Economics*, and *China Economic Review*. He has written seven books, including *Labor Economics: Theory and Evidence and Policy*. Since 1990, his research has focused on economic growth, financial markets, labor markets, and productivity in the Chinese economy. He is currently a co-editor of *China Economic Review*.

Emily Hannum is Assistant Professor of Sociology at the University of Pennsylvania, where she is also affiliated with the Population Studies Center. She conducts research on education in China, with a particular interest in socio-economic, gender and ethnic inequalities. Since 1998, she has co-directed a research project in Gansu, funded by the Spencer Foundation, the National Institutes of Health, and the World Bank, that investigates the family, school and community factors that support children's education and healthy development in the context of rural poverty.

Youxin Hu received her bachelor's degree from Nanjing University and an M. Phil. Degree from the University of Hong Kong. She is currently in the fourth year of the Ph.D. program in the Ohio State University economics department, where she is specializing in applied microeconomics.

Yifan Hu received her Ph.D. in economics at Georgetown University. Currently she is a research assistant professor at the Institute of Economics and Business Strategy of University of Hong Kong. She has worked for the World Bank, Institution of International Economics, and KPMG. Her research focuses on international economics, monetary policy and China's economy.

Jikun Huang is the founder and Director of the Center for Chinese Agricultural Policy (CCAP) of the Chinese Academy of Sciences (CAS). His research covers a wide range of issues on China's agricultural and rural development, including work on agricultural R&D policy, water resource economics, price and marketing, food consumption, poverty, and trade liberalization. He has led more than fifty research projects. In the past 15 years he has published approximately 180 journal papers, 66 of them in international refereed journals. He is co-author of ten books. He received the Outstanding Scientific Progress awards from the Ministry of Agriculture four times, the award for China's top ten outstanding youth scientists in 2002, and Outstanding Achievement Award for Overseas Returning Chinese (in 2003). He serves as a policy adviser for the Chinese government.

Ravi Kanbur is T.H. Lee Professor of World Affairs, International Professor of Applied Economics and Management, and Professor of Economics at Cornell University. He has also served on the staff of the World Bank, as Economic Adviser, Senior Economic Adviser, Resident Representative in Ghana, Chief Economist of the African Region of the World Bank, and Principal Adviser to the Chief Economist of the World Bank. Professor Kanbur's main areas of interest are public economics and development economics. His work spans conceptual, empirical, and policy analysis. He is particularly interested in bridging the worlds of rigorous analysis and practical policy making. His vita lists over 100 publications, covering topics such as risk taking, inequality, poverty, structural adjustment, debt, agriculture, and political economy. He has published in the leading economics journals such as *American Economic Review,*

Journal of Political Economy, *Review of Economic Studies*, *Journal of Economic Theory*, and *Economic Journal*.

Mingyong Lai is a professor and Ph.D. tutor in the School of Economics and Trade, Hunan University. His research focuses mainly on international trade and economic growth. He has published over 30 papers and six books in China.

Haizheng Li is Associate Professor of Economics in the School of Economics of the Georgia Institute of Technology and Special Term Professor at Hunan University. He received his Ph.D. in economics from the University of Colorado-Boulder in 1997. His research focuses on applied econometrics, primarily in the areas of labor economics, industry studies, and the Chinese economy. He has received two large research grants from the Sloan Foundation Center for Paper Business and Industry Studies (more than $450 000 including tuition waivers), and a large grant from the 985-Project of the Department of Education of the Chinese government via Hunan University. He has supported a number of graduate students through research grants. He is a member of the Advisory Board of China Economic Review, President of the Chinese Economists Society (2006–07), and has served as a consultant for the World Bank and as a Special Research Fellow of the Shanghai Development & Reform Commission in China. At Georgia Tech, he is currently Co-director of the Georgia Tech-Shanghai Summer Program, and Director of Information Technology in the School of Economics.

Zhigang Lu is an Associate Professor of Information System at the Tianjin University of Finance & Economics, China, and the chief editor of the journals CIO Forum and Digital Space. His areas of interests and economic research are e-commerce economics, information economics, and regional disparity.

Jifeng Luo is a Ph.D. candidate of Information Technology Management, College of Management, at the Georgia Institute of Technology. He received his Master's degree in Economics from the School of Economics, Georgia Institute of Technology, and Bachelor's degree from Renmin University of China. His current research focuses on information economics, pricing in online market and IT outsourcing.

Patrick McCarthy is Professor and Chair of the School of Economics, Ivan Allen College, at the Georgia Institute of Technology. Professor McCarthy is also Director of the Center for Paper Business and Industry

Studies, one of 25 Industry Centers funded by the Sloan Foundation, and is on the Advisory Board of the Sloan Funded Trucking Industry Program at Georgia Tech. He is an Associate Editor of *Transportation Research* and the *Journal of the Transportation Research Forum*. His research areas include transportation economics, regulation, industry studies, and discrete choice econometrics. He is the author of *Transportation Economics Theory and Practice: A Case Study Approach* (Blackwell Publishers 2001) and has published articles in various academic journals, including the *Review of Economics and Statistics, Economics Letters, Journal of Regulatory Economics, Journal of Health Economics, Journal of Infrastructure Systems, Journal of Transport Economics and Policy, Regional Science and Urban Economics, Annals of Regional Science,* and the *Journal of Transportation and Statistics.* He has received research grants from the AAA Foundation for Traffic Safety, the National Science Foundation, the National Institutes of Health, and the Sloan Foundation Industry Centers Program. Professor McCarthy has been a visiting professor at Duisburg-Essen University (Germany), the Athens Laboratory of Business Administration (Greece), Nanyang Technological University (Singapore), and the University of Southern California.

Sonja Opper is Gad Rausing Professor of International Business at Lund University (Sweden). She received a Ph.D. in Economics from Tuebingen University and was Associate Professor at the Department of Economics at Tuebingen University from 2003 to 2005. Her research focuses on the application of New Institutional Economics to transition countries, with an emphasis on China.

Zuohong Pan is a Professor of Economics at Western Connecticut State University. He received his Ph.D. degree from Wayne State University and M.A. and B.A. degrees from Renmin University of China. He is co-author of *Investment Banking in the U.S., The Methodology of Social Sciences,* and co-editor of *Taiwan in the 21st Century, American Studies Series.* He has also authored papers in journals including *Urban Studies, Computational Economics, Journal of Computational Intelligence in Finance, China Economic Review,* and *The International Journal of Public Administration.*

Shuijun Peng is a Ph.D. candidate in the School of Economics and Trade, Hunan University. He received his Master's degree in mathematics at Hunan University. His research focuses on growth, trade, and the environment.

Scott Rozelle is the Helen F. Farnsworth Senior Fellow and Professor, the Freeman Spogli Institute for International Studies, Stanford University. Dr. Rozelle received his B.S. from the University of California, Berkeley; and his M.S. and Ph.D. from Cornell University. Before arriving at Stanford, Rozelle was a professor at the University of California, Davis (1998–2000) and an assistant professor in the Food Research Institute and Department of Economics at Stanford University (1990–98). Currently, he is a member of the American Economics Association, the American Agricultural Economics Association, the International Association for Agricultural Economists, the Asian Studies Association, and the Association of Comparative Economics. He also serves on the editorial board of *Economic Development and Cultural Change*, *Agricultural Economics*, *Contemporary Economic Policy*, *China Journal*, and the *China Economic Review*.

Shunfeng Song received his Ph.D. from the University of California, Irvine. He is currently Professor Economics at the University of Nevada, Reno. He has published in the *Journal of Political Economy*, *Journal of Urban Economics*, *Urban Studies*, *Land Economics*, *Contemporary Economic Policy*, *China Economic Review*, *Current Anthropology*, *Review of Regional Studies*, *Socio-economic Planning Sciences*, and *Journal of Quantitative Anthropology*. He is series co-editor for Ashgate's *China Economy Series*.

Sarah Y. Tong is an assistant professor in the Economics Department and Fellow of the East Asian Institute at the National University of Singapore. She received her Ph.D. degree from the University of California, San Diego. Her main research interests include international economics, development economics, and the Chinese economy.

Meiyan Wang is Associate Professor in the Institute of Population and Labor Economics, Chinese Academy of Social Sciences. Her research interests include gender, human capital, employment, migration and labor markets in China. Her recent work has included studies of gender and education, labor market discrimination, and education and performance in the labor market. She has also conducted analyses of the China 2000 census micro-sample to investigate educational and occupational differences between rural–urban migrants and urban residents.

Sonia M.L. Wong received her Ph.D. in economics from the University of Hong Kong and is now a research assistant professor at the Institute of Economics and Business Strategy of the University of Hong Kong. She has published papers on the country's foreign exchange and banking reforms as well as the corporate governance of listed enterprises.

Helian Xu received his Ph.D. degree in Economics from the School of Economics and Trade, Hunan University in 2003. His current research is devoted to the interrelation between openness and economic growth.

Fan Zhang is an adjunct professor at the China Center for Economic Research (CCER), of which he is one of the founding members. He is a senior economist of the New York City government. He received his B.A. from the People's University of China and his Ph.D. from Wayne State University, Michigan. His main research interests are industrial organization, international trade, and urban economics.

Xiaobo Zhang is a senior research fellow of the International Food Policy Research Institute (IFPRI) and director of IFPRI's China Program. He conducts research on development strategies, governance, and public investment in developing countries. He earned a B.S. in mathematics from Nankai University, China; a M.S. in economics from Tianjin University of Economics and Finance, China; and a M.S. and Ph.D. in applied economics and management from Cornell University. He was the president of Chinese Economists Society (2005-2006).

Gongcheng Zheng is Professor, vice Chairman of the University Council, Vice Dean of the school of Labor and Human Resources and Director of the China Social Security Research Center of Renmin University of China. Professor Zheng's research fields include social security policy, labor employment and related fields. He has many publications in the above fields.

Acknowledgements

We gratefully acknowledge the Georgia Institute of Technology, Huazhong University of Science and Technology, Hunan University, and Tianjin University of Finance and Economics. Without their generous support, neither this book nor the conference from which the papers are taken would have been possible. Gongcheng Zheng wishes to acknowledge the Program for New Century Excellent Talents in University of the Ministry of Education of the People's Republic of China and to thank the Ministry of Education for its generosity in supporting the research for the paper published in this volume.

Mark F. Owens of Middle Tennessee State University provided editorial and formatting expertise for all the papers included here.

The following are reprinted from *China Economic Review*, **17**(3), with permission from Elsevier.

Z. Chen, Measuring the Poverty Lines for Urban Households in China–An Equivalence Scale Method, 239-252.

E. Hannum and M. Wang, Geography and Educational Inequality in China, 253–65.

J. Huang and S. Rozelle, The Emergence of Agricultural Commodity Markets in China, 266–80

Y. Hu, S. Opper and S.M.L. Wong, Political Economy of Labor Retrenchment: Evidence Based on China's State-Owned Enterprises, 281–99.

M. Lai, S. Peng and Q. Bao, Technology Spillovers, Absorptive Capacity and Economic Growth, 300–20.

H. Li, J. Luo and P. McCarthy, Economic Transition and Demand Pattern: Evidence from China's Paper and Paperboard Industry, 321–36.

Z. Lu and S. Song, Rural–Urban Migration and Wage Determination: The Case of Tianjin, China, 337–45.

The following is reprinted from *China Economic Review*, **16**(2), 289–304.

X. Zhang and R. Kanbur, Spatial Inequality in Education and Healthcare in China.

Introduction

It is generally recognized that despite possible upward biases in the data, in the last 25 years China has achieved a rate of economic growth unmatched in any of the world's major countries. However, this growth has been unequally shared, so that by the year 2000 China also exhibited what to many observers was an alarming degree of income inequality at the individual, sectoral, and regional levels (Yang, 2002). The 12 chapters in this book address different facets of the causes and effects of the related issues of China's growth and inequality. Each paper was originally presented at the conference of the Chinese Economists Society, 'Technology, Human Capital, and Economic Development,' held 31 July to 1 August 2004 at the Georgia Institute of Technology. After careful review and with the generous assistance of external referees, the editors selected these papers among 60 papers presented at the conference as significant contributions to the literature on China's economic growth and market development.

The book consists of two parts. Part One, Inequality in China, addresses the critical economic, social, and political issues of rising inequality. The alarming degree of sectoral, regional, and household inequality that now characterizes much of China is due in large part to the wide dispersion of economic growth rates across regions. It is also due to the movement away from a system in which health, schooling, pensions, and other human-capital and safety net programs were guaranteed by the State and state enterprises. Now, enterprises, provinces, municipalities, and government agencies can no longer rely on infusions from the central government to support vital social programs. Part Two, Market Development and Sources of Growth, focuses on several of the factors contributing to China's rapid growth and to its unequal pattern. The chapters address the ways in which specific industries, markets, and their interrelationships have affected the growth and distribution of wages, prices, and incomes in China under reform.

Part One has four chapters. In Chapter 1, Zhihong Chen addresses the question: How should poverty thresholds be calculated for China? Her answer is that equivalence scales are ideally suited for providing answers to this question, because they establish comparable poverty lines for households of different sizes and compositions and in different regions. A foundation for this study, and an important contribution to the literature on consumption behavior in China, is a specification and estimation of a consumption demand system for Chinese households, in which Chen adopts the Almost Ideal Demand System approach. Chen uses the Urban Household Survey data of China to estimate the equivalence scales for Chinese urban households and then anchors them to World Bank poverty line calculations. The methodology and the equivalence scales estimated in this chapter can be used to determine the appropriate subsidy levels for households with different demographic characteristics, given the subsidy standard specified by a poverty-reduction program.

Emily Hannum and Meiyan Wang write in Chapter 2 that two of the byproducts of China's development of a market economy have been decentralization of the administration of education and finance and increased financial burdens on families to pay for the education of their children. The authors argue that geographic origins are a significant element of educational stratification, and find that geographic disparities in education have increased over time and been an important contributor to China's rising regional economic disparities. Using 2000 census data on year and location of birth and educational attainment, they compare the links between birth province and educational outcomes across five-year birth cohorts to illuminate trends in these region-based inequalities.

Hannum and Wang show that the variation in years of schooling explained by birth province declined for cohorts born through the early 1960s, and then increased thereafter. Additional analyses using a dissimilarity index indicate that the link between geography and access to primary school has greatly increased across cohorts, as those people without access to primary school are ever more concentrated in poor areas. The link between birth province and access to subsequent levels of schooling shows mixed trends through cohorts born in the early 1960s. Thereafter, the dissimilarity index increased, substantially for junior high school and slightly for senior high school and college. Their chapter attests to the enduring significance of geography as an educational stratifier in China.

Inequality in support for social services as a source of social inequality is confirmed in Xiaobo Zhang and Ravi Kanbur's chapter. As Zhang and Kanbur emphasize, the stability of China's future economic and political progress depends in large part on a belief that it is better to be part of the economic reform than to revert to a system in which shares in the economic pie were determined more by political status than by economic success. However, in the era of market reforms, the old foundations of education and healthcare provision have eroded, and increasing competition has doomed most traditional SOEs, which formed an important foundation of the social support system under planning. They show that social inequalities in rural, urban, inland and coastal areas all have increased since the economic reforms. In particular, the rural-urban gap in illiteracy and infant mortality and the gender gap in literacy remain large.

In the fourth chapter, Gongcheng Zheng provides a view of the development of China's education system from the perspective of both an academician and policymaker. He argues that equal opportunity to obtain education is a necessary condition for the currently disadvantaged to participate in the rising standard of living available to those who have been able to attend and graduate from high-quality secondary schools and post-secondary educational institutions, which should include not only traditional academically-oriented curricula, but also courses aimed at students who wish to develop expertise in technical occupations and professions. He advocates encouraging individuals and firms to participate in the funding of education so that government funds can be used to foster the reduction of inequality of educational opportunity.

Part Two has eight chapters. In Chapter 5, Yifan Hu, Sonja Opper and Sonia M.L. Wong tackle a negative side of reform – the problem of retrenched workers in China's SOEs. They address these questions: Which SOEs successfully took on the challenge of restructuring? Are SOEs following economic reasoning in their labor decisions? Can we still observe evidence of government control in SOEs' labor decisions? Did corporatization actually tie the government's hands and end political interference in the labor decisions of corporatized SOEs compared to traditional SOEs? The two major results of their study are: (1) The degree of labor retrenchment is negatively related to enterprise performance; (2) decisions about labor retrenchment in traditional SOEs are related to the local government's fiscal position and to local reemployment conditions for laid-off workers, whereas labor decisions in corporatized SOEs are not related to these two variables. In other words, hard budget constraints appear to lead to hard decisions, and there appears to have been significant depoliticization effects for China's partially privatized, listed enterprises.

China's reforms began in agriculture, and in Chapter 6, Jikun Huang and Scott Rozelle discuss the extent to which the spark that began at the level of individual production units has spread to innovation and change in market institutions, which are critical to continued economic development in transition economies. They use several sets of price data to document the marketization of agriculture by exploring spatial patterns of market price contours over time, and they examine the extent to which market prices are integrated among China's regions and linked to world commodity markets. They show that marketization has come both from commercialization of the state sector and the emergence of a private trading sector. Markets have been integrated and transaction costs have fallen. They assert that the number of traders in agricultural markets is now so great that the constraints under which state intervention can operate have been radically altered. Local prices in the basic commodities are now determined much more by aggregate supply and demand than by regional economic conditions.

In Chapter 7, Haizheng Li, Jifeng Luo and Patrick McCarthy investigate demand patterns and structural changes in the paper and paperboard industry in China. They find that in the early stage of industrial reform, prior to 1993, the demand for paper and paperboard did not exhibit a negative price elasticity of demand. This is consistent with production and use of these products being subject to allocation by planning and directive rather than to market signals. After 1993, the markets appear to have emerged, resulting in reasonable, negative demand elasticity with respect to both domestic and international prices. Evidence from paper and paperboard industry indicate that China has become increasingly integrated with world markets.

The eighth chapter, contributed by Helian Xu, Qun Bao and Mingyong Lai, explores how export composition influenced technology spillovers to domestic production, leading to more rapid total factor productivity growth. They find that a shift away from resource- and labor-intensive exports accompanied by foreign direct investment (FDI) and a growing stock of human capital, leads to a shift in comparative advantage toward more skill-intensive manufacturing and increases the speed at which the economy can absorb technology. They conclude that policies favoring human-capital accumulation and FDI will improve efficiency and enhance growth.

In Chapter 9, Mingyong Lai, Shuijun Peng and Qun Bao analyze the connections between international technology spillovers, domestic technology absorptive capacity, endogenous technological change and the steady-state growth rate. They find that technology spillovers depend on the ability to absorb new technology, where absorptive capacity is influenced by human capital investment and degree of openness. They find that FDI is a more significant spillover channel than imports. One of the policy implications, derived from evidence of external effects on the capacity to absorb technology via FDI, is to subsidize individuals' human-capital investment.

Sarah Y. Tong and Youxin Hu provide insight into the channels and effects of technology spillovers from FDI. In Chapter 10, the authors discuss both the beneficial and detrimental effects of FDI on indigenous Chinese firms. Using firm-level data of Chinese manufacturing, they examine FDI spillover effects both within and across industries and identify differences in the impact of FDI from different countries. One of their most interesting empirical results is that FDI from countries outside the Hong

Kong–Macau–Taiwan network has a more favorable impact on productivity growth than does FDI from inside the network. This difference is likely to emanate from the greater technological level of production associated with investment from countries further away from China. They also find that FDI has a more powerful impact on productivity growth in more open segments of the Chinese economy.

In Chapter 11, Zhigang Lu and Shunfeng Song address questions concerning the rural–urban migration that has arisen in response to the immense productivity and income gap between traditional agriculture and the industrial and service sectors of the Chinese economy. Based on data derived from a survey of employees conducted in 2003 in Tianjin, they examine why some farmers migrate to cities and some do not; what are the characteristics of those who do migrate in comparison to those who choose to remain in rural areas; what factors help determine the wages of rural–urban migrants; and what evidence is there of discrimination against rural migrants in China's urban labor markets. Their empirical results indicate that urban workers earn more than migrants with similar characteristics, indicating the possibility of wage discrimination against migrants. They find evidence that the *hukou* system increases the rural–urban wage gap, and after accounting for human-capital characteristics, females earn less than males in urban employment, but not in rural employment.

In the concluding chapter, Fan Zhang and Zuohong Pan investigate the role of increasing returns to scale in explaining the pattern of regional trade in China. They test two contrasting hypotheses concerning the direction of interregional trade: is the direction trade determined primarily by factor endowments, as implied by the Heckscher–Ohlin model, or do factors on the demand side play an important role, as implied in the more recent new economic geography framework? Their results show the existence of significant home-market effects in determining production and trade patterns across regions in China. An important policy implication is that it is likely to be difficult and costly to relocate industry from center (high demand) regions to peripheral (low demand) regions. The location of industries not linked to major resource bases in the major sectors of manufacturing are likely to be spatially concentrated in the areas with higher demand for their products.

REFERENCES

Yang, Dennis Tao (2002), 'What has caused regional inequality in China?', *China Economic Review*, **13**, 331–4.

Young, A. (2000), 'The razor's edge: Distortions and incremental reform in the People's Republic of China', *Quarterly Journal of Economics*, **115**, 1091–135.

PART ONE

Inequality in China

1. Measuring the Poverty Lines for Urban Households in China: An Equivalence Scale Method

Zhihong Chen

1. INTRODUCTION

In the late 1970s, China launched an economic reform and began to transform from a planned to a market economy. One key element of the economic reform is to allow private-, individual-, and foreign-owned enterprises to compete with state-owned enterprises (SOEs). Less efficient SOEs incurred substantial financial losses in the market competition with other types of enterprises. An increasing number of urban workers in the SOEs have been laid off. Urban poverty, previously insignificant according to World Bank's estimate (1992), grew. In 1996, the government carried out an enterprise-restructuring plan. The obligations to provide welfare services such as medical care and housing were transferred from SOEs to social insurance agencies and individuals. This liberalization of the welfare system made financially disadvantaged urban groups more vulnerable. The emergence and growth of urban poverty lent urgency to the task of constructing accurate measures of poverty.

The absolute poverty line has been widely used for developing countries. The World Bank uses $32.74 per month ($1.08 a day) at 1993 international prices as a baseline.[1] But most poverty lines are for individuals only. When we consider the poverty threshold for a household, we cannot ignore the economies of scale present in any household. Family members can benefit from each other's consumption or share public goods within their household at no additional cost. Table 1.1 shows that in Chinese urban households, the average expenditure per person (calculated from the Urban Household Survey data of China) decreases with the increase of household size. That is to say, a person has to spend one dollar to afford the living expense if she lives alone, while she only needs 0.9722 dollar if she lives with another person because of the economies of scale from sharing. A fundamental

3

Table 1.1:   Expenditure Ratio of Different Household Sizes

Number of Household Members	1993	1997
1	1[ab]	1
2	0.9772	0.9667
3	0.7547	0.8330

Notes:
[a]   Expenditure of a single person has been normalized to one.
[b]   The unit of measurement is yuan/person.

question is: Given the poverty threshold for an individual, how does that threshold vary for a household with different demographic characteristics (for example, family size and region)?

Equivalence scales are ideally suited for providing answers to this question. An equivalence scale is the amount by which a household's consumption expenditure would need to be multiplied to make that household as well off as the reference household. It measures the relative cost of demographic variation and can be used to derive comparable poverty lines for households with different demographic characteristics.

This chapter uses the Urban Household Survey (UHS) data of China to estimate the equivalence scales for Chinese urban households and accordingly calculates poverty lines for different households. The more accurate poverty lines can help to better define the targets of the antipoverty program. This chapter also estimates how equivalence scales vary over time. Therefore, the corresponding poverty lines can be adjusted in a timely manner, which is especially important given the rapid changes in the Chinese economy. A useful byproduct of this study is a specification of the demand system for China.

The rest of the chapter is organized as follows. Section 2 reviews some related literature. A theoretical model for equivalence scales is delivered in Section 3. In Section 4, after the description of the data set used in this study, the empirical estimates and analysis are presented. Section 5 offers conclusions and discussion about future work.

2.   LITERATURE REVIEW

Slesnick (1998) summarized empirical approaches to measure welfare. He pointed out that welfare measurement is indelibly linked to empirical demand analysis. A fundamental welfare question is: How much additional income is required for a household with certain demographic characteristics to attain the same welfare as a reference household? The expenditure data can be used to study how demand patterns vary with the demographic composition of the household. The standard approach is to specify a functional form for the demand function and estimate the unknown parameters using regression methods. Deaton (1997) is another reference to discuss the linkage between welfare measurement and demand system analysis.

Lewbel's (1997) survey summarized the specification of demand system and the estimate of household equivalence scales. A consumer demand system is a set of equations that describe how a consumer or household with attributes z and facing prices p allocates its total expenditure x to consumption goods q. Almost Ideal Demand System (AIDS) by Deaton and Muellbauer (1980) and Quadratic AIDS by Banks, Blundell and Lewbel (1996) are two typical specifications. The simplest way to incorporate demographic effects into demand equations is to estimate a separate demand function for each value that z can take on. A more satisfactory approach is to put the demographic attributes z into the expenditure function. An equivalence scale is defined as the ratio of two expenditure functions specified from demand system analysis.

The estimate of equivalence scales is plagued with identification problems. Except for the standard econometric identification issues, the definition of equivalence scale requires the utility functions of two households to be comparable to make them equally well off. Pollak and Wales (1979) argued the equivalence scales that are calculated from demand data could not be used for welfare comparisons. Blundell and Lewbel (1991) proved that their opinion seems to be an overly negative assessment because there are three ways to resolve this fundamental underidentification. One solution is to make plausible identifying assumptions concerning the properties of equivalence scales. Blundell and Lewbel (1991) estimated an AIDS model with independence of base utility (IB) assumption, defined as the situation in which equivalence scales are independent of the base of utility u at which the cost comparison is being made. They statistically rejected IB, but also found that imposing IB restriction has almost no effect on estimated scales. Pendakur (1999) tested the hypothesis of base independence against a fully nonparametric alternative and found the preferences are consistent with the existence of a base-independent equivalence scale for some interhousehold comparisons.

Blackorby and Donaldson (1991a) constructed another adult-equivalent index by setting the utility level u in the equivalence scale $S(u, p, z)$ equal to a particular reference level of utility (such as poverty utility). This means that interhousehold comparisons need only be made for a single level of utility u^r. A method for doing this is to find poverty consumption bundles $X(z)$ for a household with attributes z to make that household have utility level u^r. According to Hussain (2003), cities could set the poverty line (benefit line) by the direct method of costing some goods and services for basic subsistence (the so-called 'basic needs' approach).

There are relatively fewer studies on the demand system of China. To my best knowledge, there is no literature on equivalence scales for urban households in China. The estimate of equivalence scales in this chapter will be a 'non-developed' comparison case in China for the existing literatures on the developed countries.

Next, I will present the theoretic model for demand system specification and equivalence scales estimate.

3.   THEORETIC MODEL

The equivalence scale is defined as the ratio of cost functions between demographically different households:

$$S(u,p,z,z^r) = \frac{C(u,p,z)}{C(u,p,z^r)} \tag{1.1}$$

or

$$\ln S(u,p,z,z^r) = \ln C(u,p,z) - \ln C(u,p,z^r)$$

where $C(.)$ is a classical cost function, u is the utility level at which two households are equally well off, p is the vector of prices, z and z^r are the vectors of demographic characteristics of households. Superscript r denotes reference household. Therefore, the specification of the demand and cost functions is the first task to calculate the equivalence scales.

The starting point is the well-known Almost Ideal Demand System (AIDS) by Deaton and Muellbauer (1980). The specified cost function gives an arbitrary first-order approximation to any cost function; it satisfies the axioms of choices exactly; it aggregates perfectly over consumers and it has a functional form consistent with known household budget data.

The basic behavioral hypothesis of consumer demand is that the consumer chooses an affordable basket of goods that maximizes his utility. Let $u = v(q,p)$ be the household's utility function, q be the quantities of n consumer goods, p be the vector of corresponding prices and the budget constraint be:

$$\sum_{i=1}^{n} q_i p_i = y .$$

The cost (expenditure) function can be written as:

$$y = \sum q_i(y, p) p_i = \sum h_i(u, p) p_i = C(u, p)$$

where $q(y, p)$ is the Marshallian demand function and $h(u, p)$ is the Hicksian demand function.

The preference of AIDS is represented via the cost of expenditure function. We write the indirect utility function as:

$$v(x, p) = \frac{\ln x}{b(p)} \qquad (1.2)$$

Where $x = y/a(p)$ is the expenditure in real terms,

$$\ln a(p) = \alpha_0 + \sum \alpha_k \ln p_k + \frac{1}{2} \sum \sum \gamma_{kj} \ln p_k \ln p_j$$

and

$$\ln b(p) = \sum \beta_k \ln p_k$$

are price indices. Therefore, the cost function is:

$$C(u, p) = a(p) e^{b(p)u}$$

or

$$\ln C(u, p) = \alpha_0 + \sum \alpha_k \ln p_k + \frac{1}{2} \sum \sum \gamma_{kj} \ln p_k \ln p_j + \prod p_k^{\beta_k} u \qquad (1.3)$$

The settings of $a(p)$ and $b(p)$ make the derivatives $\partial C/\partial p_i$, $\partial C/\partial u$, $\partial^2 C/\partial p_i \partial p_j$, $\partial^2 C/\partial u \partial p_j$ and $\partial^2 C/\partial u^2$ which at any single point can be set equal to those of an arbitrary cost function. This property makes the specified cost function an ideal approximation to any cost function.

The Marshallian demand function $q(y, p)$ is often expressed in terms of budget shares of goods in the basket. The budget share of good i is:

$$w_i = \frac{p_i q_i}{c(u,p)} = \frac{\partial c(u,p)}{\partial \ln p_i}$$

$$= \frac{\partial \ln a(p)}{\partial \ln p_i} + \frac{\partial \ln b(p)}{\partial \ln p_i} \ln x$$

$$= \alpha_i + \sum_j \gamma_{ij} \ln p_j + \beta_i (\ln y - \ln a(p)) \qquad (1.4)$$

The above equation is also known as the Marshallian share equation for good i. And the w_i s of all goods in the basket sum up to one. Usually, instead of being estimated through (1.3) directly, the cost function is calculated from the coefficients in equation (1.4).

Some empirical works suggested that linear Engel curves might not be suitable for some commodity categories. Banks, Blundell and Lewbel (1996) added a quadratic term in the logarithm expenditure to the Marshallian share equation. Their specification is called as Quadratic Almost Ideal Demand System (QUAIDS). But in this study, we choose AIDS in the end.

The aforementioned demand systems do not include demographic attributes z. Now, we can introduce variables for households with different sizes and compositions. Lewbel (1985) presented a unifying approach incorporating demographic variables into the demand system, which is based on the technique of cost function modification:

$$C(u,p,z) = f\{C[u,h(p,z)],p,z\}.$$

The demographic generalization of the AIDS model takes the form

$$C(u,p,z) = a(p,z)e^{b(p,z)u}$$

or,

$$w_i = \alpha_i(z) + \sum_j \gamma_{ij} \ln p_j + \beta_i(z)[\ln y - \ln a(p,z)]$$

And the corresponding equivalence scale is

$$\ln S(u,p,z,z^r) = \ln a(p,z) - \ln a(p,z^r) + [b(p,z) - b(p,z^r)]u$$

We follow Blundell and Lewbel (1991) to make the independence of base utility (IB) assumption, which has been justified by others such as Jorgenson and Slesnick (1987), Blundell and Lewbel (1991) and Pendakur

(1999). In this situation, the demographic variables affect the expenditure through $a(p,z)$ only and equivalence scales are independent of the base of utility u at which the cost comparison is being made. Therefore,

$$w_i = \alpha_i(z) - \beta_i \alpha_0(z) + \sum_j^n (\gamma_{ij} - \beta_i \alpha_i(z)) \ln p_j + \beta_i(\ln y - \ln a(p,z^r)) \quad (1.5)$$

and

$$\ln S(p,z,z^r) = \ln a(p,z) - \ln a(p,z^r)$$

$$= \alpha_0(z) - \alpha_0(z^r) + \sum_j^n [\alpha_j(z) - \alpha_j(z^r)] \ln p_j \quad (1.6)$$

After plugging in appropriate demographic variables, the coefficients estimated in Marshallian share equation (1.5) for n goods categories are used to calculate the equivalence scales for households with different demographic variations. In general, $\alpha_0(z)$ in (1.5) cannot be identified uniquely because it is mixed with $a_j(z)$. Blackorby and Donaldson (1991b) provided an adult good category (for example, alcohol and cigarettes). In its Marshallian share equation, $\alpha_i(z)$ can be safely assumed to be zero and therefore the incept term can be used to identify $\alpha_0(z)$.

At the base level prices, the price index $p_j = 1$ for all j, $\ln p_j = 0$

$$\ln S(p,z,z^r) = \ln a(p,z) - \ln a(p,z^r) = \alpha_0(z) - \alpha_0(z^r) \quad (1.7)$$

Given the values of equivalence scales, the poverty line for a household with a specific demographic attribute can be decided through multiplying its own equivalence scale by the poverty line for the reference household.

In an arbitrary year t, the relative equivalence scale, defined as the change of an equivalence scale for a particular household type, can be tracked by

$$\ln \frac{S_t(p_t,z,z^r)}{S_{base}(p_{base},z,z^r)} = \ln \sum_j^n [\alpha_j(z) - \alpha_j(z^r)] \ln p_{j,t} \quad (1.8)$$

Therefore, the equivalence scales in an arbitrary year can be computed. And accordingly, we can adjust poverty lines for different households in a timely manner. In the next section, empirical analyses based on the aforementioned theoretic model will be presented.

4. EMPIRICAL ANALYSES

4.1. Data

Expenditure and demographic data in this study came from the Chinese Urban Household Survey (UHS) conducted by the National Statistical Bureau (NSB) of China. This survey aims to study the condition and standard of living of urban households. It records household information about income and consumption expenditure, demographic characteristics, work and employment, accommodation and other family related matters. The dataset includes observations from ten provinces. All the provincial capitals are chosen to represent large cities while the mid-size cities and county towns are randomly selected. Within the selected cities and towns, the neighborhood and finally household are chosen by a further random selection. The sample size in each region is proportional to the region's population. Sampled households maintain transaction books that record all expenses and consumption in their households. The base year is set to 1993, the same year that the World Bank chooses as the base year to determine the individual poverty line. The sample in 1997, the latest one accessible to the author, is chosen to track the change of equivalence scales. But the methodology applies to any arbitrary year, given newer data available.

At this stage, five household types are chosen: single person without child, single parent with one child, single parent with two children, couple without child and couple with one child. Other types of households are left out in this study. The number of observations for a single adult without child and single parent with two children are relatively small. For the first group, the reason is that Chinese people rarely live alone. And the explanation for the second group is the one-child policy in China. Therefore, we should be careful with the estimation for those two groups. The household expenditure is disaggregated into four categories: food, clothing, adult goods (includes alcoholic beverages and tobacco) and others (includes household facilities, medicine, transportation and communication, recreation and education, residence, services). The fourth category includes some durable goods. But the effect of durable goods on consumption behavior will not be our concern because the total budget share of durable goods is small in our data.

Tables 1.2 and 1.3 present summary statistics by household type for 1993 and 1997 respectively. For Chinese people, most of their expenditure went to the food and clothing categories, although their total weights decreased from 1993 to 1997. As one can see, the breakdown of the budget shares of households with child/children are similar to each other in terms of food,

Table 1.2:   *Descriptive Statistics by Household Type 1993*

	All	Single	Couple	Adult and one child	Adult and two children	Couple and one child
Sample size	3707	60	688	84	36	2839
Net income	3074*	3980	3980	2808	2490	2851
Total expend.	2617	3301	3286	2498	2302	2447
Budget share food	0.49	0.594	0.564	0.503	0.534	0.469
Budget share adult goods	0.050	0.041	0.050	0.032	0.022	0.050
Budget share clothing	0.156	0.085	0.097	0.125	0.138	0.172
Budget share others (includes)	0.305	0.279	0.289	0.340	0.307	0.308
Household facilities	0.071	0.052	0.080	0.062	0.058	0.070
Medicine	0.023	0.024	0.030	0.022	0.032	0.022
Trans. and commun.	0.028	0.023	0.024	0.035	0.041	0.028
Rec. and education	0.076	0.036	0.038	0.099	0.085	0.086
Residence	0.067	0.097	0.082	0.079	0.064	0.063
Services	0.039	0.047	0.036	0.043	0.027	0.040

Note: * All values reported are the mean within stratum and the unit is yuan/year/person.

clothing, recreation and education. Households without child/children are alike, too. There is no clear pattern for the budget allocation on adult goods. Tables 1.4 and 1.5 display the consumption patterns of households in different regions for 1993 and 1997 respectively. Region 1 includes Beijing and Guangdong. Region 2 includes Chongqing, Sichuan and Jiangsu. Anhui, Hubei, Liaoning and Shanxi are put into Region 3. Region 4 includes Gansu only. The standard to make this partition can be found in Table 1.6. Households in all regions spent less on food and clothing and more on 'others' from 1993 to 1997.

Table 1.3:   Descriptive Statistics by Household Type 1997

	All	Single	Couple	Adult and one child	Adult and two children	Couple and one child
Sample size	3944	38	761	68	13	3064
Net income	5927*	7333	7314	4854	4050	5596
Total expend.	4997	5899	5813	4577	3746	4798
Budget share food	0.474	0.583	0.537	0.484	0.491	0.457
Budget share adult goods	0.038	0.052	0.036	0.017	0.019	0.039
Budget share clothing	0.127	0.069	0.089	0.119	0.111	0.137
Budget share others (includes)	0.361	0.297	0.338	0.380	0.378	0.367
Household facilities	0.056	0.049	0.061	0.044	0.035	0.055
Medicine	0.037	0.047	0.054	0.027	0.068	0.033
Trans. and commun.	0.046	0.037	0.045	0.038	0.026	0.047
Rec. and education	0.103	0.033	0.050	0.147	0.121	0.115
Residence	0.079	0.091	0.091	0.092	0.096	0.076
Services	0.040	0.039	0.037	0.032	0.033	0.041

Note: * All values reported are the mean within stratum and the unit is yuan/year/person.

4.2. Choice of Variables

Marshallian share equations (1.4) for all goods categories are estimated simultaneously to specify the demand system. In each equation, the dependent variable is the budget share of a goods category such as food and clothing. The independent variables are price indices of every goods category, the total expenditure of the household and the demographic variables.

Table 1.4: *Descriptive Statistics by Region 1993*

	1993 All	Region 1[b]	Region 2[c]	Region 3[d]	Region 4[e]
Sample size	3707	593	1217	1685	212
Net income	3074.10[a]	4952.05	3000.37	2546.91	2434.65
Total expenditure	2616.68	4107.04	2552.88	2209.16	2053.19
Budget share food	0.490	0.507	0.502	0.475	0.493
Budget share adult goods	0.050	0.027	0.047	0.056	0.075
Budget share clothing	0.156	0.114	0.132	0.186	0.170
Budget share others (includes)	0.305	0.352	0.319	0.284	0.262
Household facilities	0.071	0.082	0.081	0.062	0.055
Medicine	0.023	0.024	0.021	0.023	0.036
Trans. and comm.	0.028	0.045	0.030	0.021	0.022
Rec. and education	0.076	0.085	0.076	0.075	0.068
Residence	0.067	0.070	0.072	0.066	0.042
Services	0.039	0.046	0.039	0.037	0.039

Notes:
[a] Reported values are the means within stratum in yuan/year/person.
[b] Region 1 contains Beijing and Guangdong.
[c] Region 2 contains Chongqing, Sichuan and Jiangsu.
[d] Region 3 contains Anhui, Hubei, Liaoning and Shanxi.
[e] Region 4 contains Gansu.

As usual, the price variables used in the AIDS model estimate are price indices. The method of constructing them means the indices can catch the price variation across the time period and different households. For example, the food category in this study includes 12 specific commodities, including seven commodities with the highest expenditure shares and five commodities with the most significant expenditure change from 1993 to 1997. For household *h*, the price index of food in 1997 would be:

Inequality in China

Table 1.5: *Descriptive Statistics by Region 1997*

	1997 All	Region 1[b]	Region 2[c]	Region 3[d]	Region 4[e]
Sample size	3944	621	1216	1825	230
Net income	5926.53[a]	10118.31	5690.70	4894.67	4096.49
Total expenditure	4996.92	8467.12	4844.07	4114.54	3471.45
Budget share food	0.474	0.465	0.483	0.470	0.488
Budget share adult goods	0.038	0.020	0.037	0.043	0.052
Budget share clothing	0.127	0.089	0.117	0.146	0.128
Budget share others (includes)	0.361	0.427	0.363	0.341	0.332
Household facilities	0.056	0.073	0.060	0.047	0.056
Medicine	0.037	0.042	0.032	0.038	0.049
Trans. and comm.	0.046	0.053	0.0447	0.043	0.043
Rec. and education	0.103	0.122	0.105	0.096	0.088
Residence	0.079	0.082	0.082	0.079	0.058
Services	0.040	0.054	0.037	0.037	0.040

Notes:
[a] Reported values are the means within stratum in yuan/year/person.
[b] Region 1 contains Beijing and Guangdong.
[c] Region 2 contains Chongqing, Sichuan and Jiangsu.
[d] Region 3 contains Anhui, Hubei, Liaoning and Shanxi.
[e] Region 4 contains Gansu.

$$P_{food,h,97} = \frac{\sum_{i=1}^{12} P_{i,h,97} q_{i,h,97}}{\sum_{i=1}^{12} P_{i,93} q_{i,h,97}}$$

where $P_{i,h,97}$ is the price of commodity i paid by household h in 1997, $P_{i,93}$ is the average price of commodity i paid by all households in 1993 and $q_{i,h,97}$ is quantity of commodity i bought by household h in 1997.

Table 1.6:   *Definitions of Demographic Dummy Variables*

	Standard	Variable
Kid dummies	Kid aged 0–2 years	K_1
	Kid aged 3–6 years	K_2
	Kid aged 7–18 years	K_3
Region dummies		
Region 1: Beijing, Guangdong	(consumption expenditure $\geq$ 5000*)	R_1
Region 2: Chongqing, Sichuan, Jiangsu	(4000 $\leq$ consumption expenditure < 5000)	R_2
Region 3: Anhui, Hubei, Liaoning, Shanxi	(3000 $\leq$ consumption expenditure < 4000)	R_3
Region 4: Gansu	(consumption expenditure < 3000)	R_4

Note: The unit is yuan/year/person

When $P_{i,h,97}$ is equal to the average price paid by all households in 1997, $P_{i,97}$, this index measures the general price change from 1993 to 1997 only. When $P_{i,h,97} > P_{i,97}$, this index consists of both the price change across time and the excessive part paid by household h than other average households. By the same token, household h can have a lower price index than other average households. One advantage of this data set is that it has detailed records of quantity and expenditure for every commodity. We can construct a very accurate price index of each category for every household. This feature provides much more price variations than most data in literatures, in which usually only average price indices across households are available. Therefore, the information content of the independent variables in the regression is abundant. The total expenditure in the regression is the consumption expenditure, not including saving and investment.

The demographic attributes may include age, kids, skin color, region, etc. In this study, three 'kids' dummy variables, K_1, ..., K_3, are included, referring to the way children of increasing age affect the level of each expenditure share. The definitions of 'kids' dummy variables are in Table

1.6. As is well known, the differences in income and expenditure in different regions of China are significant. There are four region dummy variables, R_1, R_2, R_3, R_4, referring to how living in the different regions varies the level of each expenditure share. The region dummy variables are defined in Table 1.6 as well. Another dummy variable for the number of adults in the household is also included. Since each type of household includes two adults at most in the selected sample, a single dummy variable A can denote the number of adults. In our reference household, a single adult without children, $A = 0$. And $A = 1$ means that there are two adults.

4.3.   Estimation and Analyses

4.3.1.   Estimation of demand system

The simplest way to incorporate demographic effects into demand equations is to estimate a separate demand function for each household type. The Marshallian demand function for good i is defined as:

$$w_i = \alpha_i + \sum \gamma_{ij} \ln p_j + \beta_i \ln x$$

where $x = y/a(p)$ is expenditure in real terms and $a(p)$ is conducted using the Stone share weighted index. $i = 1, 2, 3, 4$ denote adult goods, food, clothing and other commodities categories respectively. Both α_i and β_i are constant for each goods category, but not functions of demographic variables.

The estimate arithmetic used in this study is the three-stage least square regression, introduced by Zellner and Theil (1962). Their method is widely used in demand analysis because it can handle the endogeneity in the simultaneous system and generate efficient estimators. Furthermore, this method can take account of restrictions on parameters in the demand system. Jorgenson (1997) provided a comprehensive reference for this method.

Table 1.7 displays the estimated coefficients of the AIDS model that omits demographic variables for five household types. The cell for each household type includes four columns. And each column is a Marshallian share equation for a goods category, connecting the budget share of this category with the prices of all goods and the total expenditure. For example, the negative sign of food price in the clothing equation indicates that the budget share of clothing will decrease when food appreciates. As we mentioned before, the observations for single adult and single parent with two children may not suffice to reveal relations between variables. In general, from the coefficient signs for each group, again, we can observe that households with child/children have similar consumption patterns. So do households without a child. This observation legitimates the use of demographic variables for the pooled data of all households.

As defined in section (4.2), the demographic variables include 'kids' dummy variables, K_1, ..., K_4, region dummy variables, R_1, R_2, R_3 and number of adults. When $K_1 = K_2 = K_3 = K_4 = 0$, the observation is a household without a child. When $R_2 = R_3 = R_4 = 0$, the household lives in region 1 (Beijing or Guangdong). Therefore, $\alpha_i(z) - \beta_i \alpha_0(z)$ in section (3.5) takes the following functional form:

$$\alpha_i(z) - \beta_i \alpha_0(z) =$$
$$\alpha_{i0} + \alpha_{i1} K_1 + \alpha_{i2} K_2 + \alpha_{i3} K_3 + \alpha_{i4} K_4 + \alpha_{i5} R_2 + \alpha_{i6} R_3 + \alpha_{i7} R_4 + \alpha_{i8} A \quad (1.9)$$

The estimated coefficients are reported in Table 1.8.

Each column of Table 1.8 is a Marshallian share equation for a goods category, revealing the effects of prices, total expenditure and demographic factors on the budget share of that goods category. The signs of coefficients, the scale of number and the elasticity computed from the estimated coefficient are comparable with those in Deaton (1997) and Gong, Soest and Zhang (2000). The coefficients of demographic variables show how they affect the level of each expenditure share. For example, the negative coefficients of the 'kids' variables in the 'food' equation reflect the fact that households with kids spend fewer budget shares on food. The positive signs of the 'kids' variables in the 'clothing' equation mean that having a kid will increase the level of budget share on clothing. These estimations are consistent with the fact we have observed in Tables 1.2 through 1.5. Similarly, having an additional adult tends to reduce the preference for food, clothing and adult goods.

4.3.2. Equivalence scales and associated poverty lines

Following Blundell and Lewbel (1991), the equivalence scales associated with the specified demand system are written as:

$$\ln S(p, z, z^r) = \alpha_0(z) - \alpha_0(z^r) + \sum_i^n (\alpha_i(z) - \alpha_i(z^r)) \ln p_i \quad (1.10)$$

$\alpha_0(z)$, $\alpha_0(z^r)$, $\alpha_i(z)$ and $\alpha_i(z^r)$ are estimated from the aforementioned demand system. For each category of goods, choices of different value combinations of dummy variables enable us to get the corresponding intercept term $\alpha_i(z)$ for all types of households with different demographic characteristics.

Table 1.7:   *Price and Income Effects in an Almost Ideal Demand System*
            Without Demographic Variables (by Household Type)

One adult

Budget share of	Adult goods	Food	Clothing	Other
Ln p(adult goods)	−0.011	−0.043	0.029	0.025
	(0.015)[a]	(0.025)	(0.011)*[b]	(0.023)
Ln p(food)	−0.043	0.075	−0.075	0.043
	(0.025)	(0.108)	(0.028)**	(0.096)
Ln p(cloth)	0.029	−0.075	0.031	0.015
	(0.011)*	(0.028)**	(0.017)	(0.024)
Ln p(other)	0.025	0.043	0.015	−0.083
	(0.023)	(0.096)	(0.024)	(0.094)
Ln expenditure	−0.016	−0.037	−0.070	0.124
	(0.023)	(0.044)	(0.025)**	(0.039)**
Constant	0.185	0.853	0.691	−0.729
	(0.192)	(0.362)*	(0.207)**	(0.322)*

Two adults

Budget share of	Adult goods	Food	Clothing	Other
Ln p(adult goods)	0.003	−0.023	0.002	0.018
	(0.003)	(0.006)**	(0.002)	(0.006)**
Ln p(food)	−0.023	0.026	−0.055	0.052
	(0.006)**	(0.025)	(0.005)**	(0.024)*
Ln p(cloth)	0.002	−0.055	0.056	−0.002
	(0.002)	(0.005)**	(0.003)**	(0.005)
Ln p(other)	0.018	0.052	−0.002	−0.067
	(0.006)**	(0.024)*	(0.005)	(0.024)**
Ln expenditure	−0.018	−0.153	−0.024	0.196
	(0.003)**	(0.010)**	(0.005)**	(0.009)**
Constant	0.207	1.867	0.329	0.207
	(0.030)**	(0.083)**	(0.040)**	(0.030)**

Notes:
[a]   Standard errors in parentheses.
[b]   * Denotes significant at 5 percent and ** denotes significant at 1 percent level.

First, we make an attempt to give a plausible base year period value of
equivalence scales as given in (1.7). Table 1.9 reports the results. Each
column of the table is for a household with a specific demographic
composition. For example, to reach the utility level that costs a single adult
$1 to attain, a couple without a child needs to spend $1.53 in total and a

Table 1.7:   *Price and Income Effects in an Almost Ideal Demand System Without Demographic Variables (Cont.)*

One adult and one child

Budget share of	Adult goods	Food	Clothing	Other
Ln p(adult goods)	0.012	−0.033	0.000	0.020
	(0.008)[a]	(0.016)*[b]	(0.007)	(0.016)
Ln p(food)	−0.033	0.220	−0.043	−0.144
	(0.016)*	(0.068)**	(0.018)*	(0.064)*
Ln p(cloth)	0.000	−0.043	0.079	−0.037
	(0.007)	(0.018)*	(0.011)**	(0.016)*
Ln p(other)	0.020	−0.144	−0.037	0.161
	(0.016)	(0.064)*	(0.016)*	(0.068)*
Ln expenditure	−0.018	−0.120	−0.048	0.186
	(0.011)	(0.028)**	(0.016)**	(0.026)**
Constant	0.191	1.474	0.550	−1.214
	(0.094)*	(0.232)**	(0.133)**	(0.217)**

One adult and two children

Budget share of	Adult goods	Food	Clothing	Other
Ln p(adult goods)	0.010	−0.044	0.016	0.019
	(0.009)	(0.023)	(0.009)	(0.022)
Ln p(food)	−0.044	0.040	−0.072	0.076
	(0.023)	(0.118)	(0.039)	(0.104)
Ln p(cloth)	0.016	−0.072	0.127	−0.071
	(0.009)	(0.039)	(0.027)**	(0.032)*
Ln p(other)	0.019	0.076	−0.071	−0.025
	(0.022)	(0.104)	(0.032)*	(0.104)
Ln expenditure	0.001	−0.062	−0.108	0.169
	(0.011)	(0.048)	(0.029)**	(0.040)**
Constant	0.015	1.017	1.146	−1.179
	(0.093)	(0.417)*	(0.250)**	(0.352)**

couple plus a child between zero and two years of age needs to spend $2.25. The equivalence scale for a couple plus a school-age (seven to 18 years old) child looks a little bit smaller than that found by others. From the coefficients of the adult goods equation, which we use to identify the equivalence scales in the base year, this type of household does spend relatively less on adult goods. According to the data, the saving rate of this type of household is relatively higher. How best to incorporate this difference that cannot be described by a demand system is an open issue after this study.

Table 1.7:   *Price and Income Effects in an Almost Ideal Demand System Without Demographic Variables (Cont.)*

Two adults and one child

Budget share of	Adult goods	Food	Clothing	Other
Ln p(adult goods)	0.007	−0.020	−0.000	0.013
	(0.001)[a]**[b]	(0.003)**	(0.001)	(0.003)**
Ln p(food)	−0.020	0.157	−0.066	−0.070
	(0.003)**	(0.009)**	(0.003)**	(0.009)**
Ln p(cloth)	−0.000	−0.066	0.087	−0.020
	(0.001)	(0.003)**	(0.002)**	(0.003)**
Ln p(other)	0.013	−0.070	−0.020	0.077
	(0.003)**	(0.009)**	(0.003)**	(0.009)**
Ln expenditure	−0.029	−0.128	−0.066	0.222
	(0.002)**	(0.004)**	(0.003)**	(0.004)**
Constant	0.307	1.576	0.748	−1.631
	(0.015)**	(0.034)**	(0.022)**	(0.036)**

Notes:
[a]   Standard errors in parentheses.
[b]   * Denotes significant at 5 percent and ** denotes significant at 1 percent level.

Poverty lines for households with different demographic compositions can be computed by multiplying the individual poverty line by corresponding equivalence scales. The results are also displayed in Table 1.9. The individual poverty line used here is $1.08 per day, determined by the World Bank.

Using the price indices of every category of goods in 1997, we can calculate the relative equivalence scales in 1997, that is, the change of equivalence scales from 1993 to 1997. Table 1.10 reports the relative equivalence scales with different choices of number of adults and age group of children. The results show that from 1993 to 1997, relative prices have changed to increase the cost of living as couples by about two percent, no matter if there is a child or not. The relative cost to be a single parent decreased a little except those having a kid in the age group 7–18. Combining the equivalence scales in the base year and relative equivalence scales in an arbitrary year, we can calculate equivalence scales in any year. Table 1.10 displays the equivalence scales in 1997 and the associated poverty lines in 1997. Again, the individual poverty line is the one determined by the World Bank. Other values set by the local government for an individual can be used as well.

Table 1.8:   *Price and Income Effects in an Almost Ideal Demand System with Demographic Variables*

	Budget share of adult goods	Budget share of food	Budget share of clothing	Budget share of other
Ln p(adult)	0.005	−0.018	0.000	0.013
	(0.001)[a]**[b]	(0.002)**	(0.001)	(0.002)**
Ln p(food)	−0.018	0.096	−0.060	−0.018
	(0.002)**	(0.009)**	(0.002)**	(0.009)*
Ln p(clothing)	0.000	−0.060	0.076	−0.016
	(0.001)	(0.002)**	(0.002)**	(0.002)**
Ln p(other)	0.013	−0.018	−0.016	0.022
	(0.002)**	(0.009)*	(0.002)**	(0.009)*
Ln expenditure	−0.021	−0.148	−0.047	0.217
	(0.002)**	(0.004)**	(0.002)**	(0.004)**
Num of Adult	0.009	0.052	0.042	−0.103
	(0.006)	(0.015)**	(0.010)**	(0.015)**
Kid (0–2)	0.008	−0.078	0.061	0.009
	(0.003)*	(0.008)**	(0.005)**	(0.008)
Kid (3–6)	0.007	−0.082	0.059	0.016
	(0.002)**	(0.005)**	(0.003)**	(0.005)**
Kid (7–18)	0.006	−0.048	0.048	−0.005
	(0.002)**	(0.004)**	(0.002)**	(0.004)
Region 2	0.006	−0.036	0.002	0.028
	(0.002)**	(0.005)**	(0.003)	(0.005)**
Region 3	0.010	−0.063	0.023	0.030
	(0.002)**	(0.005)**	(0.003)**	(0.005)**
Region 4	0.023	−0.066	0.015	0.028
	(0.003)**	(0.007)**	(0.005)**	(0.008)**
Constant	0.218	1.811	0.480	−1.509
	(0.015)**	(0.035)**	(0.022)**	(0.036)**

Notes:
[a]   Standard errors in parentheses.
[b]   * Denotes significant at 5 percent and ** denotes significant at 1 percent level.

5.   CONCLUSIONS AND FUTURE RESEARCH

Using the Urban Household Survey (UHS) data of China, this chapter presents a method to decide the poverty lines for households with different

Table 1.9:   *Equivalence Scales in Base Year 1993 and Associated*
              Poverty Lines

Adults	Child age 0–2	Child age 3–6	Child age 7–18	Equivalence scales	Poverty lines
1	0	0	0	1	$1.08
1	1	0	0	1.4555	$1.57
1	0	1	0	1.3888	$1.50
1	0	0	1	1.3251	$1.43
2	0	0	0	1.5254	$1.65
2	1	0	0	2.2468	$2.43
2	0	1	0	2.1424	$2.31
2	0	0	1	2.0427	$2.21

Table 1.10:   *Relative Equivalence Scales, Equivalence Scales in 1997*
              and Associated Poverty Lines

Adults	Child age 0–2	Child age 3–6	Child age 7–18	Relative equivalence scale	Equivalence scales	Poverty lines
1	0	0	0	1	1	$1.08
1	1	0	0	0.9977	1.4522	$1.57
1	0	1	0	0.9962	1.3835	$1.49
1	0	0	1	1.0010	1.3264	$1.43
2	0	0	0	1.0201	1.5561	$1.68
2	1	0	0	1.0178	2.2868	$2.47
2	0	1	0	1.0163	2.1773	$2.35
2	0	0	1	1.0212	2.0860	$2.25

demographic attributes, based on the equivalence scales derived from expenditure behavior study. The result provides a quantitative reference of poverty lines for the policy makers and can help to better define the targets of antipoverty programs given the limited resource. Since the equivalence scale is indelibly linked with demand system, one byproduct of this chapter is a specification of the demand system of China.

Individual cities in China have launched subsidy programs for people under the poverty line according to their budgetary capacity. The methodology and the equivalence scales estimated in this chapter can be used to decide the appropriate subsidy levels for households with different demographic characteristics, given the subsidy standard for an individual.

In the dataset used in the study, the number of single adult households is small compared to that of households including two adults. Therefore, we should be cautious of the equivalence scales choosing one single adult as reference. To measure the equivalence scale for a couple to a single adult more precisely, we can consider the collective model based equivalence scales in Browning, Chiappori and Lewbel (2003). Their work also provides a setting to avoid the interpersonal utility comparability. Given the availability of a newer Chinese dataset, we may observe more single adults because more young people choose to live alone. Such observations will help us to improve the equivalence scales estimated in the future.

NOTE

1. Source: http://iresearch.worldbank.org/PovcalNet/Introduction.html.

REFERENCES

Banks, J., R. Blundell and A. Lewbel (1996), 'Quadratic Engel curves and consumer demand', *Review of Economics and Statistics*, **79**, 527–39.

Blackorby, C. and D. Donaldson (1991a), 'Adult-equivalence scales, interpersonal comparisons of well-being, and applied welfare economics', in J. Elster and J. Romer (eds), *Interpersonal Comparisons of Well-being*, Cambridge: Cambridge University Press, pp. 164–99.

Blackorby, C. and D. Donaldson (1991b), 'Measuring the costs of children: A theoretical framework', in R. Blundell and I. Walker (eds), *Measuring Economic Welfare*, Cambridge: Cambridge University Press, pp. 51–79.

Blundell, R. and A. Lewbel (1991), 'The information content of equivalence scale', *Journal of Econometrics*, **50**, 49–68.

Deaton, A.S. (1997), *The Analysis of Household Surveys: A Microeconometric Approach to Development Policy*, Published for the World Bank, Baltimore, MD: Johns Hopkins University Press, pp. 241–69.

Deaton, A.S. and J. Muellbauer (1980), 'An almost ideal demand system', *American Economic Review*, **70**, 312–26.

Gong, X., A. Soest and P. Zhang (2000), 'Sexual bias and household consumption: A semiparametric analysis of Engel curves in rural China', The Institute for the Study of Labor in Bonn (IZA) discussion paper.

Hussain, A. (2003), 'Urban poverty in China: Measurement, patterns and policies', International Labour Office, Geneva, manuscript.

Jorgenson, D.W. (1997), *Aggregate Consumer Behavior, Welfare*, vol. 1, Cambridge: MIT Press, pp. 449–70.

Jorgenson, D.W. and D.T.S. Slesnick (1987), 'Aggregate consumer behavior and household equivalence scales', *Journal of Business and Economic Statistics*, **5**, 219–32.

Lewbel, A. (1985), 'A unifying approach to incorporating demographic or other effects into demand analysis', *Review of Economic Studies*, **52**, 1–18.

Lewbel, A. (1997), 'Consumer demand systems and household equivalence scales',
    in M.H. Pesaran and P. Schmidt (eds), *Handbook of Applied Econometrics, vol.
    II: Microeconomics*, Oxford: Blackwell Publishers Ltd.
Pendakur, K. (1999), 'Semiparametric estimates and tests of base-independent
    equivalence scales', *Journal of Econometrics*, **88**, 1–40.
Pollak, R.A. and T.J. Wales (1979), 'Welfare comparisons and equivalence scales',
    American Economic Review, **69**, 216–21.
Slesnick, D.T. (1998), 'Empirical approaches to the measurement of welfare',
    Journal of Economic Literature, **36**, 2108–65.
The World Bank (1992), *China: Strategies for Reducing Poverty in the 1990s*,
    Washington, DC: The World Bank.
Zellner, A. and H. Theil (1962), 'Three-stage least squares: Simultaneous estimation
    of simultaneous equations', *Econometrica*, **30**, 54–78.

2. Geography and Educational Inequality in China

Emily Hannum and Meiyan Wang

---

1. INTRODUCTION

Since the 1980s, education reforms in China have decentralized administration and finance and privatized costs. These changes have emerged in the context of rapid economic growth, but also rising regional economic disparities. The reforms have mobilized new resources in support of education, but have also exacerbated regional disparities in funding for schools. While analyses of trends in school finance and expenditures have emerged, there are no detailed studies of the shifting ties between geography and educational outcomes in the population.

Using micro-data from the 2000 census, we begin to address this gap by analyzing data on year and location of birth and educational attainment. We compare the link between birth province and educational outcomes across birth cohorts educated in different periods to illuminate trends in region-based inequalities.

The chapter proceeds as follows: We first place our research in a broader context of research on development and educational stratification, and develop three specific research questions. We then discuss the significance of these questions in the China context. We provide a description of data and methods, and then proceed to a presentation of results. We close with a brief discussion of the implications of our findings for research on educational stratification, in China and in other settings.

2. FRAMEWORK

A key question in the field of social stratification and mobility is whether the educational impact of ascribed characteristics, particularly social origins, gender and ethnicity, changes as a society develops. The often-cited 'industrialization hypothesis' suggests that the impact of ascription should wither away with development and educational expansion, as meritocratic status attainment processes are thought to be the most efficient means to a well-functioning economy (Treiman, 1970).

The empirical basis for this hypothesis has been mixed (Treiman, Ganzeboom and Rijken, 2003). While gender differences in education have narrowed with development in many countries, socioeconomic and ethnic gaps have proven more resistant to the purported ameliorative effects of economic development (see Hannum and Buchmann, 2005 for a discussion). For example, evidence from many countries indicates a global, long-term trend of girls' access to schooling catching up with boys' (e.g., King and Hill, 1993; Knodel and Jones, 1996; Shavit and Blossfeld, 1993; Schultz, 1993). In contrast, research from many societies finds little change in educational opportunities between social strata over the course of educational expansion (e.g., Mare, 1981; Halsey et al., 1980; Smith and Cheung, 1986; Shavit and Blossfeld, 1993). Similarly, there is little evidence that educational expansion will necessarily allow disadvantaged minorities to catch up with initially advantaged ethnic groups, at least in the short run (Buchmann and Hannum, 2001). Despite the mixed performance of the industrialization framework, no lasting alternative approach for investigating links between development and educational stratification has emerged. We use this framework to guide our research questions.

However, this chapter differs from earlier investigations of the industrialization framework in focusing on geographic origins. Many low– and middle-income countries are characterized by massive urban–rural and regional economic disparities, which tend to be much more pronounced than those in developed countries (Rodríguez-Pose and Gill, 2004). Economic disparities, in turn, tend to be reflected in disparities in social infrastructure, with more developed, more urbanized areas offering vastly better, and better-funded, education systems.

Such infrastructure disparities can have tangible implications for educational access. For example, Demographic and Health Surveys from Africa show enormous regional differences in primary school attendance, with more than 50 percentage points separating attendance ratios in different regions in some countries (ORC/Macro, 2000a).[1] Likewise, a recent study in Brazil concluded that despite considerable growth in educational attainment across all grade levels over the last twenty years, dramatic regional differences in educational opportunities endure (Rigotti and Fletcher, 2001).

A focus on geography is particularly relevant in light of recent concerns about divergence, or at least a discontinuity in the converging trend, between the regions of a large number of countries (Rodríguez-Pose and Gill, 2004) together with the rise of decentralized education policies in many countries. More decentralized education finance schemes that require local areas to provide the majority of funds for schools may be associated with greater inequality. However, as geography has not been a focus of research in educational stratification, the potential impact of policies exacerbating geographic inequality has not been assessed.

Using the case of China, we consider three questions about the impact of geographic origins on educational outcomes. First, we seek to establish whether geographic origins are a significant element of educational stratification. Second, we consider whether geographic disparities have narrowed over time, in line with the expectations of the industrialization hypothesis. Finally, we consider whether changes in geographic inequality appear susceptible to educational decentralization and regional economic disparities. We place these questions in the context of China below.

3. CHINA CONTEXT

China offers an informative setting in which to examine these questions. First, China offers a useful test case for the industrialization hypothesis because of its rapid and relatively recent improvements in quality of life indicators and educational opportunities. For example, estimates for women in a sample of seven provinces in the China Health and Nutrition Survey indicate that years of schooling rose from about two years for women age 15 in 1951 to over eight years for those age 15 in 1978. While cohorts coming of age in the early years of market transition experienced slight drop-offs in years of schooling,[2] aggregate educational indicators that extend further into the reform period suggest a resumption of educational expansion after the mid-1980s (Hannum and Liu, 2005).

Second, consistent with the discussion of low- and middle-income countries in the preceding section, China is characterized by substantial regional and urban–rural inequalities that are evident in both economic and human development indicators (Zhang and Kanbur, 2005). In education, data through the early 1980s show substantial urban–rural differences in both the provision of basic and secondary education and in educational attainments (Hannum, 1999). More recent data from the late 1990s and the year 2000 show that economically advantaged provinces continue to enjoy substantial advantages in educational provision (Zhang and Kanbur, 2005). For example, many of the more urbanized and coastal provinces have achieved an important benchmark on the way to universalizing nine years of compulsory education: nearly all primary graduates go on to secondary school. In contrast, in many of the impoverished western provinces, roughly

Table 2.1:   *Percentage of Primary School Graduates Entering Secondary School by Year and Province*

Province	Year										
	1990	1991	1992	1993	1994	1995	1996	1997	1998	1999	2000
Beijing	99	99	100	99	99	100	99	99	99	98	99
Tianjin	97	97	96	96	96	97	97	97	96	-	-
Hebei	80	82	84	86	88	90	94	99	98	98	98
Shanxi	81	83	85	84	85	89	92	95	93	-	-
Inner Mongolia	82	84	88	86	87	90	90	94	94	-	-
Liaoning	92	93	93	90	93	93	96	96	96	95	94
Jilin	86	90	91	91	95	96	95	-	-	-	-
Heilongjiang	83	86	84	83	84	93	95	94	94	94	96
Shanghai	100	100	100	100	100	100	99	100	100	-	-
Jiangsu	82	84	86	88	94	97	97	97	98	97	97
Zhejiang	85	89	92	92	95	99	99	99	99	-	-
Anhui	69	70	72	77	91	99	98	98	97	97	98
Fujian	65	71	76	81	83	92	98	99	98	97	97
Jiangxi	66	67	72	81	86	90	93	94	94	94	95
Shandong	76	79	82	83	88	94	96	97	98	98	98
Henan	66	68	68	71	79	86	91	93	95	96	95
Hubei	74	78	78	81	85	89	93	94	93	91	94
Hunan	71	77	78	84	87	91	94	96	95	95	97
Guangdong	86	87	86	88	92	95	96	96	96	96	96
Guangxi	64	65	67	70	78	86	90	91	94	-	-
Hainan	79	81	82	82	73	74	77	79	84	-	-
Chongqing	-	-	-	-	-	-	87	90	93	91	94
Sichuan	-	-	-	-	-	-	-	-	-	-	-
Guizhou	61	60	60	64	70	73	72	76	75	78	79
Yunnan	61	63	67	68	71	74	75	76	83	-	-
Tibet	62	68	63	74	87	68	67	62	65	45	55
Shaanxi	86	86	86	85	88	90	91	91	90	90	92
Gansu	81	83	83	82	84	86	87	88	87	-	-
Qinghai	89	91	90	87	86	87	88	87	91	91	89
Ningxia	86	85	88	83	89	86	90	88	88	-	-
Xinjiang	82	88	78	80	82	84	86	91	-	-	-

Source: All China Marketing Research Co., LTD (ACMR). N.D. 'China Statistical Data Compilation 1949–2000' [CD]. Beijing: International Food Policy Res. Inst. N.D. 'China Govt. Exp., Growth, and Infrastructure, 1952–2001' [Data File]. Washington DC.

one in ten primary school graduates fail to continue on; in Guizhou, the figure is close to 21 percent and in Tibet, a full 45 percent (see Table 2.1).

Finally, a particularly interesting aspect of the Chinese case is the stark policy shift in education finance in the early 1980s from a centralized system with a narrow revenue base to a decentralized system with a much more diversified revenue base in the early 1980s (Tsang, 2000: 12; Wong, 2002). As Tsang (2000: 13) succinctly summarizes, 'Before [this reform], China had a centralized public-finance system, characterized by the practice of *tong shou tong zhi* (complete collection and complete distribution) according to which a lower-level government submitted all its tax revenues to a higher-level government and received all its expenditures from the higher-level government. In 1982, the practice of *feng zou chi fang* (eating from separate pots) was introduced, by which a government at each level was responsible for its own finances.'

Decentralization coincided with rapid income growth following market transition in China, and sought to mobilize non-traditional resources in support of education (Cheng, 2003; Park et al., 1996). Consequently, educational expenditures rose while the government share in educational expenditures dropped in the 1980s and 1990s (Tsang 2000, Table 2.4). For instance, between 1990 and about 1998, the percentage of all educational expenditures from government budgets dropped from about 65 percent to about 53 percent (see Table 2.2). In contrast, the proportion of all educational expenditures comprised by tuition and fees tripled, from a little over 4 percent to about 13 percent, in the same period. Other sources of funding included levies and surcharges, enterprise and school-raised funds, social contributions, and funding from private schools and other sources; these sources comprised over one-third of educational expenditures through the 1990s.

Importantly, however, decentralization also coincided with increases in regional economic inequality. Inter-provincial income inequality increased markedly from the late 1980s at least through the year 2000, and the urban–rural gap in income and living standards remains large (Carter, 1997; Khan and Riskin, 1998; Zhang and Kanbur, 2005). In this context, while the new system succeeded in mobilizing new education resources, it also brought new geographic inequalities. The new public finance system reduced resource transfers from richer to poorer regions, increasing inequities in public spending (Piazza and Liang, 1998).

Regional disparities in funding for schools have increased as non-budgeted funding sources are more closely tied to local economic circumstances. For example, research has suggested that the highest provincial primary educational expenditures per student, in Shanghai, are

Table 2.2:   *Composition of Total Educational Expenditure by Source*

Year	BEE.[a]	LS[b]	ERI[c]	IGF[d]	SCF[e]	TF[f]	Other[g]
\multicolumn{8}{c}{Percentage of total composed by…}
1990	64.63[h]	9.63	5.83	4.70	7.98	4.21	3.02
1991	62.85	10.27	5.83	5.09	8.59	4.42	2.95
1992	62.13	10.13	5.59	5.39	8.03	5.07	3.66
1993	60.80	9.49	6.14	4.68	6.62	8.22	4.05
1994	59.38	8.92	5.99	4.08	6.55	9.87	5.23
1995	54.76	10.07	5.59	4.09	8.67	10.72	6.10
1996	53.57	10.59	5.11	3.85	8.33	11.54	7.01
1997	53.63	10.58	4.72	3.91	6.74	12.88	7.54
1998	53.09	9.46	4.37	2.00	4.81	12.54	13.73

Notes:
[a]   BEE refers to Budgetary Education Expenditures.
[b]   LS refers to Levies and Surcharges.
[c]   ERI refers to Enterprise-Run Institutions.
[d]   IGF refers to Institution-Generated Funds.
[e]   SCF refers to Social Contributions and Fundraising.
[f]   TF refers to Tuition and Fees.
[g]   Other Includes institutions run by non-governmental groups and individuals.
[h]   Classifications and translations follow Tsang (2000), Table 4. Tsang also includes
      comparable data from 1986.

Source: See Table 2.1.

now ten times greater than the lowest, and research indicates that the ratio roughly doubled in the decade of the 1990s (Park, Li and Wang, 2003). Illustrating the rising geographic gap in expenditures, Figure 2.1 shows per capita GDP plotted against per student educational expenditures for 1990 and 1997. The graph demonstrates the greater inter-provincial expenditure disparities in the latter year; the correlation between per capita GDP and per-student educational expenditures increased from 0.54 to 0.73 between 1990 and 1997.[3]

In summary, because of China's educational expansions over the past five decades, and rapid economic growth since the 1980s, it offers an informative case with which to consider the industrialization hypothesis. Because geography has played such an important role in conditioning status attainment opportunities, China offers an illustration of the potential role of geography as a significant social stratifier. Finally, because of policy choices made since the 1980s, China provides an illustration of the potential for policies linked to geographic inequality to affect educational stratification. Specifically, this chapter considers three questions: (1) Does province of birth appear significantly linked to educational stratification in

Figure 2.1: *Total Educational Expenditures per Student by Provincial per Capita GDP*

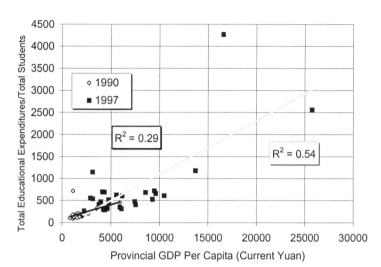

China? (2) Has province of birth declined as a stratifier across birth cohorts? and, (3) has the pace of change differed for recent cohorts coming of age under market reforms and educational decentralization?

4. DATA AND METHODS

To investigate these questions, we analyze unit-record data from a 0.95 per thousand microsample from the 2000 China population census. We conduct all analyses separately for five-year birth cohorts and compare results across cohorts to infer changes over time.

As outcome measures, we consider both a summary measure of years of schooling and levels of attainment, including primary, lower and upper secondary, and tertiary education. In both analyses, we focus on the impact of province of birth, which was reported for the first time in the 2000 census.[4]

We first conduct regression analyses of years of schooling, which we estimate from levels of schooling reported in the census.[5] We then calculate indices of dissimilarity that summarize the degree of disparity associated with location of birth for each level of schooling. For each birth cohort, we compare the distributions of those with and without a given or higher level of education. Specifically, for each birth cohort, the index of dissimilarity is calculated as $D = 0.5 \, \Sigma \, | \, [\mathbf{P}_{ie}/\mathbf{P}_e] - [\mathbf{P}_{i-e}/\mathbf{P}_{-e}] |$, where $\mathbf{P}_{ie}$ is the population

with education level *e* or higher born in province *i*, P_{i-e} is the population
with less than education level *e* in born in province *i*, P_e is the total
population with education level *e* or higher, and P_{-e} is the total population
with education less than level *e*. The value of **D** ranges from 0 to 1 (or 0 to
100) and indicates the proportion (or percentage) of either population that
would have to move for the distributions to be identical.

5. RESULTS

5.1. Years of Schooling

We consider first a summary measure of approximate years of schooling.
Figure 2.2 plots R-squared values from models of years of schooling
estimated for each five-year birth cohort. The model specification is the
same for all cohorts: a set of dummy variables for province of birth. Figure
2.2 thus depicts changes across cohorts in the variation in years of schooling
explained by province of birth.

  Figure 2.2 shows a trend of declining variation explained by birth
province from the 1946–50 cohort (R^2 equals 8.17 percent) through the
1961–65 cohort (R^2 equals 6.05 percent), who would have reached the end
of a basic nine-year school cycle around the end of the Cultural Revolution

Figure 2.2:   *Percent of Variance Explained (R-squared) by Province of*
                 Birth, Models of Years of Schooling by Age Cohort

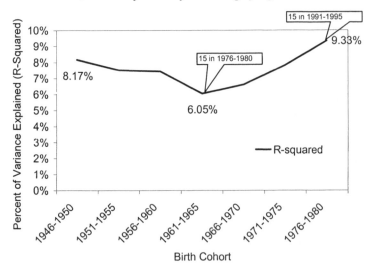

Table 2.3: *Approximate Years of Schooling Regression Results, Selected Cohorts*

Province[a]	20–24 (1976–80) Coeff.	(SE)	35–39 (1961–65) Coeff.	(SE)	50–54 (1946–50) Coeff.	(SE)
Tianjin	−1.09	(0.17)**	−0.93	(0.13)**	−0.76	(0.20)**
Hebei	−2.48	(0.12)**	−2.13	(0.09)**	−2.10	(0.15)**
Shanxi	−2.56	(0.13)**	−1.86	(0.10)**	−2.02	(0.17)**
Inner Mongolia	−2.78	(0.13)**	−2.26	(0.11)**	−2.81	(0.18)**
Liaoning	−1.92	(0.13)**	−1.93	(0.10)**	−1.21	(0.16)**
Jilin	−2.28	(0.13)**	−1.94	(0.10)**	−1.32	(0.17)**
Heilongjiang	−2.50	(0.13)**	−1.96	(0.10)**	−1.50	(0.17)**
Shanghai	−0.11	(0.16)	−0.46	(0.12)**	0.28	(0.18)
Jiangsu	−1.96	(0.12)**	−1.97	(0.09)**	−2.27	(0.15)**
Zhejiang	−2.20	(0.13)**	−2.70	(0.10)**	−3.21	(0.16)**
Anhui	−3.14	(0.12)**	−3.20	(0.09)**	−4.10	(0.16)**
Fujian	−2.75	(0.13)**	−2.92	(0.10)**	−2.87	(0.17)**
Jiangxi	−3.00	(0.13)**	−2.69	(0.10)**	−2.68	(0.17)**
Shandong	−2.31	(0.12)**	−2.48	(0.09)**	−3.03	(0.15)**
Henan	−2.66	(0.12)**	−2.21	(0.09)**	−2.58	(0.15)**
Hubei	−2.22	(0.13)**	−2.27	(0.10)**	−3.02	(0.16)**
Hunan	−2.52	(0.13)**	−2.30	(0.09)**	−2.44	(0.16)**
Guangdong	−2.22	(0.12)**	−2.38	(0.09)**	−2.23	(0.16)**
Guangxi	−3.19	(0.13)**	−2.41	(0.10)**	−2.41	(0.16)**
Hainan	−3.05	(0.17)**	−2.25	(0.14)**	−1.92	(0.25)**
Chongqing	−2.92	(0.14)**	−2.64	(0.11)**	−3.23	(0.16)**
Sichuan	−3.30	(0.12)**	−2.94	(0.09)**	−3.34	(0.15)**
Guizhou	−4.76	(0.13)**	−4.38	(0.10)**	−4.54	(0.17)**
Yunnan	−4.58	(0.13)**	−4.22	(0.10)**	−4.33	(0.17)**
Tibet	−9.06	(0.22)**	−8.41	(0.25)**	−6.87	(0.37)**
Shaanxi	−2.50	(0.13)**	−2.36	(0.10)**	−3.01	(0.17)**
Gansu	−3.90	(0.14)**	−3.58	(0.11)**	−4.97	(0.17)**
Qinghai	−5.31	(0.18)**	−4.19	(0.17)**	−5.84	(0.29)**
Ningxia	−3.59	(0.17)**	−3.33	(0.17)**	−4.43	(0.28)**
Xinjiang	−3.10	(0.14)**	−2.21	(0.12)**	−2.92	(0.21)**
Constant	12.20	(0.12)**	11.33	(0.09)**	9.29	(0.14)**
N	82 287		103 686		62 232	

Note: [a] The reference is Beijing; ** denotes $p<0.01$ and * denotes $p<0.05$.

Source: 2000 Census.

in the late 1970s. The variation explained by province of birth then increased monotonically to 9.33 percent for the most recent 1976–80 birth cohort, who would have finished a basic nine-year cycle of schooling in the early to mid-1990s.

Table 2.3 shows coefficients from three of the models that underlie Figure 2.3: the 1946–50 cohort, the 1961–65 cohort, and the 1976–80 cohort. These models illustrate the estimated disadvantages associated with individual provinces for cohorts of particular interest. Two points emerge. First, the western provinces are the most disadvantaged. For members of the most recent birth cohort, who were 20–24 years old at census time, being from Tibet was associated with an average of over nine years less education than being from Beijing, the reference category. For the same cohort, the disadvantage for those born in Qinghai was more than five years; the disadvantage was also great for those born in Guizhou (4.76 years), Yunnan (4.58 years), Gansu (3.9 years), and Ningxia (3.59 years).

Second, for highly disadvantaged western provinces other than Tibet, a comparison between the earliest and middle cohorts suggests less disadvantage for the later cohort. In contrast, a comparison between the middle and youngest cohorts suggests that this trend has reversed. For example, for the oldest cohort, having been born in Gansu was associated with an average of 4.97 fewer years of schooling than having been born in Beijing; for the middle cohort, the estimated gap was 3.58 fewer years of schooling, and for the most recent cohort, 3.90 fewer years of schooling. The exception to this pattern was Tibet. The coefficients signifying Tibet origins suggest a rising relative disadvantage for both the old-to-middle cohort and middle-to-young cohort comparisons.

5.2. Levels of Schooling

To consider further the role of geography in educational stratification, we turn to geographic disparities by level of schooling. Figure 2.3 shows indices of dissimilarity comparing the distribution across birth provinces for the population with and without a given or higher level of education, calculated by birth cohort for primary, lower secondary, upper secondary, and tertiary schooling.

Figure 2.3 suggests, first, that the distributions across birth province of those with and without access to at least primary schooling increasingly diverge, to a high dissimilarity index value of 45.75 percent for those in the most recent 20–24 year-old cohort. This trend may seem counterintuitive, given the high degree of access to primary schooling in China. It reflects the fact that, with expansion to near-universal access to primary school in many

Figure 2.3:   Index of Dissimilarity Comparing Birth Province
Distributions of Populations with and without a Given Level
of Educational Attainment, by Level and Birth Cohort

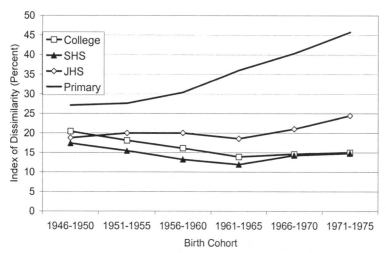

parts of China, those who lack access are, and are increasingly, concentrated in certain provinces.

For example, logit models of primary attainment for the most recent cohort show that the birth provinces that are statistically distinct from Beijing, the reference category, are the northwest and southwest provinces (with the exception of Chongqing), as well as Hainan (Table 2.4). The coefficients for the significantly distinct birth provinces imply a sizable relative disadvantage. Again comparing to Beijing, the coefficients translate to odds-ratios of attaining primary education that range from a minimal 0.0013 for Tibet to a high of 0.11 for Shaanxi and Hainan.

For subsequent levels of schooling, there have continued to be more people in all provinces who do not have access, and consequently, patterns are different. At the junior high school level, the dissimilarity index hovered between 15–20 percent for cohorts up until the early 1960s. Thereafter, the index began to rise, to a high of 24.46 percent for the most recent cohort. At the senior high school level, the index declined between the 1946–50 cohort and the 1961–65 cohort, to a low of 11.96 percent, then rose to 14.81 percent for the most recent cohort. Finally, at the tertiary level, the index declined to a low of 13.89 percent for the 1961–65 cohort, but then rose slightly to 15.01 percent for the most recent cohort.

Table 2.4: *Logistic Regression Results for Three Cohorts, Primary Attainment*

Province[a]	20–24 (1976–80) Coeff. (SE)	35–39 (1961–65) Coeff. (SE)	50–54 (1946–50) Coeff. (SE)
Tianjin	−0.05 (1.42)	−1.14 (0.53)*	−1.23 (0.51)*
Hebei	−0.06 (1.06)	−0.70 (0.47)	−1.83 (0.45)**
Shanxi	−1.01 (1.05)	−0.93 (0.48)	−1.83 (0.46)**
Inner Mongolia	−1.99 (1.02)	−2.33 (0.46)**	−3.06 (0.46)**
Liaoning	−0.83 (1.04)	−0.66 (0.48)	−1.26 (0.46)**
Jilin	−1.14 (1.04)	−0.95 (0.48)	−1.68 (0.47)**
Heilongjiang	−1.40 (1.02)	−1.47 (0.47)**	−2.19 (0.46)**
Shanghai	0.25 (1.42)	0.30 (0.67)	−1.01 (0.49)*
Jiangsu	−0.74 (1.03)	−1.04 (0.46)*	−2.43 (0.45)**
Zhejiang	0.03 (1.10)	−2.01 (0.46)**	−2.95 (0.45)**
Anhui	−1.70 (1.01)	−2.63 (0.45)**	−3.67 (0.45)**
Fujian	−1.22 (1.03)	−2.11 (0.46)**	−2.92 (0.46)**
Jiangxi	−1.60 (1.02)	−1.93 (0.46)**	−2.63 (0.46)**
Shandong	−1.03 (1.02)	−1.81 (0.45)**	−2.98 (0.45)**
Henan	−0.97 (1.02)	−1.53 (0.46)**	−2.64 (0.45)**
Hubei	−1.23 (1.02)	−1.83 (0.46)**	−3.09 (0.45)**
Hunan	−1.07 (1.02)	−1.14 (0.46)*	−2.02 (0.45)**
Guangdong	−0.88 (1.03)	−1.19 (0.46)*	−2.11 (0.45)**
Guangxi	−1.41 (1.02)	−0.72 (0.48)	−1.98 (0.46)**
Hainan	−2.25 (1.06)*	−1.77 (0.51)**	−2.73 (0.49)**
Chongqing	−1.70 (1.04)	−1.48 (0.47)**	−2.87 (0.45)**
Sichuan	−3.01 (1.00)**	−2.01 (0.45)**	−2.92 (0.45)**
Guizhou	−4.01 (1.00)**	−3.73 (0.45)**	−3.95 (0.45)**
Yunnan	−3.80 (1.00)**	−3.49 (0.45)**	−3.72 (0.45)**
Tibet	−6.66 (1.01)**	−5.82 (0.48)**	−5.47 (0.50)**
Shaanxi	−2.21 (1.01)*	−2.37 (0.46)**	−3.10 (0.45)**
Gansu	−4.10 (1.00)**	−3.54 (0.45)**	−4.28 (0.45)**
Qinghai	−4.98 (1.01)**	−4.22 (0.46)**	−4.70 (0.48)**
Ningxia	−3.88 (1.01)**	−3.70 (0.47)**	−4.11 (0.47)**
Xinjiang	−2.32 (1.02)*	−2.27 (0.47)**	−3.15 (0.46)**

Note: [a] The reference is Beijing; ** denotes p<0.01 and * denotes p<0.05.

Source: 2000 Census.

This discussion of levels of schooling introduces some complexity to the picture of geography and educational inequality in China. By the index of dissimilarity measure, primary schooling shows a rising trend in inequality across all years; for other levels, the pattern is stability or decline prior to the early 1960s cohort. After that point, disparities associated with geographic origins increased, substantially for junior high school and slightly for upper secondary and tertiary schooling.

6. DISCUSSION AND CONCLUSIONS

This chapter has considered the role of geographic origins in conditioning educational attainment in China. First, results highlight the historical and continuing link between province of birth and educational chances. The importance of geographic origins has not been fully considered in the stratification and mobility research in China due to data limitations; these analyses suggest that geography is a sufficiently important stratifier to warrant further scrutiny. Further, given that regional inequalities like those in China prevail in many other developing countries, these findings suggest the need for additional attention to geography in status attainment research elsewhere.

Turning to the question of whether geographic disparities have declined over time, with socioeconomic development and expansion of the school system in China, results are mixed. Broadly consistent with the industrialization framework, results show that the percentage of variation in years of schooling explained by birth province declined for cohorts born through the early 1960s. However, the picture was murkier when we considered the index of dissimilarity measures. These measures depicted different trends in geographic inequality by level of schooling through the early 1960s birth cohorts.

More consistent across the outcome measures was evidence of rising, or at least static, geographic inequality among subsequent cohorts. This trend emerged among cohorts educated under favorable conditions of rapid economic development; it is thus inconsistent with expectations of the industrialization hypothesis. However, the rising importance of place of birth is quite plausible in light of rising regional economic disparities, fiscal decentralization, and rising geographic disparities in educational spending under market reforms. These trends play out in wide regional gaps in the qualifications of teachers, in the cost to families, and in the quality of education experienced by children (Hannum and Park, 2006; Ross and Lin, 2006; Paine and Fang, 2006; Tsang, 2002).

Of course, the analyses presented here do not permit us to go beyond speculation about causes of rising geographic inequality. However, the results do suggest the importance of more serious attention to both the policy context and economic inequality in refining theories about development and educational stratification.

NOTES

1. For example, in Ghana in 1998, 88 percent of children ages six to 11 attended primary school in the most favored region, compared to 34 percent in the least favored region (ORC/Macro, 2000b). Likewise, in Mali, primary school attendance ranged from 71 percent in the more urban Bamako area to 17 percent in the more rural Mopti region (ORC/Macro, 2000c).
2. This downturn is not fully understood, but often attributed to some combination of push factors – shutdowns of low quality rural junior high schools as part of the upgrading that occurred in the early reform years and rising educational costs – and pull factors – the new economic opportunities that followed agricultural decollectivization in the reform period.
3. Beyond evidence of disparities in educational infrastructure, research also indicates that local economi circumstances condition children's educational opportunities, even controlling for family socioeconomic status. One analysis of 1990 census data indicates that county per capita income positively predicted rural youth's enrollment in primary school, middle school and high school, net of family characteristics (Connelly and Zheng, 2003).
4. Ideally, we would like to consider origins in these models, but the census question about birth province did not include a question about rural origins.
5. We used the following coding scheme: zero years of schooling for levels less than primary (including responses, never went to school and attended literacy classes); six years for primary; nine years for lower secondary; 12 years for upper secondary academic and technical schools; 14 years for tertiary technical; 16 years for university; and 19.5 years for graduate school.

REFERENCES

Buchmann, C. and E. Hannum (2001), 'Education and stratification in developing countries: A review of theories and empirical research', *Annual Review of Sociology*, **27**, 77–102.

Carter, C.A. (1997), 'The urban–rural income gap in China: Implications for the global food market', *American Journal of Agricultural Economics*, **79**, 1410–18.

Cheng, K. (2003), 'China's education reform: Priorities and implications', Manuscript, University of Hong Kong.

Connelly, R. and Z. Zheng (2003), 'Determinants of primary and middle school enrollment of 10–18 year olds in China', *Economics of Education Review*, **22**(4), 379–90.

Halsey, A.H., A.F. Heath and J.M. Ridge (1980), *Origins and Destinations: Family, Class, and Education in Modern Britain*, Oxford: Clarendon Press.

Hannum, E. (1999), 'Political change and the urban–rural gap in education in China, 1949–1990', *Comparative Education Review*, **43**(2), 193–211.

Hannum, E. and C. Buchmann (2005), 'Global educational expansion and socio-economic development: An assessment of findings from the social sciences', *World Development*, **33**(3), 333–54.

Hannum, Emily and Jihong Liu (2005), 'Adolescent transitions to adulthood in China', in Jere Behrman, Cynthia Lloyd, Nellie Stromquist and Barney Cohen (eds), *Studies on the Transition to Adulthood in Developing Countries*, Washington, DC: National Academy of Science Press.

Hannum, E., A. Park and K. Cheng (2006), 'Introduction: Market reforms and educational opportunity in China', in E. Hannum and A. Park (eds), *Education and Reform in China*. (Forthcoming, Routledge.)

Khan, A.R. and C. Riskin (1998), 'Income inequality in China: Composition, distribution and growth of household income, 1988 to 1995', *The China Quarterly*, **154**, 221–53.

King, E.M. and M.A. Hill (1993), *Women's Education in Developing Countries: Barriers, Benefits, and Policies*, Baltimore, MD: The Johns Hopkins University Press.

Knodel, J. and G. Jones (1996), 'Post–Cairo population policy: Does promoting girls' schooling miss the mark?', *Population and Development Review*, **22**, 683–702.

Mare, R. (1981), Change and stability in educational stratification', *American Sociological Review*, **46**, 72–87.

ORC/Macro (2000a), 'DHS EdDATA education profiles for Africa: Data from the demographic and health surveys', Development Experience Clearinghouse Document ID#: PN-ACK-134. http://www.dhseddata.com/rpt/PNACK134.pdf.

ORC/Macro (2000b), 'Ghana DHS EdDATA education profile, 1993 and 1998', http://www.dhseddata.com/rpt/ghana.pdf.

ORC/Macro (2000c), 'Mali DHS EdDATA education profile, 1995/96', http://www.dhseddata.com/rpt/mali.pdf.

Paine, L. and Y. Fang (2006), 'Supporting China's teachers: Challenges in reforming professional development', in E. Hannum and A. Park (eds), *Education and Reform in China*. (Forthcoming, Routledge.)

Park, A., W. Li and S. Wang (2003), 'School equity in rural China', Paper presented at the Education Reform in China Conference, Center for Chinese Education, Teachers College, Columbia University (New York, New York, February).

Park, A., S. Rozelle, C. Wong and C. Ren (1996), 'Distributional consequences of reforming local public finance in China', *The China Quarterly*, **147**, 751–78.

Piazza, A. and E.H. Liang (1998), 'Reducing absolute poverty in China: Current status and issues', *Journal of International Affairs*, **52**, 253–64.

Rigotti, J.I.R. and P.R. Fletcher (2001), 'Growth of educational opportunities in Brazil during the 1980s and 1990s', Paper presented at the Annual Meetings of the International Union for the Scientific Study of Population, Salvador, Brazil (August 18–24). (http://www.iussp.org/Brazil2001/s50/S53_P05_Irineu.pdf)

Rodríguez-Pose, A. and N. Gill (2004), 'Is there a global link between regional disparities and devolution?', *Environment and Planning A*, **36**(12), 2097–117.

Ross, H. and J. Lin (2006), 'Social capital formation through Chinese school communities', *Research in Sociology of Education 15: Children's Lives and Schooling Across Societies,* 43–70.

Schultz, T.P. (1993), 'Returns to women's education', in E.M. King and M.A. Hill (eds), *Women's Education in Developing Countries: Barriers, Benefits, and Policies*, Baltimore, MD: The Johns Hopkins University Press.

Shavit, Y. and H.P. Blossfeld (1993), *Persistent Inequality: Changing Educational Attainment in Thirteen Countries*, Boulder, CO: Westview.

Smith, H.L. and P.L. Cheung (1986), 'Trends in the effects of family background on educational attainment in the Philippines', *American Journal of Sociology*, **9**, 1387–408.

Treiman, D.J. (1970), 'Industrialization and social stratification', in E.O. Laumann (ed.), *Social Stratification: Research and Theory for the 1970s*, Indianapolis: Bobbs-Merrill, pp. 207–34.

Treiman, D.J., H.B.G. Ganzeboom and S. Rijken (2003), 'Educational expansion and educational achievement in comparative perspective', University of California at Los Angeles California Center for Population Research Working Paper CCPR-007-03 (http://www.ccpr.ucla.edu/ccprwpseries/ccpr_007_03.pdf).

Tsang, M. (2000), 'Education and national development in China since 1949: Oscillating policies and enduring dilemmas', Columbia University Teachers College Center on Chinese Education Publication D-1, http://www.teacherscollege.edu/centers/coce/pdf_files/d1.pdf (page numbers refer to electronic document; also published in *China Review 2000*, pp. 579–618).

Tsang, Mun C. (2002), 'Intergovernmental grants and the financing of compulsory education in China', New York: Center on Chinese Education, Teachers College, Columbia University, Retrieved 1/6/2006 (http://www.tc.columbia.edu/centers/coce/pdf_files/a1.pdf).

Wong, C. (2002), 'China national development and sub-national finance: A review of provincial expenditures', World Bank Poverty Reduction and Economic Management Unit, East Asia and Pacific Region, Report No. 22951-CHA, April 9, 2002. Washington, DC: World Bank.

Zhang, Xiaobo, Kanbur, and Ravi (2005), 'Spatial inequality in education and health care in China', *China Economic Review*, **16**, 189–204.

3. Spatial Inequality in Education and Health Care in China

Xiabo Zhang and Ravi Kanbur

1. INTRODUCTION

Since the start of the reforms in 1978, China has experienced unprecedented economic growth, which has led to spectacular reductions in income poverty (World Bank, 2000; Fan, Zhang and Zhang, 2002). However, this growth has been accompanied by dramatic increases in inequality, especially in the 1990s. In recent years, the policy debate in China has begun to reflect strong concern with this increasing inequality (UNDP, 2000; CASS, 2005). Growing disparities along different dimensions (rural–urban, inland–coastal etc.) are cited as reasons for growing social unrest, not to mention the fact the poverty reduction would have been even more spectacular had the growth not been accompanied by sharp increase in inequality. Most of the literature on inequality in China is about income inequality (Lyons, 1991; Tsui, 1991; Khan et al. 1993; Hussain et al., 1994; Chen and Ravallion, 1996; Aaberge and Li, 1997; Kanbur and Zhang, 1999, 2005; Yang, 1999; Démurger et al., 2002). Relatively little analysis is available on inequality in other dimensions of human development. For example, West and Wong (1995) discuss fiscal decentralization and increasing regional disparities in education and health status. However, their study focuses on only rural areas in two provinces, Shandong and Guangdong. The China Human Development Report (1999) highlights the negative impact of fiscal decentralization on education and health. Although it presents a human development index at the province level in 1997, it does not quantify the change in social inequality over time. This chapter is a contribution to the attempts at filling this gap in our knowledge. Using data from different sources, it presents a picture of the long-term evolution of spatial inequalities in education and healthcare in China.

There are several reasons to worry about high social inequality. First, people live in a social setting and do care about their relative positions in a society. High social inequality is often related to low happiness. Second, large social inequality often leads to more crimes and social instability, which in turn contribute negatively to the investment environment and economic growth. Third, the increasing gap of social development will reduce the trickle-down effect of economic growth on poverty reduction. For example, it is hard for an illiterate person to share the benefits of rapid economic development. All in all, social inequality is just as important as income inequality.

The chapter is arranged as follows. Section 2 provides an institutional and historical review of social welfare provision in rural areas and cities. Section 3 describes the spatial distribution of education and health development, respectively, using national level data that go back to the pre-reform period. Section 4 concludes, and an Appendix provides a description of the data used in the analysis.

2.   INSTITUTIONAL CHANGES IN EDUCATION AND HEALTHCARE PROVISION

Until the 1980s, China's distributional policies manifested a strong urban bias (Lin, Cai and Li, 1996).[1] The rationing system introduced in the 1950s enabled urban residents to have access to food, housing, education, and healthcare at much lower prices. Almost all urban residents in the working age group had guaranteed jobs in the state- or collectively owned- firms. Because these jobs were permanent, the so-called 'iron rice bowl', urban unemployment was virtually nonexistent. These jobs also provided urban residents with many benefits such as free or subsidized education and healthcare. Basically, enterprises and government agencies were responsible for providing social welfare to urban residents.

Compared to the level of social expenditure in cities, rural areas received far less. Nevertheless, the government adopted an alternative strategy in rural areas to promote basic education and healthcare. For healthcare, the focus was on preventive rather than curative healthcare measures. The communes, production brigades, and production teams had authority to mobilize the masses to engage in public health and infrastructure works. With large manpower input, the government could implement various public health campaigns, such as fighting against the four pests (rats, flies, mosquitoes and bed bugs), expanding nationwide immunization, and training indigenous rural health workers (so called 'bare-foot doctors'). By the late 1970s, 'bare-foot doctors' and clinics were set up in almost all the villages. As shown in Table 3.1, the numbers of hospital beds and healthcare personnel per thousand in rural areas rose dramatically from 0.08 and 0.95 to 1.48 and 1.81 from 1952 to 1980, respectively. In general, these

Table 3.1:   Healthcare in China, 1952–98

Year	Hospital beds per 1000 people (city)	Hospital beds per 1000 people (rural)	Healthcare personnel per 1000 people (city)	Healthcare personnel per 1000 people (rural)
1952	1.46	0.08	2.71	0.95
1957	2.08	0.14	3.60	1.22
1962	3.88	0.45	5.07	1.50
1965	3.78	0.51	5.38	1.46
1970	4.03	0.85	4.71	1.22
1975	4.46	1.23	6.70	1.41
1978	4.70	1.41	7.50	1.63
1979	-	-	-	-
1980	4.57	1.48	7.82	1.81
1981	-	-	-	-
1982	-	-	-	-
1983	4.62	1.47	8.37	1.99
1984	-	-	-	-
1985	4.48	1.50	7.81	2.06
1986	4.87	1.46	8.36	2.01
1987	5.22	1.46	8.72	1.97
1988	5.56	1.41	8.98	1.92
1989	5.71	1.38	9.08	1.89
1990	5.81	1.37	9.15	1.89
1991	5.86	1.36	9.17	1.89
1992	6.02	1.33	9.34	1.86
1993	6.06	1.30	9.24	1.83
1994	6.18	1.22	9.37	1.75
1995	6.09	1.19	9.31	1.73
1996	6.08	1.16	9.24	1.71
1997	6.10	1.14	9.25	1.72
1998	6.08	1.11	9.16	1.71

Source: China State Statistical Bureau (2000).

health measures were rather successful in controlling infectious and parasitic diseases. Mortality rates specific to infectious diseases declined noticeably in the pre-reform period (Yu, 1992).

Basic education relied largely on the communes. Agricultural collectivization created a large number of 'commune schools', making

Table 3.2:   Education in China, 1952–98

Year	Primary school enrollment rate (%)	Primary school graduates entering secondary schools (%)	Student/ teacher ratio in primary school	Student/ teacher ratio in secondary school
1952	49.2	96.0	35.6	27.4
1957	61.7	44.2	34.1	27.0
1962	56.1	45.3	27.6	24.8
1965	84.7	82.5	30.1	21.2
1970	–	71.2	29.1	22.4
1975	96.8	90.6	29.0	21.1
1978	95.5	87.7	28.0	20.5
1979	93.0	82.8	27.2	19.1
1980	93.9	75.9	26.6	18.5
1981	93.0	68.3	25.7	17.6
1982	93.2	66.2	25.4	17.6
1983	94.0	67.3	25.0	17.6
1984	95.3	66.2	25.2	18.4
1985	96.0	68.4	24.9	18.4
1986	96.4	69.5	24.3	18.4
1987	97.2	69.1	23.6	17.9
1988	97.2	70.4	22.8	16.7
1989	97.4	71.5	22.3	15.8
1990	97.8	74.6	21.9	15.7
1991	97.8	75.7	22.0	15.7
1992	97.2	79.7	22.1	15.9
1993	97.7	81.8	22.4	15.7
1994	98.4	86.6	22.9	16.1
1995	98.5	90.8	23.3	16.7
1996	98.8	92.6	23.7	17.2
1997	98.9	93.7	24.2	17.3
1998	98.9	94.3	24.0	17.6

Source: China State Statistical Bureau (2000).

access to basic education much easier. As shown in Table 3.2, the student–teacher ratio in primary schools declined from 35.6 in 1952 to 25.7 in 1980 while the ratio in secondary schools decreased from 27.4 to 17.6. By 1980 the enrollment rate among rural children reached almost 90 percent (Fan, Zhang and Zhang, 2002).

Overall, in the planned era, although health care and school conditions for rural residents were much worse than their urban cohorts due to an urban-biased policy, basic education and preventive healthcare were widely available. By the late 1970s, China's life expectancy and infant mortality rate were much higher than most developing countries, even many middle-income countries (World Bank, 2003). Despite the remarkable achievement in social equity, the collective system had well known economic drawbacks. Since the late 1970s, China has implemented a series of rural and urban reforms to introduce market incentives in order to enhance economic efficiency and dynamism. In addition, the center granted local governments more fiscal responsibility to improve their incentives to develop the local economy. Consequently, the redistributive power of central government has declined. With limited help from the center and tight budget constraints, many local governments in poor regions cut spending on social development and let individuals share more healthcare and education expenses (West and Wong, 1995). As shown in Table 3.3, the shares of both government and social spending in total health expenditure have declined dramatically.

In addition to the general fiscal reforms, rural and urban areas have undergone their own reforms. Following the rural economic reform, the communes were dissolved and households became the unit of decision-making, reducing the power of villages and directly affecting the provisions of education and healthcare. Not surprisingly, many rural health clinics have disappeared since the rural reform in the 1970s. The number of hospital beds per thousand has declined from 1.50 to 1.11 from 1985 to 1998 (Table 3.1). To fill the vacuum, in 1984 the government authorized private medical practices in rural areas. Because private medical practitioners provide their services according to patients' ability to pay, an increasing number of people have had to bear the full cost of medical care. The share of out-of-pocket expense in medical care for China as a whole increased from 16 percent in 1980 to 38 percent in 1988 to 61 percent in 2001 (Table 3.3). Table 3.4 shows that in 1998 the self-paid share in total health expenses was much greater for rural than for urban areas. After the reforms, most rural residents have been left out of healthcare coverage of any kind and paying for a health visit has become the norm. A special report in *The Economist* (2004) points out that even immunization is not free in many parts of China.

Table 3.5 compares some key indicators among several Asian countries. China's performance on literacy and infant mortality rate is more like a middle income country than many developing countries, and better than India. However, there are huge disparities in the distribution of access to

Table 3.3:   *Recurrent Health Expenditures by Source of Finance*

Year	Per capita expenditure (1980 yuan)	Government budget (%)	Social expenditure (%)	Personal expenditure (%)
1965	4.7	28	56	16
1970	5.1	27	57	15
1975	8.6	28	55	16
1980	10.9	28	56	16
1981	12.1	27	55	18
1982	13.9	26	53	20
1983	15.8	25	51	23
1984	17.3	25	50	25
1985	19.4	23	47	29
1986	22.0	22	45	32
1987	23.4	19	46	35
1988	26.3	18	44	38
1991[*]	37.7	23	38	39
1995	51.7	17	33	50
2000	95.5	15	24	61
2001	101.7	16	23	61

Note: The health expenditure data from 1991 to 2001 are converted to 1980 yuan using the national consumer price index.

Source: The data from 1965 to 1988 are from World Bank (1992), Annex Table 9.1. Information for later years are from the website of the Ministry of Health, http://www.moh.gov.cn/statistics/digest03/t28.htm.

Table 3.4:   *China's Healthcare Coverage in 1998 (yuan per capita)*

	Cities	Countryside	Total
Totally public paid	16.0	1.2	5.0
Labor related	22.9	0.5	6.2
Semi-labor related	5.8	0.2	1.6
Insurance	3.3	1.4	1.9
Cooperative	4.2	6.6	5.9
Self-paid	44.1	87.4	76.4
Other	3.7	2.7	2.9

Source: Ministry of Health (1999: 410).

health care. In rich areas, such as Shanghai, health indicators are on a par with many western countries, whereas in areas of western China, such as Guizhou, they are similar to those of African countries. According to the World Health Organization (WHO), health expenditure per capita in international dollars ranks China only at 139th, comparing to 133rd in India although China has a higher GDP per capita measured in PPP. The ranking of overall health system performance, which takes into account the fairness of access to health care and individual contribution cost, puts China at the 144th place, behind India's 112th place and far behind other Asian countries listed in Table 3.5. In a word, although China's health indicators are comparable to countries at the similar development level, the trend and distribution are more worrisome.

Although contested elections have been introduced over the past two decades partly in attempt to improve the efficiency of public goods provision, the gains are not significant for at least two reasons (Zhang et al., 2004). First, privatization has made taxation or levies on rural enterprises more difficult. Second, in many villages, the power is not shared between the party secretary and the elected village head, limiting the impact of elections. It is likely that increasing rural income inequality would translate into increasing health inequality, as villages do not have much fiscal power to provide public goods and services in poor areas under the current fiscal arrangement.

In cities, many people's livelihood is wrapped up with the fate of state-sector jobs. Unlike the simple objective of profit maximization in private enterprises, state-owned enterprises (SOEs) have to bear multiple responsibilities of efficient production and social welfare provision (Bai et al., 2001). With greater integration of China into the world market, it becomes increasingly difficult for SOEs to compete with multinationals and private enterprises because of their full range of social obligations. In the initial stage, the government could afford to subsidize the SOEs through low-interest loans. But with the increasing burden of loss, government's support to SOEs has declined. Therefore, since the mid-1990s, the government has carried out ambitious reforms to reduce the noneconomic burden of SOEs by allowing bankruptcy and more open unemployment. Since then, many SOEs have laid off workers and cut health and other benefits. To provide new impetus to the SOEs, the government has launched a series of urban reforms since the late 1980s. The central theme is to transfer welfare-provision obligations such as healthcare and housing from enterprises to social insurance agencies and individuals (China State Statistical Bureau, 1997). Although China has made progress in reforming the healthcare and pension system, a well-functioning social safety net

Table 3.5:   International Comparisons on Key Indicators

Country	GDP[a] per capita	Infant mortality rate[b]	Illiteracy rate (%)	Ranking[c] of health expend.	Ranking overall
China	3740	32	15	139	144
India	2730	68	43	133	112
Indonesia	2970	35	13	154	92
Korea, Rep.	14720	5	2	31	58
Malaysia	9100	8	13	93	49
Philippines	3790	30	5	124	60
Singapore	23700	3	8	38	6
Thailand	6230	25	5	64	47

Notes:
[a]   Expressed in current PPP dollars.
[b]   Expressed as deaths per 1000.
[c]   Ranking based on expenditure per capita in international dollars.
[d]   Ranking of overall health systems performance.

Source: Data in the second to fourth columns are for 2000 and from the World Development Indicators World Bank, (2003). The last two columns are from Annex Table 1 of the World Health Report (WHO, 2000).

Table 3.6:   Sources of Education Expenditure

Year	Total education expenditure (100 million yuan)	Government budget (%)	Social expenditure (%)	Tuition and incidentals (%)
1990	659.4	64.6	33.1	2.3
1991	731.5	62.8	34.6	2.5
1992	867.1	62.1	35.0	2.9
1993	1059.9	60.8	36.2	3.0
1994	1488.8	59.4	36.7	4.0
1995	1878.0	54.8	40.9	4.4
1996	2262.3	53.6	41.3	5.1
1997	2531.7	53.6	40.8	5.6
1998	2949.1	53.1	34.4	12.5

Source: Calculated by authors based on Table A-14, China State Statistical Bureau, (2000: 14).

is still far from being in place (Liu et al., 2001). Therefore, the liberalization of the urban welfare system may have made some disadvantaged groups more vulnerable to sudden shocks such as catastrophic illness.

Similar to healthcare, both rural and urban residents are increasingly relying on themselves to pay for education. Table 3.6 lists the sources for education expenditure, showing that the out-of-pocket education expenses have increased significantly. The government's share in total education expenditure declined from 64.6 percent in 1990, when the data were first available, to 53.1 percent in 1998, while the share of tuitions and incidental fees rose from 2.3 percent to 12.5 percent in the nine-year period. With the increasing out-of-pocket expenses on education, children in the poor families may have difficulties in finishing the basic nine-year schooling, likely leading to more uneven access to education.

This completes our discussion of the institutional changes in education and health care provision in China since the start of the reform process. Sen (1992, 2000) expresses concerns about the social inequality consequences of these policy changes for two reasons. First, social development is the end of economic development and therefore a highly uneven distributional outcome of social development is not desirable in itself. Second, considering that the rather equal distribution of human capital was regarded as a key to China's success in economic reform, the uneven social development may have a long-term negative impact on economic growth. We now turn to the evolution of inequality in health and education indicators, viewing them through the lens of spatial inequality.

3. SPATIAL INEQUALITY IN EDUCATION AND HEALTH OVER THE LONG RUN

We are interested in the evolution of social inequality in China over the long run, comparing the planned era with the more recent era of market reforms. As noted in Kanbur and Zhang (2005), although the ideal requirement for this exercise is household level survey data stretching back over fifty years, such data is simply not available for China. Analysts focusing on interpersonal inequality as revealed by household survey data have had to analyze much shorter periods or with severely restricted regional coverage – a few years for a few provinces, and mainly in the recent period. An alternative approach, as in Kanbur and Zhang (2005), is to view inequality through the lens of spatial inequality, meaning variations across provinces, subdivided by rural and urban areas. Apart from the fact that such regional inequality is interesting in its own right, the advantage of

Table 3.7:   *Regional Inequality*

Year	Gini	Year	Gini
1978	29.3*	1990	30.1
1979	28.6	1991	30.3
1980	28.2	1992	31.4
1981	27.0	1993	32.2
1982	25.6	1994	32.6
1983	25.9	1995	33.0
1984	25.6	1996	33.4
1985	25.8	1997	33.9
1986	26.8	1998	34.4
1987	27.0	1999	36.3
1988	28.2	2000	37.2
1989	29.7		

Note: *The figures for Gini coefficients are calculated based on population weighted per capita expenditure at the provincial level with a rural-urban divide.

Sources: Data for 1978–1998 and 1999–2000 are from China State Statistical Bureau (2000) and China State Statistical Bureau (2000, 2001), respectively. See Kanbur and Zhang (2005) for details of the calculation.

taking this perspective is that data are more readily available at the national level for much longer periods. As shown in Kanbur and Zhang (2005) and in Table 3.7, regional income inequality calculated at the provincial level with a rural-urban divide has increased. The Gini coefficient rose from 29.3 percent in 1978 to 25.6 percent in 1984 and then to 37.2 percent in 2000. The question for this chapter, however, is: What has happened to social inequality? We look at the spatial inequality of education and health outcomes in turn.

3.1. Educational Inequality

Focusing on the years for which census data is publicly available at the national level, we initially arrive at illiteracy rates for rural and urban areas and for females and males for the years 1981, 1990 and 2000. The illiteracy rate for 1981 is defined as the number of illiterates per hundred people who are 12 years old and above. The definition changes to 15 years old and above in the censuses of 1990 and 2000. Because the censuses do not report the aggregate illiteracy rate in coastal and inland areas, we compute it using data at the provincial level with population as weights. The upper panel of Table 3.8 presents the levels of illiteracy for overall, rural, urban, inland, coastal, females and males in China. Several striking features stand out from the table. First, the illiteracy rate has declined steadily over the years, reflecting the success of nine-year compulsory education and the high primary-school enrollment rate. Second, there exist large rural–urban and gender gaps. In 2000, the rural illiteracy rate was more than double the urban illiteracy rate. The illiteracy rate among females is more than twice as high as the male illiteracy rate, suggesting a strong gender bias against girls. The illiteracy rate in inland areas is about 15 percent higher than that in coastal areas.

Table 3.9 further displays the spread in the illiteracy rate across rural and urban areas, with the Gini and Generalized Entropy (GE) as inequality measures. The GE family of measures is discussed further in Zhang and Kanbur (2001) – the specific member of the family used in this paper is the famous Theil measure of inequality. Inequality is calculated using the population weighted values of illiteracy for spatial units. In the top panel of Table 3.9, the first two columns show that the Gini and the GE at the national level increased from 1981 to 2000. The same pattern holds true for inequalities across rural, urban, inland, coastal, female and male population. It seems that the regional variation in health outcome has enlarged over the reform period in all dimensions.

As is well known, the GE family of inequality measures can be decomposed into the sum of a within- and a between- group component, for any given partitioning of the population into mutually exclusive and exhaustive groups. Table 3.9 also presents the evolution of the between-group components of inequality. The female–male component is larger than the rural–urban and inland–coastal components.   Using the overall inequality and between-inequality, we can calculate the polarization index following the method outlined by Zhang and Kanbur (2001).[2] As shown in the last column in Table 3.9, the illiteracy rate is mostly polarized along the gender line although it has decreased from 59.0 in 1981 to 44.6 in 2000. The rural and urban areas became increasingly polarized from 17.8 in 1981 to 25.7 in 2000.

The above inequality analysis offers a snapshot for each of three years. To check whether the findings are robust over a long continuous period, we calculate regional inequality in rural illiteracy rate from 1978 to 1998, when the data at provincial level are available in various issues of *the China Rural Statistical Yearbook*. Figure 3.1 graphs the regional Gini coefficients of per capita income and illiteracy rate. As clearly shown in Figure 3.1, the regional inequality in illiteracy across rural areas has increased, consistent with the analysis based on data at the county and district level as shown in Table 3.8. The rural regional income inequality, measured by the Gini coefficient, increased from 13.7 percent to 24.1 percent in the period of

Table 3.8:   *The Levels of Illiteracy Rate and Infant Mortality Rate (IMR)*

	Illiteracy Rate			IMR		
Year	1981*	1990	2000	1981	1990	2000
National	31.9	22.2	15.1	36.6	30.5	24.1
Rural total	34.8	26.2	19.9	39.1	32.4	30.8
Female	49.1	37.1	27.9	38.1	34.9	36.7
Male	21.1	15.7	12.1	40.0	30.0	25.8
Urban total	16.4	12.0	8.7	23.6	19.1	11.0
Female	24.6	18.4	13.2	22.4	19.5	13.5
Male	8.9	6.1	4.1	24.8	18.8	10.3
Rural/Urban	2.1	2.2	2.3	1.7	1.7	2.8
Inland	33.7	23.8	16.0	44.5	35.8	26.8
Coast	29.1	19.6	13.9	24.4	17.2	13.6
Inland/Coast	1.2	1.2	1.2	1.8	2.1	2.0
Female	45.3	31.9	21.6	35.7	30.6	28.4
Male	19.2	13.0	8.8	37.6	26.8	20.5
Female/Male	2.4	2.5	2.5	1.0	1.1	1.4

Note: *The 1981 census defines the illiteracy rate using age 12 as a benchmark, while the other two censuses refer to those people 15 years old and above. Therefore, they may not be totally comparable.

Sources: See Data Appendix.

1978–98, but the Gini coefficient of rural illiteracy worsened even more rapidly, from 14.5 percent to 32.4 percent.

Figure 3.2 plots the evolution of regional inequality in the provision of primary and secondary education. We calculate the Gini coefficients of student/teacher ratios in the two sectors using provincial data. The inequalities in the two ratios show a similar pattern, except for the Cultural Revolution period (1966–76) when the middle school education system was disrupted. The regional inequality in the provision of public education has increased since the late 1970s, reflecting the fiscal decentralization policy in the reform period.

3.2.   Health Inequality

Similar to education inequality, we first look at the health outcomes using more disaggregated population census or survey data. The lower panel in Table 3.7 reports the levels of infant mortality rate (IMR), defined as the number of infant deaths per thousand births. For China as a whole, IMR declined dramatically from the 1960s to 1980s and then leveled off. With

Table 3.9:   Regional Inequality in Illiteracy Rate and Infant Mortality Rate (IMR)

Year	Illiteracy Rate			IMR		
	1981	1990	2000	1981	1990	2000
National Gini*	30.3	33.7	36.5	27.0	29.6	36.7
National Theil	14.5	18.1	21.3	11.9	14.1	22.5
Rural	11.5	12.7	13.8	10.9	12.6	17.8
Urban	17.3	17.5	23.9	7.3	8.0	13.7
Rural/Urban	2.6	4.7	5.5	1.3	2.4	8.1
Rural/Urban total	17.8	26.0	25.7	11.1	16.7	35.9
Inland	13.0	17.5	19.8	9.6	9.9	19.5
Coast	16.5	18.0	23.6	3.7	4.8	11.5
Inland/Coast	0.2	0.4	0.2	3.8	5.4	4.6
Inland/Coast total	1.7	2.4	1.1	31.6	38.1	20.6
Female	4.8	7.0	9.8	11.3	14.5	23.2
Male	8.6	12.8	16.7	12.3	13.6	18.8
Female/Male	8.6	9.3	9.5	0.0	0.2	1.2
Female/Male total	59.0	51.4	44.6	0.3	1.6	5.1

Note: *The GE measure is parameterized so as to make it the Theil measure of inequality. National inequality in illiteracy and infant mortality rate (IMR) are calculated using population at the provincial level with a rural–urban and gender divide. Rural–urban, female–male, inland–coastal polarization indexes are defined as the ratio of between-group GE to within-group GE. For a discussion of polarization measures, see Zhang and Kanbur (2001).

Sources: See Data Appendix.

careful adjustment, Banister and Hill (2004) even find that the mortality risks of girls at the national level in infancy increased from 1990 to 2000. IMR in rural areas was significantly higher than in cities and the gap widened from 1.5 in 1981 to 2.1 in 2000. The ratio of female to male IMR increased dramatically from 0.9 to 1.3 over the same period. More seriously, female IMR in rural areas rose from 34.9 to 36.7 in the period of 1990–2000. These probably reflect an outcome of family planning policy, as rural residents in general prefer to have boys.

Using the data set, we can further examine the regional distribution of IMR. As shown in the lower panel of Table 3.8, overall regional inequality increased from 1981 to 2000, so did the within-rural, within-urban, and between rural-urban inequalities. It seems that the regional variation in health outcomes has enlarged over the reform period in both rural and urban areas.

Figure 3.1:   *Twenty Years of Rural Inequality in Income and Illiteracy Rate*

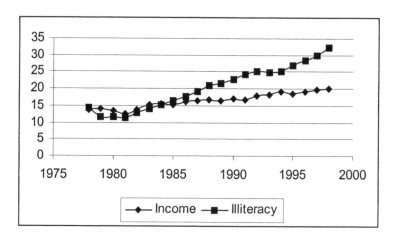

Notes: The income inequality measure is the Gini coefficient, calculated by authors based on population weighted per capita expenditure at the provincial level in rural areas. The illiteracy inequality measure is also the Gini coefficient, calculated from population weighted province level data on rural illiteracy rates.

Sources: China (2000) and *China Rural Statistical Yearbook* (China State Statistical Bureau, various issues).

Figure 3.2:   *Regional Inequality in Student/Teacher Ratio*

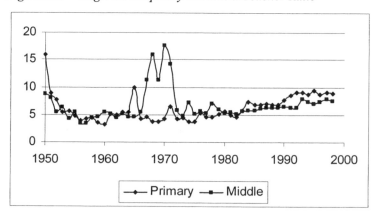

Note: The figure reports regional Gini coefficients of student–teacher ratios in primary and secondary schools calculated by authors based on population weighted provincial data from China State Statistical Bureau (2000).

To understand the driving forces behind the observed changes in health outcome, we further investigate the distribution of healthcare provision. Based on the data in Table 3.1, we graph the urban–rural ratios of healthcare personnel and hospital beds per thousand people in Figure 3.3. Figure 3.3 shows that the density of healthcare personnel and facilities in cities has been much higher than that in rural areas. For example, in 1980, hospital beds and healthcare personnel per 1000 people in cities were 4.57 and 7.82, respectively, compared to 1.48 and 1.81 in rural areas. Moreover, as shown in Figure 3.3, the gap between rural and urban areas has grown. The enlarging difference in access to healthcare appears to be a contributing factor to the widening gap in IMR between rural and urban residents.

While Figure 3.3 provides a rural–urban comparison at the national level, Figure 3.4 graphs the regional distribution of the above two variables using data at the provincial level. Regional inequality declined steadily in the planned era but leveled off since the late 1970s. The picture in Figure 3.4 is in contrast to the increasing trend of rural–urban disparity shown in Figure 3.3. This is probably due to the fact that the provincial level data used in Figure 3.4 does not have a rural–urban divide, masking the large variation in this dimension within a province.

Figure 3.3:   *Urban–Rural ratios in Hospital Beds per Thousand People and Healthcare Personnel per Thousand People*

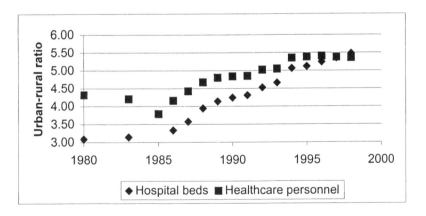

Note: The vertical axis measures the urban–rural ratios of hospital beds per thousand people and healthcare personnel per thousand people, based on data at the national level reported in Table 3.1.

Figure 3.4:   Regional Inequality in Healthcare

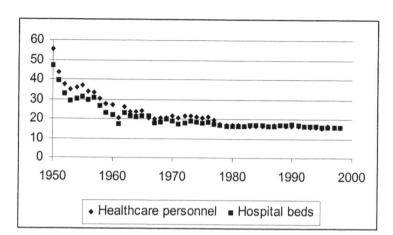

Note: The vertical axis represents regional Gini coefficients of healthcare personnel and hospital beds per thousand people calculated by authors based on provincial data from China State Statistical Bureau (2000).

4.   CONCLUSIONS

In this chapter, we have described the institutional and historical background on the public provision of education and healthcare and examined the patterns and evolution of social inequality. In the era of market reforms, the old foundations of education and healthcare provision have eroded. First, the increasing fiscal decentralization has reduced the central government's redistributive power. Many local governments, in particular those in poor regions with insufficient revenues, have largely withdrawn from their role in investing in human development. Second, increasing competition has doomed SOEs, as it is difficult to serve well the dual task of profit maximizing and welfare provision. As a result, a large number of SOEs have laid off employees and reduced welfare benefits. Third, weak governance at the village level makes it difficult to finance public infrastructure in rural areas. Fourth, governments cannot mobilize vast manpower in public works as they did in the planned era, because labor must be adequately compensated in the market economy.

With this background, we examine the spatial patterns of social development indicators. Not surprisingly, the changing distribution in outcomes of education and public health has reflected the evolution of underlying institutions in the process of economic transformation. Social inequalities in rural, urban, inland and coastal areas all have increased since the economic reforms. In particular, the rural–urban gap in IMR is increasing and the gender gap in literacy is still large.

It has been argued by many observers that to ensure long-term sustainable development, China should adopt a broad-based development strategy. A healthy and well-educated labor force is a key asset to ensuring China's success in incorporating the challenges of WTO accession. However, the increasing economic integration will greatly intensify market competition, which will likely further weaken the central government's ability to redistribute wealth among provinces, and it will reduce the role of SOEs as social welfare providers. In addition, the increasing shocks associated with global integration may further worsen social inequality. Moreover, increasing social inequality may increase social instability, which in turn affects economic growth. The facts of social inequality presented in this paper call for more attention to improving the mechanisms of education and healthcare provision and reforming the fiscal arrangement between local and central governments so as to ensure more equitable education and health outcomes. In other words (UNDP, 1999), the state should play a more 'substantial and vigorous role' in providing education and health care.

NOTES

1. This bias still exists today, but in different forms (for example, government invests more in urban than in rural areas; universities post higher admission scores for rural students; and there are still visible and invisible restrictions on migration from rural to urban areas).

2. The polarization index is defined as the ratio of between-inequality to within-inequality.

REFERENCES

Aaberge, R. and X. Li (1997), 'The trend in urban income inequality in two Chinese provinces, 1986–90,' *Review of Income and Wealth*, **43**(3), 335–55.

Bai, C., D.D. Li, Z. Tao and Y. Wang (2001), 'A multi-task theory of state enterprise reform', The William Davidson Institute Working Paper 367, University of Michigan.

Banister, Judith and Kenneth Hill (2004), 'Mortality in China', *Population Studies*, **58**(1), 55–75.

Banister, J. and X. Zhang (2005), 'China, economic development and mortality decline', *World Development*, **33**(1), 21–41.

Chen, S. and Martin Ravallion (1996), 'Data in transition: Assessing rural living standards in southern China', *China Economic Review*, **7**(1), 23–56.

China National Working Committee on Children and Women (2001), *Report of the People's Republic of China on the Development of Children in the 1990s*, Beijing: China State Council.

China State Statistical Bureau (SSB) (various issues), *China Rural Statistical Yearbook*, Beijing: China Statistical Press.

China State Statistical Bureau (SSB) (1997), *China Development Report*, Beijing: China Statistical Press.

China State Statistical Bureau (SSB) (2000), *Comprehensive Statistical Data and Materials on 50 Years of New China*, Beijing: China Statistical Press.

China State Statistical Bureau (SSB) (2000, 2001), *China Statistical Yearbook*, Beijing: China Statistical Press.

Chinese Academy of Social Sciences (CASS) (2005), *Blue Report on Social Development in China*, Beijing: China Social Science Literature Publishing House.

Demurger, Sylvie, J.D. Sachs, W.T. Woo, Shuming Bao, Gene Chang and Andrew Mellinger (2002), 'Geography, economic policy and regional development', *Asian Economic Papers*, **1**(1), 146–97.

Economist, The (2004), Special report: China's health care', 21 August.

Fan, S., L. Zhang and X. Zhang (2002), 'Growth, inequality, and poverty in rural China: the role of public investments', International Food Policy Research Institute (IFPRI) Research Report 125, Washington, DC.

Hussain, A., P. Lanjouw and N. Stern (1994), 'Income inequalities in China: Evidence from household survey data', *World Development*, **22**(12), 1947–57.

Kanbur, R. and X. Zhang (1999), 'Which regional inequality: The evolution of rural–urban and coast–inland inequality in China', *Journal of Comparative Economics*, **27**, 686–701.

Kanbur, R. and X. Zhang (2005), 'Fifty years of regional inequality in China: A journey through revolution, reform and openness', *Review of Development Economics*, **9**(1), 87–106.

Khan, A.R., K. G., C. Riskin and R. Zhao (1993), 'Sources of income inequality in post-reform China, *China Economic Review*, **4**(1), 19–35.

Lin, J.Y., F. Cai and Z. Li (1996), *The China Mmiracle: Development Strategy and Economic Reform*, Hong Kong: The Chinese University Press.

Liu, G., X. Wu, C. Peng and A. Wu (2001), 'Urbanization and access to health care in China', paper presented at the International Conference on Urbanization in China: Challenges and Strategies of Growth and Development, June 26–28, Xiamen, China.

Lyons, T.P (1991) 'Interprovincial disparities in China: Output and consumption, 1952–1987', *Economic Development and Cultural Change*, **39**(3), 471–506.

Ministry of Health (1999), *China Heath Yearbook 1999*, Beijing: People's Health Publishing Press.

Sen, A. (1992), 'Life and death in China: A Reply', *World Development*, **20**(9), 1305–12.

Sen, A. (2000), *Development as Freedom*, New York: Random House, Inc.

Tsui, K. (1991), 'China's regional inequality, 1952–1985', *Journal of Comparative Economics*, **15**(1), 1–21.

United Nations Development Programme (UNDP) (2000), *China Human Development Report 1999: Transition and the State*, Oxford University Press.

West, L.A. and C.P.W. Wong (1995), 'Fiscal decentralization and growing regional disparities in rural China: Some evidence in the provision of social services', *Oxford Review of Economic Policy*, **11**(4), 70–84.

World Bank (1984), *China: The Health Sector*, Washington, DC: World Bank.

World Bank (1992), *China: Long-term Issues and Options in the Health Transition*, Washington, DC: World Bank.

World Bank (2000), *China: Overcoming Rural Poverty*, Washington, DC: World Bank.

World Bank (2003), *World Bank Development Indicators*, Washington DC: World Bank.

World Health Organization (WHO) (2000), *World Health Report*, Geneva: World Health Organization.

Yang, D.T. (1999), 'Urban-biased policies and rising income inequality in China', *American Economic Review (Paper and Proceedings)*, **89**(2), 306–10.

Yu, D. (1992), 'Changes in health care financing and health status: The Case of China in the 1980s', *Economic Policy Series, No. 34, International Child Development Centre*, UNICEF.

Zhang, X. and R. Kanbur (2001), 'What difference do polarisation measures make? An application to China', *Journal of Development Studies*, **37**(3), 85–98.

Zhang, X., S. Fan, L. Zhang and J. Huang (2004), 'Local governance and public goods provision in rural China', *Journal of Public Economics*, **88**(12), 2857–71.

DATA APPENDIX

The data for per capita expenditure, population, hospital beds, healthcare personnel, school enrollment, teacher–student ratios and education expenditures prior to 1999 are gathered from China State Statistical Bureau (2000). The information on per capita expenditure and population for 1999 and 2000 are from *China Statistical Yearbook* (China State Statistical Bureau, 2000 and 2001).

The healthcare coverage data in 1998 are from *China Health Yearbook 1999* (Ministry of Health, 1999) and the sources of the data on health expenditures are World Bank (1992) and the website of Ministry of Health, http://www.moh.gov.cn/statistics/digest03/t28.htm.

The illiteracy and IMR data are compiled from published provincial and national statistical volumes of the population censuses of 1981, 1990 and 2000. The official data report illiteracy and IMR rates at the provincial level with a rural–urban and gender disaggregation for each province. When we calculate regional inequality in illiteracy and IMR, we use the corresponding population as weights. The annual rural illiteracy data at the provincial level from 1978 to 1998 is from *China Rural Statistical Yearbook* (China State Statistical Bureau, various issues).

Banister and Zhang (2005) find that the infant mortality rates reported from the census are lower than those from a large annual survey conducted by China's Ministry of Health, which is specially designed to get unusually complete death reporting. This survey estimated that China's infant mortality rate was 50.2 infant deaths per thousand live births in 1991 and 32.2 in 2000 (China National Working Committee on Children and Women, 2001, p. 28). The *World Development Indicators* (World Bank, 2003) report the higher figure from the second source, as shown in Table 3.5.

If we compare the survey results in 1991 and 2000 with the census results in 1990 and 2000, and if we assume that the infant mortality survey data are accurate, we can conclude that infant deaths may have been underreported with only about 61 percent reported for 1990 in the 1990 census and over 70 percent reported in the 2000 census. However, without access to the survey data at the disaggregate level, we cannot make use of them for inequality measures. To the extent that the two data series share similar trends, the impact on the accuracy of the inequality measures may not be that serious.

4. From a Welfare to a Mixed-Plural Education System: Chinese Welfare Education and Investment in Human Capital

Gongcheng Zheng[1]

1. INTRODUCTION

I am very grateful to the organizers for giving me an opportunity to attend this conference. I feel very inspired by the speeches of the famous professors Chow[2] and Heckman.[3] However, I would like to explain the circumstances of human capital investment in China from an educational development angle and communicate my main point of view on this problem. The rest of this chapter is as follows. Part 2 describes how China has passed beyond the pure welfare education era and has come into a new era of mixed-plural education that has continued since reforms and opening policies were established. Part 3 describes the basic characteristics of the mixed-plural education system. Part 4 explains the problems concerning a mixed-plural education system. Part 5 discusses some actions that have been, or are being taken by the Chinese government to solve the problems. Finally, Part 6 provides some suggestions for educational development in China.

2. THE CHANGE FROM A WELFARE TO A MIXED-PLURAL EDUCATION SYSTEM

I have always believed that education is the essential premise for people who want to have a better society and also the basic reason for the development of a country. China began its massive investment in human capital in the 1950s after the People's Republic of China (PRC) was established. At that time, a pure welfare education system was established. During the planned economy era the education system in urban China included both general education and technology training for the employees as parts of public welfare. Even educational institutions sponsored by enterprises were a part of public welfare because the state-owned enterprises had exclusive and close relationships with official finances. In addition, the rural education system was set up by rural collectives that were always supported by the state. Under this system, students generally received education at very low cost or even free of charge. For a long time in China, the tuition and miscellaneous fees for compulsory education were kept under $1 and in senior secondary schools they were kept under $2. Even in higher education the government had complete responsibility for tuition. Students did not need to pay any fees but could get different levels of allowances.

From the 1950s through the 1970s, Chinese government appropriations for education occupied about 2 percent of GDP with the lowest level reaching 1.7 percent (Yu, 2002). The proportion is a little larger if the educational investments for children of the collective economy in rural areas are included. Relative to the economic development level at that time the government attached great importance to education and made a large impact. It was this education system characterized by low, or even no, cost for students that improved the national education level rapidly in China.

According to related statistics, illiterates and semi-literates occupied over 80 percent of the Chinese population in 1949. Receiving an education had become a special right of the children from well-off families. According to statistics from the census of 1982, the proportion of illiterates and semi-literates had declined to 30 percent as a result of the improvements between the 1950s and 1970s. The average years of education attained increased from 5.01 years to 7.93 years over this time (Li and Zheng, 2003). The accumulation of human capital profited not only from standard forms of education, but also non-standard education such as night schools.

Since economic reforms and the opening of the economy, especially in the 1990s, China has gradually turned its pure welfare education system into a mixed-plural education system. This transformation is due to several factors. On the one hand, the national demand for education increased steadily and rapidly due to the market economy reforms. The belief that study had no use during the Cultural Revolution period was swiftly reversed so that pursuing an educational degree was seen as important. With these changes, it was very difficult for the Chinese government to meet educational demands. As a result, schools began to charge tuition and miscellaneous fees not only for non-compulsory education, but also for compulsory education. Moreover, some schools also created enterprises and other profitable institutions for overcoming the insufficiency of educational funds. On the other hand, since the reforms and opening of the economy, the national demands for education have taken on different forms. Besides general education, non-standard degree education and various non-degree educational forms have experienced unprecedented development.

The development of educational investment has gone through a transition from the traditional mode where the government appropriated money for education and enterprises invested in human capital, to the present mode in which the whole society, including families and individuals, are all educational investors. Even the schools themselves have become profitable institutions. This highlights the manner in which China has turned its original pure welfare education system into a mixed-plural education system since the 1990s. As a result of the mixed-plural education system, the Chinese national education level has been further improved. According to Census statistics from the year 2000, the average years of schooling among the rural labor force increased from 5.01 in 1982 to 7.33 in 2000. The average among the urban labor force increased from 7.93 years to 10.2 years over the same span and the proportion of illiterates declined to 6.72 percent (Li and Zheng, 2003).

According to the National Bureau of Statistics, the total number of students in China was about 225.6 million in 2002, including 501 000 postgraduates, nine million undergraduates, 94.2 million students in secondary school and 121.6 million pupils.

3. THE BASIC CHARACTERISTICS OF THE MIXED-PLURAL EDUCATION SYSTEM

The educational system in China today is a mixed-plural system that has plurality in educational investors, institutions and demands. The details of the system are as follows:

3.1. Diversity/Plurality of Educational Investors

The government, enterprises, families and individuals, and society, as well as the educational institutions themselves, invest in for-profit institutions or turn to domestic and foreign loans. The diversity of educational investors has no doubt brought about the massive increase in educational investment and rapid development of the education industry compared to the past situation involving purely public investors. According to 'Penetrating Analysis of the Chinese Education and Human Resource Problem', the Engle index among rural residents has declined to 47.7 percent. This means the residents are in the well-off phase. The same figure among urban residents is 37.9 percent, which means the residents are in the affluent phase. In the family consumption structure, expenditures on education and culture occupied 12.6 percent of the total family expenditure. This is second only to expenditure on food and exceeds expenditure on housing and clothing. The consumption structure implies that families could devote increasing resources to human capital investment in their members (Yin and Wu, 2004).

3.2.   Diversity/Plurality of Educational Institutions

In China now there are private and non-standard educational institutions to go along with the public and standard institutions. Although public and standard institutions are still the mainstay of the educational system, private schools, including primary schools, secondary schools, and colleges, and also non-standard training institutions have developed rapidly. According to the Ministry of Education (2004), by 2002 there were 62 000 private schools of all types (including 1335 institutions of higher education, 133 of which meet the qualifications for providing degree education) and 11 million students in China. As a typical example of a private educational institution, the New Oriental School (NOS) was set up by Mr Yu Minhong in 1993 with no support from the government. The NOS expanded and strengthened itself rapidly through students' tuition. The number of enrolled students increased from 15 000 in 1995 to 200 000 in 2001 and to 350 000 in 2003. In a word, the NOS has grown through individual investment in education, and has become a successful example of private education in a market economy (Luo, 2004).

3.3.   Diversity of Educational Patterns

The structure of the education system now takes many forms and is composed of degree education and non-degree education, knowledge education and skill education, standard education and non-standard education, domestic education and international education. This diversification of educational patterns is a direct reflection of the diversification of national demands for education. It is impossible for the pure welfare education system to meet the diverse national demands for education.

3.4.   Complexity of Educational Situations

Different education types emerge and mix with each other for diversification. For example, the public schools now generate revenue by charging tuition in addition to getting financial support from the government. Non-traditional types allow a student to receive the complete and standard higher education, without being released from production.

In summary, the nature of the education system today is not only diverse but also mixing. The trend of diversity can certainly not be reversed, but the situation of mixing on the basis of division does need to change through further reform actions such as rectifying relations, specifying responsibility and enacting some pertinent policies.

4. PROBLEMS WITH THE MIXED-PLURAL EDUCATION SYSTEM

There are also problems with the plural education system. Some of these problems are as follows:

4.1. Educational Investment is Insufficient and the Structure is Unreasonable

As Table 4.1 illustrates, the ratio of total outlays for education to GDP increased to 5.4 percent in 2002 from 2.5 percent in 1985; and the government appropriation proportion was increased to 3.41 percent in 2002 from 2.5 percent in 1985. Based on these figures and some related data, we can draw the following conclusions about the devotion of educational outlays in China.

First, although the outlays for education increased rapidly, the total quantity is actually not sufficient. In China, except for a few colleges such as Beijing University, and some authorized key primary and secondary

Table 4.1: Educational Outlays as a Proportion of GDP

	1985	1990	1995	2000	2001	2002
Total educational funds						
(Billions of yuan)	22.7	65.9	187.8	384.9	463.8	548.0
(Percent of GDP)	2.5	3.6	3.2	4.3	4.8	5.4
Government appropriations for education						
(Billions of yuan)	22.5	54.9	141.2	256.3	305.7	349.1
(Percent of GDP)	2.5	3.0	2.4	2.9	3.2	3.4

Sources: China Statistical Yearbook 2002, 2003, and 2004 edited by the National Bureau of Statistics of China.

schools in medium and large cities, many other schools are insufficiently financed or seriously lack financial support.

Second, increases in government appropriation of funds for education have been relatively slow, which means the increase is mainly driven by non-governmental finance. As the significant national education investor, the government should enhance its educational commitment.

Third, outside of the government appropriation, the commitments from social organizations and families or individuals increased greatly. The greatest increase was from families and individuals. As the second significant body of education investors, the enterprises did not behave so well. A survey shows that the human capital investment by over 30 percent of enterprises is so little that it is basically symbolic– an average level of ten yuan per capita. The average outlay for education and training for about 20 percent of the enterprises is between ten and 20 yuan per capita and most of the enterprises operating at a loss have nearly stopped investment in human capital. In addition some capable enterprises also have abandoned, or prepared to abandon, the pre-job training and medium–long-term training plan. In recent years 45 percent of the affiliated vocational education institutions of state-owned enterprise have been repealed and 47 percent have been amalgamated (Erdong, 2003).

Fourth, the structure of educational investment is unreasonable and the emphasis on basic education is not enough. Generally speaking, basic education should depend on the support of financial funds. In addition, Chinese law stipulates exactly that nine years of compulsory education should be achieved. However, the total amount of educational funds is not only insufficient, but it is also not reasonably distributed. At present, the funds for basic education from the government occupy only about 58 percent of the total basic education commitment; while the same figure in higher education is about 50 percent. Taking the situation in 2000 for example, the outlays used in higher education are about 25.54 percent of the total government expenditure for education. In non-compulsory education, such as technical secondary schools and senior secondary schools, this figure is about 40 percent; while that in the compulsory phase (elementary and junior high schools), is only about 30 percent.[4] Moreover, some related statistics show that per capita public education funds for the pupils and secondary school students has been declining since 1999, with the average level of rural pupils at below 28 yuan (Cheng). According to a survey of the basic education funds in 50 counties published by the National Audit Office in July 2004, the outlays for personnel took 87.3 percent of the public education funds in 2002. The debt of basic education had reached 3.898 billion yuan at the end of June 2003 with more than 80 percent of primary and secondary schools in some counties running in debt. There were still 19 counties in the sample that owed teachers salaries amounting to 202 million yuan, or 17.7 percent of the whole salary payable.[5] The lack of investment in basic education has resulted in a phenomenon that educational institutions in some areas now charge the students for random items, which further increases the cost of basic education, especially for rural residents.

Fifth, the Chinese government lacks effective measures to mobilize nongovernmental resources. Although there has been much beneficial investment in education from the social organizations and enterprises, and individuals have done more since the reforms and opening of the economy, the government still lacks effective measures to mobilize these nongovernmental resources. For instance, one could enjoy a related, tax-free, preference by donating to educational institutions according to the Donation Act. However, this stipulation cannot actually be put into effect because the specific policy has not been enacted, which practically restrains the nongovernmental resources from being invested in education.

4.2. The Inequity in Education is Obvious

Because China itself is in a transitional period, and is also reforming its educational system from a welfare to a mixed-plural education system, the lack of laws, the inapplicability of a management system, and the imperfection of related accessory mechanisms all result in obvious inequity in education. This will hinder the healthy and sustained development of educational undertakings and directly distort the human capital investment behaviors of the whole society to some extent. As a result, the failure and inefficiency of educational investments is inevitable.

The distribution of public educational resources is extremely inequitable. For a long time, the government financial expenditure for education placed more emphasis on urban areas than rural areas; more on authorized key schools than on non-key schools; more on degree education than on non-degree education; and more on knowledge-based education than on skill-based education. The example of compulsory education clearly illustrates the difference between urban and rural areas. More than 75 percent of all nine-year students are in rural schools, but educational appropriations use only about 50 percent of the total funds for the junior secondary schools and elementary schools. Among all kinds of schools, whether elementary schools, secondary schools, or universities, the authorized key schools usually are the main focus of educational funds, while the conditions of the other schools have not been improved for a long time. The Chinese government pays more attention to degree education, and has not given the necessary support to non-degree vocational technical education, since the reforms and opening of the economy. As a result, the vocational technical schools have withered rapidly. These examples show that the unequal distribution of education resources has led to poor results.

In addition, the educational opportunities for people of different groups are inequitable. It has long been true that the people in cities are provided with more educational opportunities than those in rural areas. National census data from 1982 and 2000 show some evidence of this. In 1982 the average length of education among the rural workforce (population between 16 and 64 years old) was about 5.01 years, which is a primary school level. The same figure for the urban workforce was 7.93 years, which is at the level of two years of secondary school. In 2000, the average length of education among the rural workforce increased to 7.33 years, or to the level of one year of secondary school; while the same figure for the urban workforce increased to 10.2 years, or to the level of one year of senior secondary school (Li and Zheng, 2003). Even with the uniform system of entrance exams, urban young people have a far greater chance to enroll than rural young people. All these facts imply that there exists a great gap in education and human capital between urban and rural areas in China.

There is also gender inequity in education. Rural residents display an obvious preference for males rather than females in terms of educational investment and it follows that the chance of receiving an education is less for females than for males.

Additionally, with the emergence of massive numbers of peasant workers, obvious inequities also exist between the floating population and the local settled population. The children of the floating population who want to enroll in urban schools are charged additional high fees and cannot get treatment equal to that of local residents. This affects the children of millions of peasant workers. Moreover, the peasant workers with floating status cannot enjoy the skill training necessary for urban workers.

4.3.   The Tendency Towards Market-Oriented Education is Worrisome

The direct effect of the reforms to the market economic system in China has been to move the educational system toward a more market- and efficiency-oriented system. This transition has reached an alarming situation due to the lack of corresponding policies and criteria. On the one hand, the phenomenon of random charges exists in almost all levels and kinds of schools and it has become a social problem in China. Accordingly, the educational systems have even been considered as trades of staggering profit. In some places schools charge for the compulsory education for which the government should be primarily responsible. Children born into poor families have to stop their schooling because they are not able to afford the high fees, which is still the usual case. On the other hand, the burden of educational investment to families and individuals becomes increasingly heavy due to increased spending on education. One example is college tuition. In 2001, the average tuition was 3985 yuan per person per year, which equates to more than 50 percent of GDP per capita in the same year. By comparison, the same figure in the US is 15 percent (Wen). The tuition and miscellaneous fees for graduates are about 30 000 yuan, or 400 percent of GDP per capita and they continue to increase.

Under the market-based background, public schools begin to establish profitable institutions. Different kinds of non-degree education and non-standard education have become an important source of educational outlays for the operation and improvement of colleges and universities in China. The field of continuing education is in chaos. At present, the educational system in China is actually influenced both by planning and by the market. The excessive market and efficiency orientation has impaired natural fairness, welfare, and the criterion of national education. This results in the deprivation of the right for some people to be educated and thus impairs the people's basic living standard.

4.4. The Low Level of Human Capital Coexists with Inefficient Human Capital Use

The average years of education for Chinese people is at the middle or low level relative to other developing countries. According to the Ministry of Education, the gross enrollment rate in colleges increased to 17 percent in 2003 and continued to rise in 2004. However the National Bureau of Statistics reports that only 4.4 percent of the total population has attained an education above the junior college level; 11.7 percent at the senior secondary school level; 35.3 percent at the junior secondary school level; 32.7 percent at the primary school level; and 9.2 percent were illiterate. Given these low human capital levels, immature labor markets, and the unreasonable income distribution, the efficient use of human capital is very low. In recent years, graduates have had difficulty finding employment. In 2003, the employment rate for graduates was 70 percent, which is also the decided aim in 2004 (He, 2004). This employment rate was obtained only after many measures were taken to promote employment which clearly shows that the use of Chinese human capital is not efficient.

According to information from the Ministry of Labor and Social Security Department published on 12 July 2004, the ratios of the number of job seekers to jobs for different levels of job applicants, including junior secondary school or below, senior secondary school, junior college, college, and master or above, were 0.96, 0.92, 0.91, 0.87, and 1.42 respectively (Liu,

2004). The ratios imply that there were 100 students of secondary school level to compete for 96 positions; 100 postgraduates for 142 positions; but 100 undergraduates for only 87 positions. Undergraduates as a group have the most difficultly finding jobs. These figures also indicate that human capital is not used efficiently in China.

5.   ACTIONS BY THE CHINESE GOVERNMENT

The Chinese government pays a great deal of attention to the problems in the educational system. In recent years, actions have been taken or are being taken to promote the development of education and to accelerate the transformation from human resource to human capital. The government has undertaken the following policies and measures to address problems with the system.

5.1.   Increased Financial Allocations to Education

On this aspect, the government continuously increased financial allocations to educational funds by an average growth rate of 16.7 percent per year between 1997 and 2003 (Ministry of Education, 2003). In 2005, the Chinese government will devote 4 percent of GDP to finance educational funds, and the goal is to reach 5 percent of GDP in 2010.

5.2.   Taken the Equity of Education into Account and Adopted Appropriate Actions

First, the government must pay more attention to rural education and practice actual measures to improve it. Since 2002, the financial budget for rural compulsory education has increased in successive years. Also, central finance promotes the transformation of rural compulsory education from peasant-run to government-run through the transfer of pay and by transforming administrative fees into taxes. At the same time, the government has implemented 'The National Compulsory Education Project in the Poorly-Off Areas', the 'Reconstruction of Dangerous Building Project for Rural Primary Schools and Secondary Schools', the 'Basic Educational Establishment Building Project in Western Areas', and 'The National Compulsory Education Subvention Plan for Poorly-Off Students'. In addition, the government now provides textbooks for pupils and secondary school students in poverty. All these related actions have begun to rectify serious inequities in the distribution of educational resources between urban areas and rural areas.

Secondly, owing to the National Standing Committee's inspection of executing minor protection act in 2003, the Chinese government confirmed definitely that the local government should form an overall plan for compulsory education that includes children of the floating population. The children of the floating population whose main body is peasant workers have begun to share the same educational opportunities.

5.3. Brought Vocational Education into the National Education Revitalization Plan

The Ministry of Education of China will make strenuous efforts to promote the development of vocational education, cultivate high quality and skillful talents, and diversify adult education and continuous education, which have been brought into the national education revitalization plan. The Ministry of Labor and Social Security has also begun to take some actions, such as strengthening the skill training to laborers through governmental commitment and functional adjustment of the unemployment insurance system. It has also made a large-scale training plan for peasant workers. We can speculate accordingly that vocational skill education will become a very important part of the plural education system of China.

5.4. Intensified the Welfare Elements of Compulsory Education and Built the Educational Cost Share-in Mechanism

The main goal of the Chinese government recently has been to ensure that every young person of the right age has the opportunity to receive compulsory education. This has been nearly achieved in cities since even the poorest families could get educational subsidies from the municipal government. In rural areas, it has basically carried out the transformation from peasant-run to government-run education through establishing an administrative mechanism based at the county level. In addition, the Chinese government put a 'One-Fee System' into practice among public compulsory education in all the provinces. A 'One-Fee System' means that students can only be charged once based on a strict check of incidental and textbook expenses. With this policy the government expects to stop random charges in primary and secondary schools. Free compulsory education has been realized in some cities and the compulsory education system is starting to regain its natural welfare character.

At the same time, the Chinese government is attempting to establish the cost share-in mechanism of non-compulsory education, including higher education and other non-compulsory education. This mechanism requires that financing channels and schemes be decided according to the educational cost, and that families and individuals share some necessary costs as the preconditions for the students to receive non-compulsory education. With the establishment of the cost share-in mechanism educational charges will be standardized and systematized.

6. SUGGESTIONS FOR EDUCATIONAL DEVELOPMENT IN CHINA

China takes employment as the essence of people's livelihood, and education is no doubt the groundwork for employment because the level of education objectively determines the developmental opportunity for individuals and the national education level determines the future of the country. Therefore, it is a necessary condition for a country to be strong and prosperous that the government attaches importance to, and develops, its education system. As far as the Chinese educational undertaking is concerned, I want to offer some suggestions as follows:

First, under the principle of scientific development philosophy, it is necessary for the state to take national education as a priority and promote it.

Second, education, although a kind of human capital investment, should maintain the characteristics of equity and welfare. Education possesses special particularities, such as lagging returns, which determine that education should be dominated by the state. Ensuring everybody an equal opportunity for education is an important embodiment of safeguarding human rights. Therefore, the state needs to maintain the equity and welfare of education, especially of compulsory education, with public resources. Only if these actions are taken can the people, especially the poorest people, be released from worrying about their children's educational future. And education, the groundwork of people's livelihood, would be solidified permanently.

Third, a broad educational philosophy and a guideline for coordinated and balanced development should be set. We need not only the traditional knowledge education, degree education, and standard education, but also the skill education, non-degree education and non-standard education that are all in great demand. Therefore, it is very necessary to set a broad educational philosophy, and promote rapid development of all kinds of vocational skill education, non-degree education and non-standard education according to the guidelines of coordinated and balanced development. Provided that the whole population attaches importance to education and could receive education during their lifetime, the country would achieve great development.

Fourth, the Chinese government needs to increase its commitment and give prominence to education. The financial outlays for education should reach 4 percent of GDP as soon as possible and reach 5 percent earlier than is currently planned. Compulsory education should be the main focus and keystone for the distribution of the financial outlays for education. The government should be responsible for guaranteeing the general suitability and absolute equity of compulsory education. At the same time, the government should give proper support to non-compulsory education after distinguishing its differences.

Fifth, continue to combine the government and the people in the education system. Historically the government has taken sole responsibility for education, but as both the demands for education and the diversity of those demands are steadily expanded, it is necessary to track along the road of combining the government with the people. The government should not only increase its devotion to education, but also mobilize the people, society, and enterprises to invest in education through corresponding policies and institutional guarantees. Examples of such policies include annulling the proviso for educational investment, attracting domestic and foreign capital to jumpstart the education industry, guiding the enterprises to become the main body of continuous educational investment for laborers by tax privilege, safeguarding the due rights and interests of private education institutions with regulations, and encouraging all circles to endow educational undertakings. Only by sufficiently mobilizing the enthusiasm of the people, enterprises and society to participate in education can we achieve greater and better development of the educational cause.

Sixth, differentiate the problems by type of institution, administrative levels, and school levels and then provide solutions to them. The Chinese educational system is facing an era of great development with the transition from welfare education to a mixed-plural education system. There are many challenges and problems to be settled in the transitional process. In my point of view, differentiating them by types, levels and classes will be the most effective method of addressing the problems. On the one hand, classification of responsibilities by administrative levels should be established. The government surely acts as a guarantor of educational welfare. However in addition, the local government should be established as the first guarantor, and the central government should be established as the last. On the other hand, the different types of educational institutions should be treated differently whether they are public or private, knowledge-based or skill-based, degree or non-degree, and standard or non-standard because they have different goals. For example, the public colleges where continuous education and adult education are held should not be profitable institutions. Sorting by institution types helps to institutionalize the operating behaviors of educational institutions. In addition, clearly differentiating the goals between education levels is also necessary. Doctorial education should be the most rigorous; master's level education should be somewhat less rigorous; undergraduate education should be somewhat more general; senior secondary school education should focus on broad skills; the nine-year compulsory education should focus on basic skills; and the kinds of continuous education and adult education should depend on the social and nongovernmental resources.

In conclusion, education is the essential premise for all people who want to have a foothold in society and also the basic foundation for the development of a country. The financial support from the government, human capital investment from enterprises, and educational commitment for children from families have all become important sources of human capital investment in China. Owing to a steadily increasing financial commitment from the government, the welfare aspects of the system have been maintained. Educational devotion from families and individuals increases steadily, which further shows the importance of human capital investment. Chinese education is now in its crucial period and there are many challenges and difficulties to which the government needs to respond urgently through adopting a better development philosophy and further reforming the system.

NOTES

1. The author wishes to acknowledge the Project for New Century Excellent Talents in Universities of the Ministry of Education of the People's Republic of China and to thank the Ministry of Education for its generous support for this research.
2. G. Chow is an economics professor at Princeton University in the USA.
3. J. Heckman is a famous economist, professor at the University of Chicago, and winner of the Nobel Prize in 2000.
4. The author calculates these figures by referring to outlay for education in all sorts of schools in the *China Statistical Yearbook, 2001* (edited by National Bureau of Statistics of China, 2001).
5. Result of survey on the basic education funds in 50 counties publicized by the National Audit Office, on the official website 22 June 2004.

REFERENCES

Cheng, G. (2003), 'The per capita public educational fund for pupils and secondary school students has taken on a tendency to decline', China Youth Online Website, 27 August.

Erdong (2004), 'Enterprises' human capital investment is seriously insufficient', *Market Newspaper*, 29 November.

He, Q. (2004), 'The bottleneck for Chinese development – the distorted distribution of educational resource', Guangming Website, 13 July.

Li, S. and J. Zhang (2003), *Would Education be Able to Supply the Adequate Human Resources for All-Around Well-Off Society?*, Xinhua Press.

Liu S. (2004), 'Report of Ministry of Labor and Security shows that there are more chances for the junior secondary school level than the college level', *The Chinese Youth Newspaper*, 23 July.

Luo J. (2004), 'Yu Minhong – seeking hope from desperation, that life will be splendid', *People of Beida*, 27 January.

Ministry of Education (2003), 'Ministry of Education responded to the reporters on compulsory education and educational commitment', *People's Daily*, 3 November.

Ministry of Education (2004), 'The circumstances of educational reform, development and financial commitment', 6, January.

Ministry of Labor and Social Security Department (2004), published on 12 July.

National Audit Office (2004), on the official website, 22 June.

National Bureau of Statistics of China (2001), *China Statistical Yearbook*, China Statistical Press.

National Bureau of Statistics of China (2003), *Summary of China Statistical Yearbook, 2003*, China Statistical Press, p. 23.

National Bureau of Statistics of China (2003), *Summary of China Statistical Yearbook, 2003*, China Statistical Press, p. 174.

Wen, Z. (2004) 'Tuition will increase again and how much is the cost for training an undergraduate to the end?', *The China Youth Daily*, 23 July.

Yin, H. and H. Wu (2004), 'Educational expenditure has become the second item for urban Chinese residents', *Xinhua Net*, 17 February.

Yu, B. (2002), 'Education: Achilles' heel?', *The 21st Century Business Herald*, 31 December.

PART TWO

Market Development and Sources of Growth

5. Political Economy of Labor Retrenchment: Evidence Based on China's State-Owned Enterprises

Yifan Hu, Sonja Opper and Sonia M.L. Wong

1. INTRODUCTION

In the transformation economies of the post-Soviet era, enterprises often found themselves with a significant stock of surplus labor created by central labor allocation and full employment guarantees under the socialist system. Employment restructuring thus became one of the major objectives of enterprise reform in all of these economies. To improve their performance, enterprises not only had to adjust their product assortment in response to consumer preferences and rapidly changing market conditions, but also had to optimize factor inputs. Labor reforms usually started with the promulgation of flexible labor regulations and laws. Highly variable progress within employment restructuring suggests that the formal provision of market-oriented labor laws and regulations serves as a necessary, but not sufficient, condition for successful labor restructuring. Labor retrenchment commonly encounters complex and multifaceted constraints, with political–economic constraints among the crucial determinants of their success (Fleisher and Yang, 2003).

Among China's state-owned enterprises (SOEs), inertia in the labor retrenchment effort has been marked. SOEs were granted some formal autonomy in labor decisions in the mid-1980s but did not undertake any significant labor restructuring until the mid-1990s. Although SOE profits fell by 50 percent between 1994 and 1996, they failed to restructure in any significant sense. In fact, the size of the total SOE work force increased slightly (see Table 5.1).

Many observers have identified continuing government interference in labor decisions as a major cause of China's slow SOE labor restructuring. Groves et al. (1995) offer evidence that increasing de facto managerial independence from political control in labor decisions was positively related

Table 5.1: *Main Indicators of State-Owned Enterprises in China, 1990–2002*

	Main Indicators of State-Owned and State-Holding Industrial Enterprises					
	[a]No. of firms	[b]Gross industrial output value	[c]Value added of industry	[d]Total profit	[e]No. of workers	[f]Labor productivity
1990	74 775	12 570		388	10 346	12 150
1991	75 248	13 934	4 019	402	10 664	13 066
1992	74 066	16 711	5 193	535	10 889	15 346
1993	80 586	22 088	7 281	817	10 920	20 227
1994	79 731	25 301	7 903	829	11 214	22 562
1995	87 905	25 890	8 307	666	11 261	22 991
1996	86 982	27 289	8 742	413	11 244	24 270
1997	74 388	27 859	9 193	428	11 044	25 225
1998	64 737	33 621	11 077	525	9 058	37 118
1999	61 301	35 571	12 132	998	8 572	41 497
2000	53 489	40 554	13 778	2 408	8 102	50 055
2001	46 767	42 408	14 652	2 389	7 640	55 508
2002	41 125	45 179	15 935	2 633	7 163	63 073

Notes:
[a] All data before 1994 include SOEs only.
[b] Data are expressed in units of 100 million RMB. The gross industrial output value in 1995 was calculated in accordance with new stipulations.
[c] Data are expressed in units of 100 million RMB.
[d] Data are expressed in units of 100 million RMB.
[e] Data are expressed in units of 10 000 workers.
[f] Data are in terms of yuan per person per year. The overall labor productivity between 1994 and 1995 is incomparable because of a new definition of gross industrial output value.

Source: *China Statistical Yearbook* (various issues).

to labor productivity and enterprise performance in China's SOEs from 1980 to 1989. This result confirms the existence of political control in SOEs' labor decisions. Dong and Putterman (2002) further establish that hardening budget constraints, without relieving SOEs of their social burden, was a major proximate cause of rising redundant labor in the early 1990s. Bai et al. (2002) argue that China delayed ownership reforms of SOEs because the central government wanted to use SOEs as policy tools to provide exaggerated levels of employment when alternative institutions for social welfare provision (unemployment benefits) had yet to be established.

Because of increasing financial losses and growing enterprise debts incurred by SOEs, in 1997 China's central government pledged to reverse SOEs' money-losing trends within a three-year period, with labor retrenchment as one of the reform measures. More importantly, while western-style outright privatization was not feasible for ideological reasons, the central government took a major step in intensifying corporatization and partial privatization of large-scale SOEs within the framework of the Modern Enterprise System (*xiandai qiye zhidu*), the core objective of which was to separate government from enterprises (*zhengqi fenkai*) so as to reduce direct political interference in SOE's decision-making. Pursuant with these strategic SOEs reforms, the government took several steps in order to deal with the expected increase of laid-off workers. Core measures included an increase in financial assistance, extended labor reemployment services for displaced workers, and financial support to strengthen the newly established social security system (Dong, 2003).

Within four years (1997–2000), the state sector's work force decreased by more than 30 million workers (about 27 percent), and labor productivity increased by 100 percent (see Table 5.1). In spite of significant progress in labor retrenchment as signaled by aggregate data, however, little systematic research has been conducted to examine the underlying causal patterns and determinants of the recent restructuring wave. There are many questions that deserve attention, such as: Which SOEs successfully took on the challenge of restructuring? Are SOEs following economic reasoning in their labor decisions? Can we still observe evidence of government control in SOEs' labor decisions? Did corporatization actually tie the government's hands and end political interference in the labor decisions of corporatized SOEs compared to traditional SOEs?

Based on data obtained from a World Bank survey, this chapter investigates the major driving forces of labor restructuring among China's corporatized and traditional SOEs from 1998 to 2000. Specifically, we examine how the degree of labor retrenchment is related to a set of business-related and political–economic determinants. To the best of our knowledge, our study is among the first micro-level studies to investigate the causal pattern of labor restructuring during the most recent SOE reforms. Empirical evidence on this issue will provide some insights on the nature of labor policies and on the nexus between government and these two types of SOEs in China's increasingly market-oriented economy. An understanding of these issues in China is critical, since the government is determined to maintain SOEs as an important part of the economic system and labor restructuring in China's SOEs is still an unfinished endeavor. Furthermore, our comparative analysis of labor decisions in both traditional and corporatized SOEs will also shed some light on the unresolved but important issue of whether China's corporatization strategy with only partial privatization actually accomplished the intended separation of government and enterprises. If we can still observe evidence of government control of labor decisions in corporatized SOEs, this would indicate that corporatization is an insufficient means to separate government from enterprises. If, on the other hand, our results show evidence of political control only in traditional SOEs, this would support China's corporatization without privatization strategy as a feasible depolicitization method, at least in the critical labor restructuring decision. In this sense, our study also nurtures the ownership debate around the question of whether full-scale privatization or corporatization is necessary for successful SOE reforms.[1]

The chapter is structured as follows. The next section provides a brief account of China's labor market reforms since 1978 and the specific institutional background of SOEs' employment restructuring in the late 1990s. Section 3 discusses the potential determinants of an SOE's labor policies and sets out our hypotheses. Section 4 presents our estimation model and results. Section 5 concludes.

2.   LABOR MARKET REFORMS AND SOE REFORMS: THE INSTITUTIONAL BACKGROUND AND STATUS QUO

Before reform, labor in China was directly allocated to SOEs. In return, SOEs had to fulfill production quotas specified by production plans and had to provide workers with comprehensive benefit packages including subsidized housing, education, health care, and retirement pensions. Following the introduction of industrial reforms in the early 1980s, a 'dual-track transition' of the labor market was instituted. Free labor markets were developed in the newly emerging non-state sector, while SOEs continued to perform the dual tasks of producing goods and providing social welfare and only gradually acquired the formal right to make independent employment decisions according to their production needs (Bai et al., 2002).

A first important breakthrough in the liberalization of the labor system was achieved in 1986, when the labor contract system (*laodong hetongzhi*) was introduced on a pilot basis to replace socialist-style lifelong employment in SOEs. In addition, SOEs' directors/managers acquired the right to conduct entrance examinations to screen promising job applicants, to refuse ill-qualified applicants and to institute a probation period for new hires. To stave off opposition of the new system, it was first applied only to new hires; it became universal only in 1996. As a consequence, the move toward contract-based labor proceeded slowly. By the end of 1995, only 40 percent of SOE employees were working under the new system, while complete implementation of the system was not realized until 2000 (China's Labor Statistics Yearbook, various years).

In 1992 the 'regulations for the transformation of enterprise mechanisms of state-owned enterprises' were promulgated. Article 17 gave management the formal rights to make decisions autonomously about 'conditions and type of employment as well as the number of employees' for the first time. Central plans for labor allocation were abolished in 1993.

The implementation of China's Labor Law in 1995 was probably the most important legal reform, as this law formally grants all enterprises, including SOEs, legal rights to restructure and to eliminate excessive labor. The liberalizing effect of the law rests on three crucial provisions, which facilitate adjustment and restructuring decisions: (1) the general application of labor contracts with time limits (Article 19); (2) agreements on probation periods (Article 21); and, most important, (3) the right to cut down on manpower when an enterprise runs into economic difficulties (Article 27). In particular, the latter provision introduces new flexibility for timely labor adjustments in response to an enterprise's order situation and profitability. As labor relations between employers and employees are legally specified, and labor contracts can be terminated by both sides, the law formally finalized the break with China's 'iron rice bowl'. Authority over labor decisions was formally transferred from the state to enterprise managers in all enterprises, including SOEs.

Despite a wide range of policy measures introduced to reform SOEs, up to the mid-1990s the dismissal of state employees remained a rarity, and most SOEs still provided non-wage welfare benefits (Dong, 2003). Zhang (1994) reports that only 2 percent of SOEs made use of their formal rights to terminate labor contracts. Based on a panel data set of 681 SOEs in four provinces (Jiangsu, Sichuan, Shanxi, and Jilin), Dong and Putterman (2002) confirm that SOE managers' ability to perform downward adjustment of the labor force remained seriously limited until 1994. Bodmer (2002) documents the degree and the effects of labor reforms in Chinese SOEs up to 1994 and concludes that reforms relevant to employment decisions remained very limited in scope. In conclusion, ample evidence shows that a large proportion of SOEs have failed to restructure and remain burdened by excess manpower and low productivity.

The lack of effective labor restructuring up to the mid-1990s has been largely attributed to the continued political control of SOEs' decision-making (Groves et al., 1995; Bai et al., 2002; Dong and Putterman, 2002). Unlike most of the other transitional economies, China's government, until mid-1990s, did not follow the so-called property-approach in reforming the state-owned sector but relied on a distinct reform path of the market-oriented approach which relied on fostering market development and granting decision-making autonomy for managers/directors of SOEs in order to turn SOEs into competitive economic entities. The results were not encouraging, however. Continuing soft budget constraints and multi-level principal–agent relationships weakened both the management's incentives and capacity to react to market signals. Political interference lingered in decision-making of China's SOEs, particularly in labor decisions, either due to the efforts of political elite to preserve their traditional base of political support (Opper et al., 2003) or as a mechanism to control agency problems (Bai et al., 2002; Chang and Wong, 2004).

In the late 1990s the heavily indebted and ailing state sector forced the government to address the labor redundancy problem. Two strategies have been adopted. First, the central government allowed SOEs to reduce part of their surplus labor. The government's commitment to improving SOE performance through labor restructuring is illustrated by its increasing provision of financial assistance and labor reemployment services for displaced workers. Secondly, the government launched the corporatization and partial privatization of large-scale SOEs within the new framework of the Modern Enterprise System. Based on the legal foundation established by China's Company Law in July 1994, enterprises were transformed into shareholding enterprises either as limited liability companies or stock companies. Enterprises registered under the law gained the status of independent legal business entities modeled after the Western-style corporation in which the Board of Directors and managers enjoy control rights over operational and strategic enterprise decisions, whereas shareholders exert their property rights through shareholder meetings. In order to reduce arbitrary political interference in company decisions, the law specifies no privileges for the state as a shareholder and grants equal rights to state and non-state shareholders. Although the state maintained a dominant shareholding in most of the corporatized SOEs, the state's decision-making rights were formally reduced because the state representatives have to share their control rights with other shareholders and are supposed to rely on the general shareholder meetings to exert the state's shareholder rights. Increasing profit incentives are introduced through non-state shareholders who usually act under harder budget-constraints and hence have a stronger profit orientation. According to the government's reform intention, corporatization of SOEs should improve SOE's performance by simultaneously introducing stronger profit motives and reduced political control in comparison to the traditional SOEs.

3. WHEN DO STATE-OWNED ENTERPRISES RESTRUCTURE? SOME POLITICAL ECONOMY CONSIDERATIONS AND HYPOTHESES

In a neoclassical world, an enterprise's labor input would be calculated based on a production function, input prices, and expected sales, while flexible labor markets would guarantee smooth adjustment processes. SOEs, however, seldom operate as independent business entities responding only to market forces. This is because politicians tend to use them to enhance their political support (Buchanan et al., 1980; Shleifer and Vishny, 1994).[2] This tendency is particularly strong in socialist systems and is especially pronounced in China because China's danwei-socialism guaranteed urban SOE workers not only lifetime employment but also a wide range of benefits such as inexpensive housing, free medical care, and diverse types of subsidies and in-kind payments (Naughton, 1997). SOE workers were thus naturally reluctant to accept market-based labor reforms. Dong and Ye (2003) offer evidence that employees of loss-making enterprises in China tended to cling to their jobs, preferring to take wage cuts than to change jobs. Workers frequently expressed their discontent through protests and strikes (Lee, 1998) as well as through 'collective inaction' in the form of noncompliance, absenteeism, and evasion (Whyte, 1987; Zhou, 1993; Lee, 1998). Protests and strikes often compelled the government to pressure enterprise managers to hire extra workers or to refrain from imposing additional layoffs, whereas collective inaction generated direct pressure on managers because managers' performance is dependent on workers' cooperation (Whyte, 1987; Lee, 1998).

The Chinese Communist government, on the other hand, is inclined to continue danwei-socialism to secure social support (Opper, et al., 2002). Although the theory of political business cycles has been developed largely with reference to democratic political systems, the general idea that politicians' survival rests on public support also holds for autocratic regimes. Even China's one-party regime needs to respond to major interest groups, such as the urban working class, if political stability and the immediate survival of the political leadership are to be secured.[3] Using SOEs to keep redundant labor seemed particularly important during the early transition period when a sustainable social security system was not yet in place and the newly emerging private sector lacked the capacity to absorb excessive labor (Bai et al., 2002).

The political use of SOEs as an employment tool is mainly due to a beneficial cost–benefit calculus. Despite the political benefits, the use of SOEs as an employment provision tool is not without costs. The most obvious constraining factor will be the distraction from enterprise performance caused by over-employment. Politicians benefit from the asymmetric distribution of costs and benefits when making political use of SOEs. While politicians and affected workers receive most of the benefits of intervention directly and without delay (for example for politicians, increased support from favoured groups and for workers job security), the costs of political interference are socialized over the whole population via tax increases or bank loans. In some cases, costs are even transferred to future generations by increasing state debts. Hence, the inclination for politicians to actually use SOEs as an employment provision tool is high.

Nonetheless, the social burdens in the form of budgetary deficits and non-performing bank debt may accumulate and eventually place a limit on the political uses of enterprises. In China, the governments had to extend an increasing amount of subsidies to the loss-making SOEs. During the period 1996–99, the total amount of subsidies was 103.94 billion yuan, which was 44 percent of the income taxes collected from SOEs. At the end of 1990s, the state-owned banking sector, which had been charged with the responsibility of providing funding for SOEs, was laden with non-performing loans as high as 40 percent (Wong and Wong, 2001). These financial burdens exerted strong pressure on the government to reduce the level of excessive employment in SOEs in order to reverse SOEs' money-losing trend.

The second cost-component in using SOEs as an employment device includes execution and monitoring costs, which in turn are affected by two determinants. The first are the formal control rights of the government and the second is the incentive of SOEs to comply with the government's wishes. Regarding the formal control rights of government, Sappington and Stiglitz (1987) conclude that the state's residual rights of control reduce politicians' transaction costs when intervening in SOEs. In an extension of this argument Shleifer (1998) makes the case that residual rights of control reduce the costs involved in changing the pattern and strategy of political interventions. The execution and monitoring costs of intervention would therefore vary with the relative amount of state shares. Governments tend to enjoy a more favorable cost–benefit calculus in traditional SOEs, in which the governments hold 100 percent of the shares and hence enjoy full control rights, than in corporatized SOEs, where the state shareholders have to share their control rights with other shareholders (Shelifer and Vishny, 1994).

Given the same capacity for politicians to exercise political control over enterprise decisions, the incentive of SOEs to comply with the government's wishes is another determinant of the execution and monitoring costs. Bai et al. (2002) formally build a theoretical model, which demonstrates that government has to provide weak profit incentives to managers in SOEs in order to induce the managers to keep excessive labor. Their study implies that an increase in profit incentives for SOEs may lead to higher resistance to a political request to use SOEs to provide excessive employment. Shleifer's and Vishny's (1994) model on political interventions in enterprise decisions further suggests that partial privatization of SOEs may increase the costs of political interference, since non-state owners tend to have stronger profit motives and will therefore ask for compensation for negative performance effects. This incentive-argument further strengthens the assumption that governments tend to enjoy lower costs when interfering in traditional SOEs and corporatized SOEs.

Based on the above theoretical considerations, we discuss and develop hypotheses on three major political-economic determinants that are likely to have affected the payoffs for using SOEs as employment provision in the late 1990s: We take into account enterprise performance and government fiscal conditions as central determinants of the costs of intervention, and local absorption capacity for laid-off workers as a major determinant of the expected political benefits from interference. Since traditional and corporatized SOEs are associated with different cost–benefit ratios, due to differing shareholding and incentive structures, we differentiate between these two types of SOEs when formulating our hypotheses.

3.1. Enterprise Performance

With the central government's call to turn around the loss-making state sector, governments and managers of both traditional and corporatized SOEs came under increasing pressure to improve enterprises' performance in the late 1990s. One of the most commonly adopted and effective short-term strategies is the cutting of redundant labor because this can reduce labor costs without affecting production capacity and sales (Denis and Kruse, 2000; Kang and Shivdasani, 1997). Such an adjustment mechanism is applicable to both types of SOEs.

We expect a negative relation between enterprise performance and labor retrenchment in traditional SOEs for two reasons. First, poorly performing SOEs usually imply a higher burden in terms of subsidies and bad loans and thus incur higher costs when used as employment provision tools. Second, the central government's specific objective of the three-year program was to turn the loss-making SOEs into profit-making ones. As a consequence, special incentives were created for local governments to allow the poorly performing SOEs, particularly the loss-making ones, to cut more excessive labor while the good performers had to maintain a higher amount of excess labor. This strategy helped to improve the profitability of the loss-making SOEs and increased the total number of profit-making SOEs, while the government could still provide a certain amount of excessive employment.

The reasoning of local governments given above is also applicable to the corporatized SOEs. Though governments tend to enjoy less control and therefore have a lower capacity to directly influence decision-making in these enterprises, the introduction of non-state shareholders and the liability for profits and losses should boost the profit incentives of managers and shareholders in corporatized SOEs. Subsequently, enhanced profit incentives should increase the extent of labor restructuring in poorly performing corporatized SOEs.

Our hypothesis on the relation between enterprise performance and labor retrenchment in traditional and corporatized SOEs is

II1:   The degree of labor retrenchment is negatively related to firm performance in both traditional and corporatized SOEs.

3.2. Government's Fiscal Position

The fact that government interference in labor decisions affects government budget position by increasing expenditures (e.g. subsidies to SOEs) and decreasing revenues (e.g. tax income) suggests that a government's fiscal capacity will limit its ability to fund excessive employment (Sheifer and Vishny, 1994).[4] A tight fiscal position (i.e. a high budget deficit) might increase the government's willingness to accept politically unpopular labor retrenchment, since labor shedding and the concomitant improvement in financial performance brings financial release via tax increases and subsidy reduction (Li, 1998). On the other hand, governments with favorable fiscal conditions can afford to keep more excess labor.

As we discussed earlier, governments enjoy favorable execution and monitoring costs in traditional SOEs because of their full ownership and the managers' relatively weak profit incentives. As a result, we expect that the government can flexibly adjust its interventions in accordance with the current status of the fiscal budget conditions. Governments, on the other hand, face relatively unfavorable conditions for interventions in corporatized SOEs due to lower direct control rights and stronger resistance from profit-oriented non-state shareholders against the provision of excessive employment. As a result, we expect that local governments are not able to flexibly influence labor decisions in corporatized SOEs in accordance with the current budget conditions. We therefore expect:

H2:   The government's budget is negatively related to the degree of labor retrenchment in traditional SOEs but not related to the degree of labor retrenchment in corporatized SOEs.

3.3.   Absorption Capacity of Laid-Off Workers

While early models of political business cycles assumed that a government's incentives and expected benefits from inducing political cycles do not vary over time, more recent research has revealed that the expected benefits for manipulating the economy should be negatively correlated with the level of the government's political security and the size of the support base (Schultz, 1995). As low reemployment possibilities for surplus workers increase workers' resistance to labor retrenchment and weaken a government's political security and support base, a government will benefit more (politically) by funding a certain level of excess labor if reemployment possibilities for surplus worker are low. In contrast, a government will benefit less (politically) by funding a certain level of excess labor if reemployment possibilities are high. The local absorption capacity for surplus labor actually turned out to be the government's major political concern in China. Under the slogan 'making a channel before the water comes', the government sought to ensure the existence of alternative employment chances before workers were laid-off from SOEs (Hassard et al., 2002).

The expected negative relation between labor retrenchment and local re-employment conditions reflects a government's calculus to maintain social stability. Whether we can observe this negative relation once again depends crucially on the amount of execution and monitoring costs involved. Due to favorable cost conditions in traditional SOEs, we hypothesize a strong dependence on the local labor market in traditional SOEs. On the other hand, local governments are less likely to influence the labor retrenchment decisions of the corporatized SOEs in accordance with the local re-employment conditions because of their relatively unfavorable intervention cost conditions. We therefore hypothesize:

H3:   The absorption capacity of labor market is negatively related to the degree of labor retrenchment in traditional SOEs but not related to the degree of labor retrenchment in corporatized SOEs.

4.   DATA AND METHODS

4.1.   Data and Variables

4.1.1.   Data sources and sample enterprises

The empirical data for our research comes from a World Bank survey of China's enterprises. It covers 323 SOEs, of which 197 are traditional and 126 are corporatized. The sample enterprises are randomly drawn from ten sectors in five cities. A summary of enterprise distributions across sectors and cities is shown in Table 5.2.

In Table 5.2, the five cities are Beijing, Chengdu, Guangzhou, Shanghai, and Tianjin, covering the capital city (Beijing), the municipalities in the highly developed eastern coastal belt (Guangzhou, Shanghai, and Tianjin) as well as the central region (Chengdu). The chosen locations also represent different levels of market reforms, with Shanghai and Guangzhou representing the most developed regions in economic liberalization and financial development, and Tianjin and Chengdu representing a national base of SOEs concentrating in heavy industry.

The ten sectors include five service sectors – accounting, advertising and marketing, business logistics, communication, and information technology – and five manufacturing sectors – apparel and leather goods, consumer goods, electronic equipment, electronic components, and vehicles and vehicle parts. The chosen sectors represent fast-growing and relatively technologically advanced portions of China's industry.

The data set provides us with a broad variety of enterprise-level data, which allows us to measure the most important business-related determinants of labor policy choices. We complement the data set with socioeconomic regional data to cover potential political–economic determinants of employment restructuring. The socioeconomic data are derived from China's Labor Statistics Yearbook and the China Statistical Yearbook.

4.1.2.   Dependent variables

We construct the labor retrenchment rate variable as a direct measure with which to investigate how SOEs are tackling the surplus labor issue. The variable is defined as the ratio of a labor reduction in the current period to the total work force of the preceding period. Accordingly, the labor retrenchment rate is positive if an enterprise reduces the number of workers it employs in the current period and negative if it increases the number.

Table 5.2: Sample Distribution (323 State-Owned Enterprises)

Sectors[*]/ Cities	Beijing	Chenngdu	Guangzhou	Shanghai	Tianjin
Accounting services (15)	2	5	2	3	3
Advert. and mkt. (20)	1	4	2	10	3
Apparel/ Leather goods (50)	11	12	6	12	9
Business logistics services (52)	9	13	12	10	8
Comm. services (20)	5	1	6	4	4
Consumer products (18)	1	8	1	5	3
Electronic comps. (37)	18	10	1	2	6
Electronic equip. (39)	10	8	3	8	10
Info. tech. services (22)	3	2	6	4	7
Vehicles/ Vehicle parts (50)	8	15	7	11	9
Total (323)	68	78	46	69	62

Note: * Number of observations in each sector is in parentheses.

4.1.3. Explanatory variables

Enterprise performance. We employ two alternative variables – sales revenue and profit – to measure enterprise performance. These variables are deflated by industrial price indices created by the *China Statistical Yearbook* and are transformed into logistic form.

We first estimate a baseline model using the current value of the two performance variables alternately as the determinant. We use current performance because labor adjustments, in comparison with capital adjustments, are usually short-term responses that can react more quickly and directly to performance.

Local government's fiscal position. To approximate the government's financial leverage, we focus on the ratio of the balance of the government's budget (total government revenue minus total government expenditure) to gross domestic product (GDP). It is assumed that governments with a budget deficit are more likely to refrain from employing SOEs as employment provision tools than governments with a balanced budget or a surplus.

Absorption capacity for laid-off workers. We use two proxies to capture the local absorption capacity for laid-off workers. First, we calculate the current ratio of reemployed laid-off workers to laid-off workers who have not been reemployed. Second, we use employment growth rates in the private sector, including foreign-involved enterprises. The private sector was formally promoted as a convenient channel for absorbing redundant workers and farmers in late 1990s and is closely correlated with local growth and development. The two proxies for reemployment chances are constructed at the city level.

4.1.4. Control variables

Some factors can jointly affect labor retrenchment and our explanatory variables. We introduce five control variables to capture possible confounding effects. The first control variable is enterprise age. Older enterprises with a long tradition in the planning apparatus are subject to stronger political control and interference owing to their established and stable network relationships with the government administration. At the same time, age is likely to be negatively related to the extent of an SOE's work force adjustment, because older SOEs tend to have a higher level of organizational inertia. We therefore introduce the variable of SOE age to eliminate the possible confounding age effect.

We also use an SOE's total work force in the previous year to control for SOE size. A large work force may be connected to a higher degree of underemployment and therefore to higher potential for labor retrenchment than a smaller work force. On the other hand, SOE size may be negatively related to the degree of labor retrenchment because there is a cost advantage for the government in using larger SOEs to provide employment. Assuming that a local government decides 5000 positions for underemployed workers need to be secured. The first option would be to bargain with ten enterprises, each with 5000 employees, to convince each to keep ten percent of its redundant workers. The second option would be to bargain with 100 enterprises, each with 500 employees, to convince each to keep 10 percent of its redundant workers. Clearly, transaction costs would be much higher for option two. This assumption is consistent with the finding that the privatization of large enterprises in Central Eastern European countries is shaped by political–economic determinants, while progress in the privatization of small enterprises is unaffected by such determinants (Opper, 2004). We therefore introduce the size of an SOE's work force in the previous period to capture the conflicting effects associated with SOE size.

The third control variable is unionization rate, defined as the proportion of workers joining unions in different regions, to capture the bargaining position of workers vis à vis the government and managers. According to Olson (1968) we may expect that underemployed workers could articulate their interests more effectively and could weaken a government's public support base if they were better organized. Although China's labor unions have historically been subordinated to the interests of the Chinese Communist Party and therefore lack an independent voice comparable to that of unions in capitalist economies, unions are nevertheless the only organization in China that hold a pro-worker stance. We therefore control for the unionization rate to remove the possible confounding effect.

We also introduce a set of industrial dummies as control variables in our specification. On the one hand, industrial sectors may be burdened with underemployment to varying degrees because the government has fostered various national and local industrial policies since 1989. On the other hand, industrial sectors may be correlated with our hypothesized political-economic determinants. For example, different industries are likely to be associated with different market competition conditions and varying enterprise performance. Finally, year dummies are introduced to capture potential year-specific business cycle effects.

4.2. Model Specification

We use the following model to estimate the determinants of labor retrenchment:

$$Y_{it} = \alpha + \beta\, X_{it} + \delta\, CONTROL_{it} + \eta\, Sector + \theta\, Year + \varepsilon_{it} \qquad (5.1)$$

where i and t represent enterprise i and period t respectively; ε_{it} is the error term. Y is a measure of labor retrenchment ratio, and the vector X contains variables for enterprise performance, government fiscal condition and absorption capacity of laid-off workers. *CONTROL* is a set of control variables including the lagged labor sizes, firm age and unionization rate as described in Section 4.1. While *Sector* represents a set of industry dummies to control the variation across industries, *Year* denotes year dummies to capture the business cycle and macroeconomic development over years.

We estimated Equation (5.1) by using robust OLS,[5] which weighs the sample outliers to make the estimation less sensitive to measurement errors. We also used White-corrected standard errors to deal with potential problem of heteroskedasticity. The robust OLS regression results serve as our benchmark estimators.

4.3. Endogeneity Issues

An important estimation issue we might face is the potential endogeneity of enterprise performance. An underlying assumption of our model is that weak enterprise performance leads to labor retrenchment. However, as performance determines labor decisions, labor decisions could also affect enterprise performance. We recognize that endogeneity, or reverse causality, could be an important concern in studies analysing the linkage between performance and labor retrenchment, but we expect it is less of a problem to our specific analysis. Specifically, for the first performance variable of sales revenue, a reduction in an enterprise's excessive labor might not affect the sales volume in the short run because excessive labor is less likely to affect production capacity or promotional activities. For the second performance variable of profit, a reduction in labor redundancy is likely to improve the enterprise's profit, so the effect of labor reduction on profit is positive, which is the opposite of our hypothesized negative effect of profit on labor reduction in our model. In sum, the endogeneity problem might not cause a serious identification problem for our estimation. Thus we directly use the current values of two performance variables in our regressions as the benchmark cases.

Although the endogeneity problem of performance variables might not be serious in our case, we nevertheless attempted to deal with this issue by using instrument variables that were highly correlated with firm performance but uncorrelated to labor retrenchment. We used two sets of instrument variables for our study. First, a natural candidate for the instrument is the one-year lagged enterprise performance, since the pre-determined variable is highly correlated to the current performance, but unaffected by the current labor decision. Meanwhile a competition variable is also correlated with the current performance but unaffected by the current labor decision. Accordingly we applied two instruments – the one-year lagged performance and competition variable proxied by the entry cost of a firm's major business lines – as our first attempt to deal with endogeneity.

Second, we used a set of more general instruments to further examine the robustness of our results. Our instruments include five variables: (1) wage as an indicator of productivity;[6] (2) the ratio of engineers to total employees as an indicator of a firm's technological level; (3) debt–equity ratio as an indicator of a firm's finance source and capital structure; (4) location in an industry park as an indicator of the cluster effect on firm performance; and (5) entry cost as an indicator of competition environment. We expect these five variables to be highly correlated to firm performance but less likely to labor retrenchment rate.

5.   EMPIRICAL RESULTS

5.1.   Descriptive Statistics and Sample Data

Tables 5.3 and 5.4 show the descriptive statistics of variables included in our regression model. Three facts stand out in comparing statistics from traditional and corporatized SOEs. First, for corporatized SOEs, the number of workers and amount of capital, on average, are 1180 workers and 247 million RMB, while traditional SOEs have almost twice as many workers and twice as much capital. Consistent with the official policy of 'seizing the big and relieving the small' (*zhua da fang xiao*), partial privatization and corporatization in China was first confined to relatively small SOEs. Second, corporatized SOEs are much younger than traditional SOEs, with an average age of 20.97 and 28.39 years, respectively. Finally, the return on assets (ROA) of corporatized SOEs is three times that of traditional SOEs, although the value of sales and profits in corporatized SOEs is less than that of traditional SOEs.

Between 1998 and 2000, the sampled SOEs cut on average 4.3 percent of their work force per year, whereas the degree of labor reduction in traditional SOEs was slightly higher (4.7 percent) than in corporatized SOEs (3.8 percent). The difference in work force reduction between traditional and corporatized SOEs is consistent with the fact that corporatized SOEs usually succeed in reducing redundant labor when they undergo corporatization.

The fiscal position to GDP ratio on average is negative, although the size of the budget deficit is moderate (around 1.44 percent). The deficit size is moderate when compared to international standards, but may still turn out to be a critical constraint for local bureaucrats and governments whose performance is judged mainly by local economic indicators, including fiscal conditions. Furthermore, local governments have no access to cross-regional transfer payments if the local tax base deteriorates and their chances to obtain additional funding from the state-owned banking sector weakened in the late 1990s when the central government strengthened its control over the state-owned banks, which had accumulated a high

Table 5.3: Summary Statistics (by SOE Type)

Variable Name	All SOEs	Traditional SOEs	Corporatized SOEs
Labor Retrenchment			
Labor retrenchment	4.37[a]	4.71	3.80
rate (%)	(896)[b]	(562)	(364)
	[20.84][c]	[19.67]	[22.69]
Enterprise Production and Performance			
No. of employees	1 180	1 412	805.5
	(944)	(583)	(361)
	[5 000]	[6 191]	[1 815]
Capital in 1000 RMB	247 173	324 173	126 114
	(962)	(588)	(374)
	[1 793 799]	[21 289 970]	[847 683]
Age of enterprise in	25.5	28.39	20.97
years	(966)	(590)	(376)
	[20.5]	[20.72]	[19.23]
Sales revenue in 1000	102 217	125 726	64 564
RMB	(947)	(583)	(364)
	[487 394]	[594 325]	[224 597]
Profit in 1000 RMB	19 975	23 084	14 981
	(927)	(583)	(353)
	[177 922]	[215 738]	[88 140]
Return on asset (ROA)	1.55	0.89	2.62
ratio	(938)	(580)	(358)
	[10.96]	[8.55]	[13.94]

Notes:
[a]   Denotes the mean.
[b]   The number of observations is in parentheses.
[c]   The standard deviation is in brackets.

proportion of bad loans through SOE loans (Wong and Wong, 2001). The average annual labor absorption rate and the employment growth rate in the private sector are 45.21 percent and 42.72 percent, respectively, which reflects a relatively favorable socioeconomic environment for labor reform over the survey period. The unionization rate is generally high, with around 60 percent of the local work force being organized in trade unions. The Pearson correlation test confirms that all correlations are lower than the threshold value of 0.7, which suggests that we can rule out serious estimation errors due to multicollinearity.

Table 5.4:   *Summary Statistics (by City)*

| | | Socioeconomic Environment | | | |
City	Beijing	Chengdu	Guangzhou	Shanghai	Tianjin
Govt fiscal position	−3.19	2.76	−2.00	−2.66	−3.02
Reemply. ratio for laid-off workers	55.05	43.63	42.38	56.11	26.29
Private sector employ. growth	27.83	24.07	18.88	17.20	14.06
Union rate	54.97	54.27	41.70	73.37	71.67

Notes: *Figures are ratios.

5.2.   Regression Results

Table 5.5 presents the results of our regression analyses of the determinants of labor retrenchment among China's SOEs.[7] Three facts stand out. First, we notice that enterprise performance is significantly and negatively correlated with the degree of labor retrenchment. This finding is consistent with *H1*.

Second, the fiscal position of the local government is negatively related to the degree of labor retrenchment in traditional SOEs but not in corporatized SOEs. *H2* is therefore supported. The lack of labor decision dependence on government fiscal conditions in corporatized SOEs suggests that this type of corporatized SOEs enjoys autonomy in labor decisions, whereas labor decisions in traditional SOEs are still influenced by the local government.

Third, for traditional SOEs, both proxies for the local labor market situation, the reemployment ratio and the growth of employment in the private sector are positively related to the degree of labor retrenchment; in particular, the coefficient of the local absorption ratio is significant. On the other hand, the coefficients for corporatized SOEs are not only statistically insignificant but also negative. Overall, our estimates therefore lend support to *H3*. As we assume that the absorption capacity of the local labor markets

Table 5.5:　Robust OLS Estimation on Labor Retrenchment, 1998–2000

Dependent Variable: Labor Retrenchment Rate	Traditional SOEs		Corporatized SOEs	
Enterprise Performance				
Ln (Sales)	−3.059*** [a]		−4.128***	
	(0.716) [b]		(1.051)	
Ln (Profit)		−1.784***		−2.416***
		(0.474)		(0.923)
Political–Economic Factors				
Fiscal position to	−0.901***	−1.171***	−0.619	−0.270
GDP ratio	(0.284)	(0.304)	(0.583)	(0.669)
Reemployment ratio for laid-off	0.179**	0.021	−0.044	−0.074
workers	(0.089)	(0.065)	(0.088)	(0.097)
Employment growth in private	0.006	0.056	0.065	0.152
sectors	(0.077)	(0.073)	(0.143)	(0.169)
Control Variables				
One-period lagged	3.726***	3.359***	4.968***	3.013**
Ln (Labor)	(0.985)	(0.879)	(1.244)	(1.163)
Ln (Age)	1.942*	1.978	4.766**	6.721***
	(1.137)	(1.339)	(1.918)	(2.493)
Unionization	−0.161*	−0.028	0.111	0.082
	(0.094)	(0.094)	(0.131)	(0.162)
Sectoral dummies	Yes		Yes	
Year dummies	Yes		Yes	
Constant	8.908	−6.880	0.920	−13.327
	(9.027)	(10.616)	(12.691)	(14.672)
Observations	559	416	334	270
Adjusted R^2	0.16	0.14	0.21	0.20

Notes:
[a]　The symbols ***, ** and * represent significance level at 1, 5 and 10 percent, respectively.
[b]　The numbers in parentheses are White-corrected standard errors.

is the government's major political concern in defense of social stability across the country, this result once again suggests that labor decisions of traditional SOEs are related to government objectives, while labor decisions of corporatized SOEs are unrelated. The relationship between reemployment chances and labor retrenchment seems fairly robust. Using other proxies such as changes in the official local unemployment rate and the percentage of registered laid-off workers from SOEs in the reemployment market, our estimation results are confirmed, which underscores the critical role of the local employment situation in traditional SOEs' labor retrenchment.

With respect to our control variables, we notice that the initial employment level is positively and significantly associated with the labor retrenchment rate, which might suggest that the labor redundancy problem is more serious in large enterprises, resulting in their need to cut more labor to survive during the economic transition. In contrast to our expectations, enterprises obviously do not suffer from organizational inertia with increasing age. We find a positive effect of enterprise age on labor retrenchment for both traditional and corporatized SOEs, though estimates for traditional firms are only significant at conventional levels in one case. Finally, the labor union variable exhibits no significant effect on labor retrenchment for either traditional or corporatized SOEs, which suggests that unionization is not an effective avenue by which workers can resist labor reduction.

Table 5.6 reports the estimations of the models, which include the first set of instrument variables. We first tested the validity of the instruments by using the over-identifying test (Davidson and MacKinnon, 1993). The p-values of the test are 0.71 and 0.16 respectively for two performance variables in traditional SOE group; and the p-values are 0.86 and 0.62 in corporatized SOEs. Therefore we cannot reject the null hypothesis that the instruments are valid in the four cases. As shown in Table 5.6, we found similar results as those in Table 5.5 that labor retrenchment of both types of firms is significantly and negatively affected by firm performance; and labor cuts in traditional SOEs are also significantly and negatively associated with government fiscal position but positively associated with local labor absorption rate for laid-off.

Table 5.6 presents the estimation results based on the second set of instrument variables. We also test the validity of the instruments before applying them in the regressions. The p-values for two performance variables for traditional and corporatized SOE groups are 0.94, 0.12, 0.49 and 0.18 respectively, which imply these instruments are valid in all four cases. Table 5.6 again shows results consistent with those in Table 5.5. In sum, the regressions with instrument variables suggest our results of the benchmark models are robust.

Table 5.6:   *Robustness Check Using Instrument Variables*

Dependent Variable: Labor Retrenchment Rate	Traditional SOEs		Corporatized SOEs	
Enterprise Performance				
Ln (Sales)	−3.050***		−3.904***	
	(0.902)[ab]		(1.264)	
Ln (Profits)		−1.230**		−1.594*
		(0.567)		(1.152)
Political–Economic Factors				
Fiscal position to GDP ratio	−0.914***	−1.178***	−0.578	−0.123
	(0.295)	(0.332)	(0.593)	(0.648)
Reemployment ratio for laid-off workers	0.177**	−0.051	−0.031	−0.039
	(0.088)	(0.067)	(0.088)	(0.103)
Employment growth in private sectors	−0.004	0.053	0.112	0.383**
	(0.076)	(0.091)	(0.147)	(0.172)
Control Variables				
One-period lagged Ln (Labor)	3.709***	2.771***	4.745***	2.645*
	(1.134)	(1.025)	(1.437)	(1.516)
Ln (Age)	2.015*	1.289	4.656**	3.415**
	(1.154)	(1.342)	(1.933)	(1.427)
Unionization	−0.156	−0.074	0.123	0.043
	(0.095)	(0.114)	(0.140)	(0.169)
Sectoral dummies	Yes		Yes	
Year dummies	Yes		Yes	
Constant	8.556	−0.100	−4.334	−13.768
	(9.569)	(10.053)	(12.912)	(15.654)
Observations	555	339	327	221
Adjusted R-squared	0.16	0.17	0.20	0.28
First Stage Regression				
Endogenous Variables: Ln (Sales)/Ln (Profit)				
Instruments: Lagged Ln (Enterprise Performance, Ln (Entry Cost)				
Adjusted R^2	0.89	0.75	0.86	0.75

Notes:
[a]   The symbols ***, ** and * represent significance level at 1, 5 and 10 percent, respectively.
[b]   The numbers in parentheses are White-corrected standard errors.

Table 5.6: Robustness Check Using Instrument Variables (Cont.)

Dependent Variable: Labor Retrenchment Rate	Traditional SOEs		Corporatized SOEs	
Enterprise Performance				
Ln (Sales)	−1.296		−4.046***	
	(1.499)		(1.457)	
Ln (Profits)		−1.608**		−3.829**
		(1.512)		(1.911)
Political–Economic Factors				
Fiscal position to GDP	−1.212***	−1.375***	−0.367	0.142
ratio	(0.362)	(0.440)	(0.727)	(0.882)
Reemployment ratio	0.242*	0.073	−0.157	−0.063
for laid-off workers	(0.129)	(0.137)	(0.133)	(0.144)
Employment growth in	−0.167	−0.144	0.028	0.085
private sectors	(0.128)	(0.130)	(0.154)	(0.174)
Control Variables				
One-period lagged	5.128**	0.981	5.337***	3.451*
Ln (Labor)	(2.031)	(1.905)	(1.531)	(1.863)
Ln (Age)	0.062	1.559	5.918**	8.133**
	(1.917)	(1.983)	(2.850)	(3.534)
Unionization	−0.184	−0.097	0.086	0.136
	(0.140)	(0.149)	(0.166)	(0.195)
Sectoral dummies	Yes		Yes	
Year dummies	Yes		Yes	
Constant	−8.952	−15.556	3.650	−8.754
	(13.044)	(14.034)	(14.918)	(17.251)
Observations	261	188	232	185
Adjusted R^2	0.34	0.16	0.25	0.23
First Stage Regression				
Endogenous Variables: Ln (Sales)/Ln (Profit)				
Instruments: Wage, Engineer Ratio, Debt–Equity Ratio, Location in				
Industrial Park, Ln (Entry Cost)				
Adjusted R^2	0.10	0.21	0.14	0.12

Notes:
a.   ***, **, and * represent significance level at 1, 5 and 10 percent respectively.
b.   The numbers in parentheses are standard errors.

6. CONCLUSION

This study examines the determinants of the restructuring of China's SOEs in the late 1990s, which was eventually implemented to speed up employment restructuring after two decades of only gradual and often hesitant reforms. Our study yields two major findings. First, we find that the degree of labor retrenchment is negatively related to enterprise performance. This finding suggests that China's recent adjustment processes have been driven at least partly by economic forces. In this sense our study suggests that to some extent enterprise restructuring is possible without full-fledged privatization.

Second, we offer evidence that decisions about labor retrenchment in traditional SOEs are related to the local government's fiscal position and to local reemployment conditions for laid-off workers. In contrast, labor decisions in corporatized SOEs are not related to these two variables.

The significant relationship between political–economic determinants (as measured by local reemployment chances and fiscal constraints) and labor retrenchment suggests that local governments still employ traditional SOEs to generate and maintain local employment if this is deemed necessary to support social stability. Corporatized SOEs with non-state shareholders, on the other hand, seem to enjoy greater autonomy in labor decisions, as a direct relationship between the enterprise's labor policies and the political–economic conditions could not be substantiated. The differences diagnosed between traditional and corporatized SOEs in terms of labor retrenchment support the idea that the depoliticization of enterprise decision-making – one of the major enterprise reform objectives in formerly centrally planned socialist economies – can actually be achieved through partial privatization. The results are consistent with theoretical arguments of Shleifer and Vishny (1994), which suggest that the existence of private owners and their individual interests in profit maximization reduces the bargaining power of politicians and thereby increases the costs of political interference in enterprise decision-making. They are also consistent with Wong et al. (2004), who found significant depoliticization effects for China's partially privatized listed enterprises. Though one could argue that our findings on the depoliticization of labor decisions in corporatized SOEs could not be generalized to all other enterprise decisions, we believe that the labor retrenchment issue could still serve as a crucial test case for the depoliticiation of enterprise decision-making due to its imminent role in the government's efforts to secure social stability.

Skeptics might also claim that the greater freedom of corporatized SOEs could simply reflect a selection bias in the sense that the government only corporatized those SOEs that were not needed as policy tools. In fact, the selection effect is consistent with the observation that China's central government delayed SOEs' ownership reforms to preserve SOEs as tools of employment provision. Based on our results, we are unable to determine whether the government voluntarily refrains from using corporatized SOEs as policy tools or whether it is simply unable to exert effective control owing to resistance from private investors. In light of our recent empirical findings on the persistence of political control over decision-making in China's partially privatized listed enterprises (Opper et al., 2002; Wong et al., 2004; Chang and Wong, 2004), and particularly given the fact that the state still retains a controlling share in corporatized SOEs, we have doubts that our results could be attributed entirely to a selection bias. Instead, we expect that our findings rather reflect the complementary effect of both mechanisms.

NOTES

1. For an overview article, see Shirley (1999).
2. Politicians are particularly apt to intervene in labor decisions, since employment opportunities and wage levels provide convenient tools by which to redistribute wealth from the common pool to the favored parties (Nordhaus, 1975: Frey and Schneider, 1978).
3. In the mid and late 1990s local governments even offered extra payments to workers at enterprises and areas with frequent outbreak of social unrest (Hassard et al., 2002).
4. Empirical studies on privatization suggest that a government's policymaking decisions depend to some extent on the tightness of fiscal budget constraints. State withdrawal, in general, is more likely to occur during an economic crisis when financial conditions are dire and public debt is regarded as excessive (World Bank, 1995).
5. See, for example, Huber (1964).
6. The marginal productivity of surplus labor is very low, if not zero. Subject to non-economic constraints such as interference from political superiors and resistance from workers, managers have incentive to cut as much surplus labor as they can, if they want to improve enterprise performance. As wage is unlikely to be a determinant of retrenchment decision for surplus labor, the level of wage is therefore unlikely to be related to the extent of labor retrenchment.
7. As we discuss above, we include sector and year dummies in the regressions to control for firm-specific and year-specific effects. To save space, we do not report the estimated coefficients of these dummies

REFERENCES

Bai, C.-E., D. Li, Z. Tao and Y. Wang (2000), 'A multitask theory of state enterprise reform', *Journal of Comparative Economics*, **28**(4), 716–38.

Bodmer, F. (2002), 'The effect of reforms on employment flexibility in Chinese SOEs, 1980–94', *Economics of Transition*, **10**(3), 637–58.

Buchanan, J.M., R.D. Tollison and G. Tullock (eds) (1980), *Toward a Theory of the Rent-seeking Society*, College Station, TX.

Chang E. and S.M.L. Wong (2004), 'Political control and firm performance in China's listed firms', *Journal of Comparative Economics*, **32**, 617–36.

China State Statistical Bureau, various years, *China Labor Statistical Yearbook*, Beijing: China Statistics Press.

Davidson, R. and J. MacKinnon (1993), *Estimation and Inference in Econometrics*, New York: Oxford University Press.

Denis, D.J. and T.A. Kruse (2000), 'Managerial discipline and corporate restructuring following performance decline', *Journal of Financial Economics*, **55**, 391–424.

Dong, K. and X.F. Ye (2003), 'Social security reform in China', *China Economic Review*, **14**(4), 417–25.

Dong, X.-Y. (2003), 'China's urban labour market adjustment: A summary of literature review', Working paper, University of Winnipeg.

Dong, X.-Y. and L. Putterman (2002), 'Soft budget constraints, social burdens, and labor redundancy in China's state industry', *Journal of Comparative Economics*, **31**, 110–33.

Fleisher, B.M. and D.T. Yang (2003), 'China's Labor Market', Paper presented at the conference on 'China's Market Reforms' organized by Stanford Center for International Development, Stanford University, September 19–20.

Frey, B. and F. Scheider (1978), 'An empirical study of politico-economic interaction in the United States', *The Review of Economics and Statistics*, **60**(2), 174–83.

Groves, G.T., Y. Hong, J. McMillan and B. Naughton (1995), 'China's evolving managerial labor market', *Journal of Political Economy*, **103**(4), 873–92.

Hassard, J., J. Morris and J. Sheehan (2002), 'The elusive market: Privatization, politics and state-enterprise reform in China', *British Journal of Management*, **13**, 221–31.

Huber, P.J. (1964), 'Robust estimation of a location parameter', *Analysis of Mathematical Statistics*, **35**, 73–101.

Kang, J.-K. and A. Shivdasani (1997), 'Corporate restructuring during performance decline in Japan', *Journal of Financial Economics*, **26**, 29–65.

Lee, C.K. (1998), 'The labor politics of market socialism: Collective inaction and class experiences among state workers in Guangzhou', *Modern China*, **24**(1), 3–33.

Li, D. (1998), 'Changing incentives of the Chinese bureaucracy', *AEA Papers and Proceedings*, **88**(2), 393–97.

Naughton, B. (1997), 'Danwei, the economic foundations of a unique institution', in X. Lü and E.J. Parry (eds), *Danwei. The Changing Chinese Workplace in Historical and Comparative Perspective*, Armonk, NY: M.E. Sharpe.

Nordhaus, W. (1975), 'The political business cycle', *Review of Economic Studies*, **42**, 169–90.

Olson, M. (1968), *The Logic of Collective Action: Public Goods and the Theory of Groups*, Schocken, NY.

Opper, S., S.M.L. Wong and R. Hu (2002), 'Party power, market and private power: CCP persistence in China's listed companies', in K. Leicht (ed.), *The Future of Market Transition, Research in Social Stratification and Mobility*, vol 19, pp. 103–36.

Sappington, D.E. and J.E. Stiglitz (1987), 'Privatization, information, and incentives', *Journal of Policy Analysis and Management*, **6**, 567–81.

Schultz, K.A. (1995), 'The politics of the political business cycle', *British Journal of Political Science*, **25**(1), 79–99.

Shirley, M. (1999), 'Bureaucrats in business: The roles of privatization versus corporatization in state-owned enterprise reform', *World Development*, **27**(1), 115–36.

Shleifer, A. (1998), 'State versus private ownership', NBER Working Paper Series, Working Paper 6665.

Shleifer, A. and R.W. Vishny (1994), 'Politicians and firms', *The Quarterly Journal of Economics*, **109**(4), 995–1025.

Wong, R.Y.C. and S.M.L. Wong (2001), 'Competition in China's domestic banking industry', *Cato Journal*, **21**, 19–41.

Wong, S.M.L., S. Opper and R. Hu (2004), 'Shareholding structure, de-politicization and enterprise performance: Lessons from China's listed companies', *Economics of Transition*, **12**(1), 29–66.

World Bank (1995), *Bureaucrats in Business. The Economics and Politics of Government Ownership*, Washington, DC: World Bank.

Whyte, G. (1987), 'The politics of economic reform in Chinese industry: The introduction of the labour contract system', *China Quarterly*, **111**, 365–89.

Zhang, Z. (1994), 'Harmonize and perfect the relationship between enterprise and labor', *Jingji Cankao* May 1, 31–42.

Zhou, X. (1993), 'Unorganized interests and collective action in communist China', *American Sociological Review*, **58**, 54–73.

6. The Emergence of Agricultural Commodity Markets in China

Jikun Huang and Scott Rozelle

1. INTRODUCTION

Although the initial reforms in China and other successful transition nations centered on improvements to property rights and transforming incentives (McMillan, Whalley and Zhu, 1989; Fan, 1991; Lin, 1992), the other, equally important task of reformers was to create more efficient institutions of exchange (McMillan, 1997). Markets – whether classic competitive ones or some workable substitute – increase efficiency by facilitating transactions among agents to allow specialization and trade and by providing information through a pricing mechanism to producers and consumers about the relative scarcity of resources. But markets, in order to function efficiently, require supporting institutions to ensure competition, define and enforce contracts, ensure access to credit and finance and provide information (McMillan, 1997). These institutions were either absent in the Communist countries or, if they existed, were inappropriate for a market system. In assessing the determinants of the success and failure of 24 transitions during their first decade of reform, Rozelle and Swinnen (2004) demonstrate that improved institutions of exchange were absolutely essential for nations to make progress. A study by de Brauw et al. (2004) has shown the positive effect that market development had on the efficiency of China's agricultural producers and their welfare during the 1980s and early 1990s. The continued success of transition nations during the second decade of reform and beyond almost certainly will also depend on continued market development. Somewhat surprisingly, despite the importance of market performance in the reform process there is little empirical work on the success that China (or any other transition nation) has had in building markets.

In part in response to the lacunae of research on the performance of markets in China's rural economy, our main goal is to bring together a number of simple and revealing facts on the emergence of China's markets.

To do so we will have two specific objectives. First, after briefly documenting the market-reform policy environment that has unfolded during the reform era, we examine several sets of price data by looking at spatial patterns of market prices contours over time. Second, we examine the extent to which market prices are integrated among China's regions.

In order to examine such a broad topic, it is necessary to limit the scope of the analysis. To do so, we restrict ourselves to China's main staple commodities – rice, maize and soybeans. These commodities – especially maize and soybeans – are ideal since the quality differences among regions are relatively narrow, a characteristic that facilitates integration analysis. Data on these commodities are available over time and across space. Data quality, however, restricts most of our analysis to after the mid-1990s.

2. COMMODITY PRICE AND MARKETING POLICIES

Although ever since the start of transition in the late 1970s China's leaders pursued price and marketing reform with different degrees of enthusiasm, there has been a steady shift towards more liberalization (Huang et al., 2004). The key characteristic of the reform strategy, however, was gradual. For example, the initial price and market reforms in the late 1970s were aimed only at raising farm level procurement prices and gradually liberalizing the market. These reforms included gradual increases in the agricultural procurement prices toward market prices and reductions in procurement quota levels. In the initial years, however, there was little effort to move the economy to one in which resources and factors were allocated according market price signals.

As the right to private trading was extended to include surplus output of all categories of agricultural products after contractual obligations to the state were fulfilled, the foundations of the state marketing system began to be undermined (Sicular, 1995). After a record growth in grain production in 1984 and 1985, a second stage of price and market reforms was announced in 1985 aimed at radically limiting the scope of government price and market interventions and further enlarging the role of market allocation. Other than for rice, wheat, maize and cotton, reformers gradually began to eliminate planned procurement; government commercial departments still existed, but they could only continue to buy and sell at the market. For grain, incentives were introduced through the reduction of the quota volume and increase in procurement prices. In subsequent years, although mandatory procurement of rice, wheat, maize, soybean, oil crops and cotton continued, to provide incentives for farmers to raise productivity and to encourage sales to the government, quota procurement prices were raised over time (Huang et al., 2004).

True to the spirit of gradualism, as grain production and prices stabilized in the early 1990s, plans to abolish the grain ration system led to a new round of reform (Rozelle et al., 2000). Urban officials discontinued sales at ration prices to consumers in early 1993. Although the state compulsory quota system was not eliminated, in most parts of China in the mid-1990s, leaders once again lowered the procurement level. The share of grain compulsory quota procurement in total production kept at only 11 percent in 1995–97. Local government grain bureaus and stations were encouraged to trade on their own accounts as a way to increase the marketing of agricultural commodities and increase the incomes of grain bureau officials (Park and Rozelle, 1998). Moreover, despite the announcement of seemingly retrenchment-oriented polices, such as the 'Rice Bag' responsibility system, at the local level private traders emerged as an economic force that was difficult, even with considerable policing effort, to suppress. In fact, it was documented that a great number of efforts to restrict the flow of grain were not successful (Park et al., 2002). Market flows continued as the share of total government procurement in domestic production fell; trade was driven by the profits that traders could earn by shipping grain from low to high priced areas (Huang et al., 2004).

In the early 2000s, marketing reforms were launched once more (Huang et al., 2004). Restrictions on marketing were removed, new efforts to commercialize the grain bureau were begun and government intervention in grain prices (that had been given to farmers in certain regions of the country) was eliminated. In short, a new effort was made to push the policy environment to be even more market-oriented. Hence, while it took more than 20 years to achieve, gradually China's policy environment became one that condoned the market and sought to influence production primarily through the signal generated by market prices. What is unclear, however, is how effective the policies were in creating a functional market system – one that was relative efficient and integrated. It is to this question that we turn in the rest of the chapter.

3. DATA

To assess the nature of China's markets in the last ten years, we use data from a number of different sources. First, we use a set of price data collected by China's State Market Administration Bureau (SMAB – Dataset 1). Nearly 50 sample sites from 15 of China's provinces report prices of agricultural commodities every ten days. This means there are 36 price observations available for each market site for each commodity each year. The prices are the average price of transactions that day in the local rural periodic market. The Ministry of Agriculture assembles the data in Beijing and makes them available to researchers and policy makers. Unfortunately, after 2000, the quality of the data has deteriorated (which we, fortunately, do not have to depend on, since other data sources – discussed below – are available).

Using the SMAB data, we can examine rice, maize and soybean prices from 1996 to 2000 (except for maize that was only available through 1998). The three crops are produced and consumed in nearly every province in China. Rice price data are available for 31 markets. Because of quality differences among rice varieties in different regions of China, we look at price integration among markets within four regions, South China (South), the Yangtze Valley (YV), the North China Plain (and Northwest China – NCP) and Northeast China (NE).[1] For the provinces included in the sample, rice prices are available for over 90 percent of the time periods. Prices for maize and soybean data are available for 13 and 20 markets, respectively.[2] Product homogeneity in the case of maize and soybeans makes it possible to examine price integration among markets across a broader geographic range. We compare our results for the late 1990s (1996 to 2000) to results from 1988 to 1995 that were produced with the same data and published in Park et al. (2002).[3]

The second source of data on China's domestic market (Dataset 2) comes from a price data set collected by the Jilin Province Grain and Oil Information Center (GOIC). For maize, on a weekly basis between August 10 1998 and February 24 2003, prices are reported for 15 of China's main maize production and consumption provinces, including Heilongjiang, Jilin, Liaoning, Hebei, Shandong, Jiangsu, Zhejiang, Shanghai, Hubei, Sichuan, Hunan, Fujian, Guangdong and Guangxi. Since September 7 1998, there is a price from Liaoning for Dalian, the main port from which exports to foreign and other domestic markets (by ship) leave.

To examine maize markets robustly in the northeast regions of the country and between major producing and consuming regions of the country in the post-WTO accession period, we use another set of data collected by the Jilin Province GOIC (Dataset 3). The data in this dataset were first available after October 26 2001; they continue through February 25 2003. This dataset is more detailed than data in Dataset 2 for two reasons. First, it is more spatially disaggregate. The dataset includes prices from three markets in Heilongjiang; three markets from Jilin; three markets from Liaoning (including two in production regions and Dalian); and market sites in Guangdong, Fujian, Jiangsu and Hubei. Dataset 3 also reports data more frequently, typically twice a week (every third day, then every fourth day).

The data from the Jilin Grain and Oilseed Price Information Center (Datasets 2 and 3) appear to be of relative higher quality compared to the price series in Dataset 1. For example, there are fewer missing observations. There are also relatively few inconsistencies in the data. In Dataset 1, corrections frequently need to be made to the data to account for missing observations and to adjust for prices when they are written down in price 'per jin' even though the data category is supposed to be price 'per kilogram'.

The soybean data come from the same source, the Jilin Provincial GOIC, but are collected a bit differently (Dataset 4). Soybean data are only available on a monthly basis. There are data for 20 markets. Similar to the maize data in Datasets 2 and 3, the soybean data series are complete and overall the quality of the data appears to be high.

4. PRICE TRENDS AND SPATIAL PATTERNS OF MARKET EMERGENCE

In this section, we use our price data to sketch a descriptive picture of China's agricultural markets. To do so, we first plot the data over time and examine how prices move together in markets in the same geographic region and in markets separated by long distances. Next, we examine how price data points from different markets across space (but during the same time period) relate to one another graphically (which is done by tracing out transportation gradients in China's rice, maize and soybean markets). To put the results in perspective, we examine these over time and compare those of China with those of the US. Our assumption is that if prices in markets in different parts of China move together and if they create spatial patterns similar to those found in more market-oriented economies (like the US), then our data are suggesting that China's markets are becoming increasingly integrated and efficient.

4.1. Price Trends

4.1.2. Maize
Using Dataset 3, it can be shown that prices in different markets closely track one another in Northeast China (Figure 6.1). In the figure, we plot the Dalian domestic price versus the prices in the two Heilongjiang market sites (chosen because they are the furthest Northeast markets from Dalian). While varying over time, the Dalian domestic price remains between

Figure 6.1:   *Maize Prices in Heilongjiang, Liaoning and Dalian*
                  (RMB/mt), October 2001 to February 2003

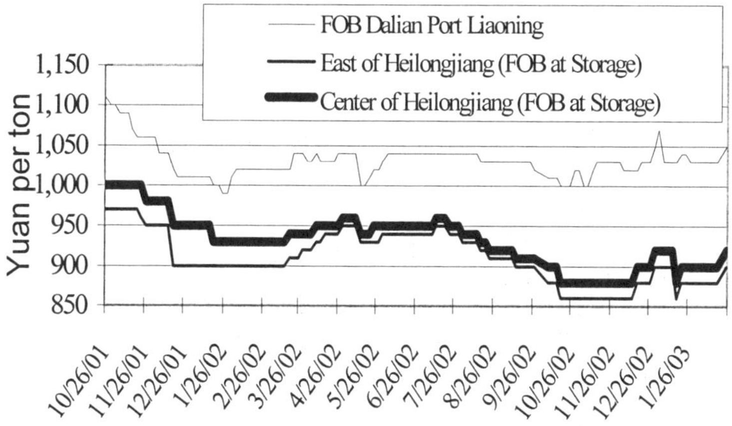

Source: Dataset 3.

US$120/mt and US$130/mt from December 2001 to February 2003. During the same period, the prices in both Heilongjiang markets move almost in perfect concert with one another; maize prices in Heilongjiang are around US$110/mt to US$115/mt. Most importantly, visual inspection shows that although the market in Dalian and those in Heilongjiang are more than 1000 kilometers apart and prices vary by US$12/mt to US$17/mt, the prices in many periods are moving together. When the prices in Dalian move up (down), the prices in Heilongjiang tend to move up (down).

Similar patterns of price movements are found to exist between the two markets in western and central Liaoning and Dalian (not shown in the figure). In fact, the prices in the two Liaoning producing areas track each other even closer than the markets in Heilongjiang, a finding that perhaps is not surprising given the fact that Liaoning is a smaller province with better transportation and communication infrastructure. The co-movements of prices among the producing areas in Liaoning and the consumption center of the province, Dalian, also are easily perceptible. The narrower price gaps among producer (lower trend lines) and consumer areas (higher trend line) are a reflection of the closer distance (than when compared to Heilongjiang–Dalian figure – Panel A).

Using Dataset 1, the patterns of movement across further points of China display similar patterns of close movements of prices (Figure 6.2, Panels A and B). While prices have moved together since the mid-1990s between Dalian and Guangdong and between Dalian and Fujian, the tracking among markets appears to be even closer in recent years. Almost every turning point in Guangdong and Fujian can be found in the Dalian market. The close movement of prices occurs even though the primary way grain moves between the two sets of markets is by ocean. With the advent of private shipping and commercial trading, there are now many shipping lines and trading companies that move grain between the Northeast and South China's main consumption areas. The results from Figure 6.2, Panels A and B, when linked with those from Figure 6.1, demonstrate that prices in Heilongjiang appear to depend on shifts in feed demand and corn availability in Guangzhou and Fujian.

4.1.2. Soybeans

Using Dataset 4, we find soybean prices similarly move together for pairs of markets both in the same region and across more distant locations. The bottom two price series in Figure 6.3 trace the price trends for soybeans in Heilongjiang and Jilin. The two series are almost indistinguishable from one another with Heilongjiang prices slightly lower from almost the entire period. The Guangdong price series, the top line in the figure, also shows that prices move in concert with one another inside China's domestic market even though the markets are thousands of kilometers apart. In only two short periods – early 2000 and late 2002 – does the gap between the two markets deviate from a fixed margin which is almost equal to the transport price between the Northeast and the South.

Prices appear to be even more integrated in the South (not shown in figure). The prices in Guangdong, Fujian and Shanghai throughout the entire period are so close that it is difficult to distinguish the individual price series. Although we are unable to draw conclusions that are based on descriptive statistics with any degree of statistical confidence, the patterns of price movements would seem to indicate that China's markets are highly integrated; it is hard to imagine that planners could generate such closely shifting sets of prices.

4.1.3. Cross-commodity trends

In addition to observing co-movements of maize prices between regions over time during the post-WTO accession period, our data (Dataset 3) also shows that prices of different feed types move together (Figure 6.4). In south China, early rice is frequently used as a feed, albeit in the view of most livestock producers, a slightly inferior one. However, even though the price of maize is higher than feed rice across China, the ratio of maize to feed rice is almost identical in markets in different province. Figure 6.4 illustrates that even though the ratio of maize to feed rice varies over time in

Figure 6.2: *Maize Prices in Guangdong, Fujian and Dalian (RMB/mt),*
1996 to February 2003
Panel A. Guangdong and Dalian Maize Prices

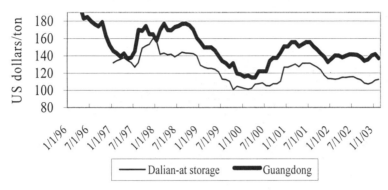

Panel B. Fujian and Dalian Maize Prices

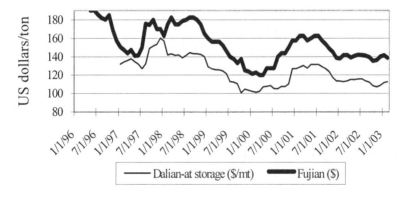

Source: Jilin Oil and Grain Information Center.

Guangdong and Fujian, the trend of the ratios in each of the province almost perfectly tracks one another.

Figure 6.5 shows that the same co-movement of prices occurs in the case of different soybean-based products within the soybean market. The prices of soybeans and soybean meal almost perfectly track one another for the entire sample period between 1999 and 2003. Interestingly (although not shown), when the price of soybean oil is added, after 2000, oil prices (albeit higher) also move together with soybean and soybean meal. Before 2000, restrictions in the import market for oil kept the soybean oil price abnormally above the price of soybeans and soybean meal.

Figure 6.3: Soybeans Prices in Heilongjiang, Jilin and Shanghai,
January 1999 to September 2003

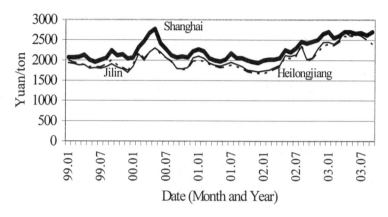

Source: Dataset 4.

Figure 6.4: The Ratio of Corn to Feed Rice (Paddy) Prices in Guangdong
and Fujian Provinces between October 2001 and February
2003

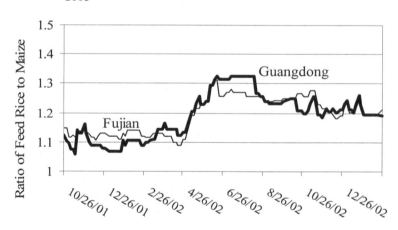

Source: Dataset 3.

Figure 6.5:   *Comparisons of China's Average Soybean and Soybean Meal Prices (RMB/mt), January 1999 to September 2003*

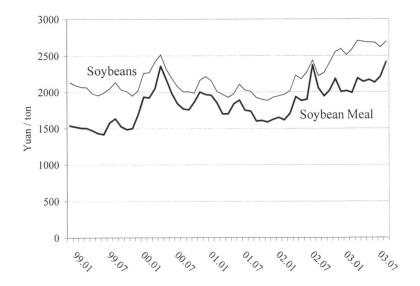

Source: Dataset 4.

4.2.   Price Patterns Across Space

We also can use our data descriptively and in conjunction with relatively simple multivariate analysis to examine price behavior across space, holding time constant. If China's markets function well, then there should be well-defined relationships across space. At any given point of time, the price in the consumption center should be the highest, while the price in the most remote production location lowest. If all prices are plotted as a function of their distance from the consumption center, the plot of these points traces out a 'transportation gradient'. It is called the transportation gradient because in the absence of other distortions, the fall of the line reflects the rising transportation costs. Higher per kilometer transport costs and distance-varying distortions and other costs also will increase the steepness of the line. Thus, the nature of the transportation gradient can be used to measure the efficiency of a marketing/transportation system. In examining transportation gradients, the less steep the slope, the more efficient commodities move across space (everything else held equal).

Figure 6.6:   *Changes in Maize Prices across Northeast China as Markets*
                 Increase Distances from the Port of Dalian, 2000-2003

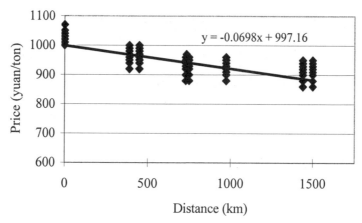

Source: Dataset 3.

A simple plotting of the relationship between the price of maize in
Dalian and those in Liaoning, Jilin and Heilongjiang during the post-
accession period (after December 2001) illustrates a price contour that is
consistent with the existence of well-functioning markets (Figure 6.6).
Since the main demand center in the Northeast and point of export for
maize to foreign markets and the point of transshipment to south China is
Dalian, one would expect that in an integrated marketing system, as a
market became more remote, the price should fall according to a well-
defined 'transportation gradient'. Indeed, the price in a market 1000
kilometers away from Dalian (e.g., the Jilin market) is, on average, about
RMB 70/mt lower than the price in Dalian. In percentage terms, this means
the price of Jilin maize is about 6 percent lower than the price of maize in
Dalian.[4]

The patterns of the price data (that is, the transportation gradients) are
even more evident when using Dataset 1 to look at the case of rice (Figure
6.7). In Figure 6.7 the points at the origin are those in one of four of China's
main consumption points and the rest of the points are prices in the markets
that are in the supply points of the marketing areas that service the
consumption points. Specifically, in southern China the main demand point
is Guangzhou and the supply points are markets in the southern China
marketing region (e.g., Guangdong's rural area, Hunan, Fujian, Guangxi
and Yunnan). In the Yangtse River Basin the main consumption point is

Figure 6.7:   Changes in Rice Prices across China as Markets Increase Distances from Port Cities, 2000

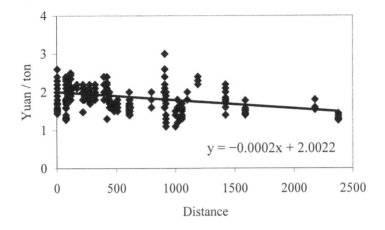

Source: Dataset 1.

Shanghai and the other marketing points are in supply regions up the Yangtse River. In northern China the main consumption center is Beijing/Tianjin and the marketing points are in supply regions up the Yellow River Basin. In the northeast the main consumption center is Dalian and the main marketing points are in Liaoning and Heilongjiang. When data are arranged like this, rice prices in China's four marketing regions trace out a well-defined transportation gradient.[5]

When looking at average transportation gradients for 1998 to 2000 for maize, soybeans and rice in China (and the US), three findings suggest that China's markets are indeed performing relatively efficiently.[6] First, and interestingly because they build the case for robustness, the magnitudes of the transportation/transaction costs are similar to those reported in Park et al. (2002). Unlike our regression-based method (see footnote 6 and Table 6.1), Park et al. (2002) used a completely different methodology, a method that uses a maximum likelihood estimator examining the price differences between markets when traders arbitrage away price difference between markets. Second, the transportation gradients for all crops are falling over time. Although we cannot pinpoint the exact source of the fall in the transportation gradient, as in Park et al. (2002), the patterns are consistent with a marketing environment in which there is an improving infrastructure and more competitive markets. Finally, the results show that the transportation gradients in China are similar to those found in the US. When

Table 6.1:   *Percentage Change in Price for Every 1000 Kilometers of Distance from the Port, 1998 to 2000*[*]

	Maize	Soybeans	Rice
China			
1998	−4	−10	−10
1999	−4	−11	−9
2000	−3	−8	−7
US			
1998	−5	−3.5	N/A

Note:
[*]   The figures in the tables can be thought of as the average transportation gradient for each year. It is the coefficient on the 'distance variable' (a variable that is measuring the distance in 1000 kilometers from the port of the location of the market) from regressions that explain commodity-specific prices for each year (in logs) as a function of the distance variable and a series of period dummies (one for each week of the year). In other words, the coefficient is the average percent change in price for each 1000 kilometers that a marketing site is removed from the port, holding constant the average price change for all sites during each week of the year. Regression results available from authors upon request.

Sources: China rice, soybeans and maize prices (1998) are from Dataset 2. Maize for 1999 and 2000 are from Dataset 1. The US data come from the Chicago board of trade website.

plotting similar data and running similar regression on corn in the Mississippi valley we find pattern of spatial price spread similar to those in China – especially in the case of maize. While we are not suggesting that China's commodity markets are as efficient in all dimensions as those in the US, it does appears as if the marketing reforms (as well as aggressive investment in roads and other infrastructure projects in the past decade – Luo et al., 2005) have dramatically improved the ability of traders to move agricultural commodities (at least maize) around China at costs that rival those of the US.

5.   MARKET INTEGRATION IN CHINA

This section uses more formal tests of market integration. Cointegration means that although many developments can cause permanent changes in the individual elements of a tested series (e.g., grain prices in this chapter), there is some long-run equilibrium relation tying the individual components together. Here, the Engle–Granger cointegration approach is applied to test China's market integration.

According this approach (assuming that one is using stationary price series), one price series is then regressed on another using ordinary least squares:

$$P_t^i = \alpha + \lambda t + \beta P_t^j + e_t \qquad (6.1)$$

where *t* is the common trend of the two price series and e_t is the error term. The residual, e_t, is then used in the augmented Dickey–Fuller test:

$$\Delta e_t = \delta e_{t-1} + \sum_{j=2}^{N} \gamma \Delta e_{t-j} + \xi_t \qquad (6.2)$$

If the test statistic on the δ coefficient is less (more negative) than the relevant critical value from the Dickey-Fuller table, the null hypothesis is rejected and the two series are said to be cointegrated of order (6.1). According to Engle and Granger, this implies that the two markets are integrated. The analysis assumes that markets are integrated when the absolute value of the test statistic is greater than three (implying significance at the 10 percent level).

5.1. Results

The cointegration analysis shows that China's markets have continued to develop in the late 1990s, especially when the results are compared with the market integration research of the late 1980s and early 1990s (Table 6.2). In the middle part of the reform era (1988–95), a time when markets were starting to emerge, some 20–25 percent of markets showed signs of prices moving together (Park et al., 2002).

Using the results from the early 1990s as a baseline, the current analysis shows that during the late 1990s China's markets continued along their path of maturation. The co-movement of prices among pairs of markets in the sample shows a significant increase in the share of market pairings that are integrated. In the case of maize, for example, prices in paired markets moved together in 89 percent of the cases, up from 28 percent in the early 1990s (Table 6.2). The share of market pairs showing price integration also increased for soybeans, japonica rice, and indica rice. The integration is especially notable because in many cases the paired markets are more than 1000. kilometers apart. For example, in many years soybean and maize prices were found to be integrated between markets in Shaanxi and Guangdong Provinces and between Sichuan Province and southern Jiangsu.

Table 6.2:   Percentage of Market Pairs in Rural China that Test Positive for Integration Based on the Dickey–Fuller Test, 1988–2000

Commodity	1989–1995	1996–2000
Maize	28	89
Soybeans	28	68
Japonica Rice (Yellow River Valley)	25	60
Indica Rice (Yangtze Valley and South China)	25	47

Note: Results are for two periods from the same dataset. For results for 1989–95 for maize and rice, see Park et al. (2002). Rice results are for the whole country in 1989–95. Results for soybeans for 1989–95 and all results for 1996–2000 are from the authors.

Source: Database 1.

Despite significant progress in integration, the results also show pairs of markets that are not integrated. For example, in a third of cases japonica rice prices moved in one market but not in another. One explanation is an institutional breakdown or infrastructure barrier (a policy measure or a weak link in the transportation or communication infrastructure) that is fragmenting China's markets for certain commodities, as shown in Park et al. (2002). But since every province in China produces and consumes rice, it is also the case that if supply in one region during one period is just equal to demand and if regional price differentials stay within the band between regional 'export' and 'import' prices, then moderate price movements in another area might not induce a flow into or out of the region that is in equilibrium. For that reason, despite the nontrivial number of cases in the late 1990s in which market prices in pairs of markets do not move together, it must be concluded that the impacts of WTO accession on China's agriculture will increasingly be experienced across wide regions of the nation from coastal to inland areas.

Although we do not show the results here for brevity, the shift towards integration has apparently continued. For example, for the case of maize, using Dataset 3, almost 100 percent of all pairs of markets are integrated after 2000. The same is true for soybeans (using Dataset 4).

5.2.   Other Studies Finding Increased Market Performance

The only truly systematic attempts at trying to measure both the improvements in markets and their returns (in terms of impact on producer welfare) are in de Brauw et al. (2004). These papers develop measures of increased responsiveness and flexibility within a dynamic adjustment cost framework to estimate the return to market liberalization reforms, holding the incentive reforms and other factors constant. The authors find that the behavior of producers in China has been affected by market liberalization, but that the gains have been relatively small. Gains in responsiveness (that are measured by price elasticities of factor demand for variable inputs – in this case, fertilizer) between the early and late reform periods are attributed to the gradual market liberalizing changes of the late 1980s. Farmers also have increased their speed of adjustment of quasi-fixed factors (which in the case of China's agriculture includes labor and sown area) to price changes (and other shifts in exogenous factors) between the early and late reform period. The work in de Brauw et al. (2004) also measures the effects on overall welfare of the increased flexibility and responsiveness and finds that the magnitude of the gains in efficiency from increased responsiveness and flexibility in the late reform period is positive and significant.

6. CONCLUSIONS

In this chapter, we have shown in a number of ways the steady improvement in agricultural commodity markets that have occurred in China during the past decade. Regardless of using descriptive statistics or more formal techniques, our results are consistent with the emergence of markets for rice, maize and soybeans. Moreover, markets are robust, even when looking across long distances and at different time periods. Transaction (or at least transportation) costs also appear to have fallen.

Although people that visit rural China are not surprised, such a picture of markets may be surprising when juxtaposed against the policy background. Even during the late 1990s China's leaders were taking a cautious, gradual approach to reforming markets. Our results show that despite the gradualist strategy, during this time commodity markets have steadily strengthened in rural China.

The power of markets to continue to integrate perhaps more than anything shows the power of China's gradual method of transition. As argued by McMillan (1997), China's market reform has really been one of entry-driven competition. In the case of China entry has come from both the commercialization of the state and the emergence of a private trading sector. In doing this, China enfranchised millions of individuals to be involved in commodity trade. While this has produced the rise in integration and fall in transaction costs that has been documented in the chapter, it also has eroded the power of the state to control the markets with the traditional command and control methods. Our results suggest that if the nation's leaders want to control markets in the future, they are going to have to devise new ways to intervene, ones that use indirect methods instead of trying to suppress traders. There are now just too many traders to deal with as shown by the integration trends that continued to increase even when the nation tried to stop trading.

Indeed, one of the real lessons of our work is that both China's leaders and domestic and foreign traders and other observers should realize that rural China now has commodity markets that are much less distorted than previously. This fact will become of significance in future international trade talks as China attempts to be declared a 'market economy', a status that will benefit it in its ability to defend itself against anti-dumping cases. Of course, for poverty alleviation and other purposes this is often a two-edged sword. When prices rise (for whatever reason) in consumption centers, integrated markets mean that farmers all over China, even those in more remote areas, will benefit. However, if prices fall (for example, from increased trade liberalization), the downward effects of price shifts will also be experienced throughout the nation.

NOTES

1. Park et al. (2002) have a complete explanation of the nature of China's rice economy and the quality differences that exist among the different regions. We follow their regional breakdown in our analysis.
2. Since we use data over time, we need to convert prices to a real basis. Nominal prices from our data set are deflated using monthly consumer price indices calculated and reported by the China National Statistical Bureau. Deflation facilitates transaction cost comparisons across time and allows us to disregard transaction cost increases within periods associated with inflation.
3. To produce the results, we run co-integration tests on each pair of markets using the data for each year. So, in other words, we use 36 observations (since the price data are available every ten days) and count the number of pairs of markets that are co-integrated in a statistically significant way (see next endnote and text for explanation of testing). For example, for the case of soybeans, for the late 1990s (1996 to 2000), this means that we are   examining the extent of integration between 190 (20*19/2) pairs of markets in each of five years, which equals a total of 950 pairs of markets. Hence, since we found that prices in 646 markets were integrated (according to the testing procedure), we report that 68 percent of markets are integrated in the late 1990s. Since we only use 36 observations per test, and since co-integration tests typically perform better with longer time series, by splitting our data into annual increments, we are biasing the results against accepting integration. We do this in order to make our analysis comparable to Park et al. (2002) which follows a similar procedure.
4. China's customs data demonstrate overwhelmingly that most of China's maize is exported from Dalian (more than 90 percent over the past five years). By far most of the maize from the north part of the nation that moves to the south part of the nation also flows through Dalian.
5. See Park et al. (2002) for a complete discussion of the major channels of flow of China's rice trade. According to extensive interviews with rice traders between 1995 and 2001, the largest flows of rice from each of the four clearly designated regions end up in the major consumption centers in Guangzhou, Shanghai, Beijing and Dalian.

6.   An average transportation gradient (which are reported in Table 6.1 for maize, soybeans and rice for China for 1998–2000 and for maize and soybeans for the US for 1998) is the coefficient on the 'distance variable' (a variable that is measuring the distance in 1000 kilometers from the port of the location of the market) from regressions that explain commodity-specific prices for each year (in logs) as a function of the distance variable and a series of period dummies (one for each week of the year). In other words, the coefficient is the average percentage change in price for each 1000 kilometers that a marketing site is removed from the port, holding constant the average price change for all sites during each week of the year. Regression results available from authors upon request.

REFERENCES

de Brauw, A., J. Huang and S. Rozelle (2004), 'The sequencing of reforms in China's agricultural transition', *Economics of Transition*, **12** (3), 427–66.

Fan, S. (1991), 'Effects of technological change and institutional reform on production growth in Chinese agriculture', *American Journal of Agricultural Economics*, **73**, 266–75.

Huang, J., S. Rozelle and M. Chang (2004), 'The nature of distortions to agricultural incentives in China and implications of WTO accession', *World Bank Economic Review*, **18**(1), 59–84.

Lin, J.Y. (1992), 'Rural reforms and agricultural growth in China', *American Economic Review*, **82**(1), 34–51.

Luo, Renfu, Linxiu Zhang, Chengfang Liu and Scott Rozelle (2005), 'Tracking public goods invesment in rural China', Working Paper, Center for Chinese Agricultural Policy, Institute of Geographical Sciences and Natural Resource Research, Chinese Academy of Sciences.

McMillan, J. (1997), 'Markets in transition', in D. Kreps and K.F. Wallis (eds), *Advances in Economics and Econometrics: Theory and Applications*, vol. 2, Cambridge: Cambridge University Press, pp. 210–39.

McMillan, J., J. Whalley and L. Zhu. (1989), 'The impact of China's economic reforms on agricultural productivity growth', *Journal of Political Economy*, **97**(4), 781–807.

Park, A. and S. Rozelle (1998), 'Reforming state–market relations in rural China', *Economics of Transition*, **6**(2), 461–80.

Park, A., H. Jin, S. Rozelle and J. Huang (2002), 'Market emergence and transition: Transition costs, arbitrage, and autarky in China's grain market', *American Journal of Agricultural Economics*, **84**(1), 67–82.

Rozelle, S. and J. Swinnen (2004), 'Success and failure of reform: Insights from the transition of agriculture', *Journal of Economic Literature*, **42**, 404–56

Rozelle, S., A. Park, J. Huang and H. Jin (2000), 'Bureaucrat to entrepreneur: The changing role of the state in China's transitional commodity economy', *Economic Development and Cultural Change*, **48**(2), 227–52.

Sicular, T. (1995), 'Redefining state, plan, and market: China's reforms in agricultural commerce', *China Quarterly*, **144**, 1020–46.

7. Economic Transition and Demand Pattern: Evidence from China's Paper and Paperboard Industry

Haizheng Li, Jifeng Luo and Patrick McCarthy

1. INTRODUCTION

China's economic transition since 1979 is characterized by rapid economic growth, gradual transformation into a market system, and increasing integration into the world economy. The complex economic dynamics during the transition period affects every aspect of the economic system, including industry demand structure. Understanding the demand for a particular industry is important for policy makers and for the industry stakeholders; as an emerging international market, China is also of special interest to foreign producers and investors who are ready to tap into the Chinese market.

Moreover, the economic transition and market reforms may add new features to industry demand, and thus poses new questions in studying the demand structure. Over the period of 1979–2001, continuing economic growth and economic reforms have dramatically changed the Chinese economy, providing an opportunity to investigate the demand dynamics. If the economy becomes increasingly market oriented and open, it is expected that the demand responses to price and to international markets would increase. Some studies, such as Young (2000), however, indicate that the Chinese economy has become fragmented internally as a result of economic reform. The demand dynamics for a particular product group will at least shed light on the overall degree of market mechanism in the Chinese economy.

This chapter investigates the demand for paper and paperboard products in China. The paper and paperboard industry represents Chinese traditional industries. A common feature of a traditional industry in China is that most firms in this industry were state-owned or other publicly owned and thus operated under the government planning system that did not use profits or return on investment as a metric for success. The economic reforms forced state-owned enterprises to adopt more market oriented approaches and are increasingly employing market-related criteria to evaluate the success of the enterprise. This change is having a greater impact on traditional industries (with inefficient organizational structures) relative to 'new economy' industries, such as information technology (IT), which suffer considerably less from these 'legacy costs'. Moreover, traditional industries are facing increasing competition from international producers as China gradually opens its markets. Therefore, given the combined effects of increasing international competition and market reforms, the demand pattern has important implications for any traditional industry.

At the same time, China possesses a huge market potential for paper and paperboard products. Chinese total paper and paperboard consumption is currently ranked second in the world, only behind the US. The consumption of paper and paperboard products in 2001 reached 42.6 million metric tons, increasing at an average annual rate of 10.38 percent over the last 20 years.[1] By comparison, the average growth rate of the US paper and paperboard consumption over the same period is 1.85 percent.[2] China's imports of paper and paperboard products grew at an average annual rate of 12.7 percent for the period 1979–2000, and the share of imports in the consumption increased from 9 percent to 17 percent for the same period. In 2001, China imported 5.57 million tons of paper and paperboard products, almost double the amount in 1995.

However, in comparison with the worldwide average of per capita consumption of 53.8 kg and the US per capita consumption of 331.7 kg, China's per capita paper and paperboard consumption remains very low, at 28.4 kg in 2000. Therefore, as the Chinese economy grows, spurred on by continuing economic reforms and an increasingly literate population, the demand for paper and paperboard products will increase rapidly. In addition, with the entry into World Trade Organization (WTO), China's import tariffs are expected to fall from between 12 and 15 percent to 5 percent for most paper and paperboard grades over the next few years. Overall, there is every expectation that China will be one of the major markets for international pulp and paper producers.[3]

Currently China's small-scale mills and outdated technologies limit its ability to satisfy the growing demand. Its capacity and output are scattered among numerous small mills. On average, Chinese paper mills produce less than 6500 tons/year, while the world average is over 40 000 tons/year and the average in developed countries is well above 100 000 tons/year. Only 44 of China's 4748 mills produce more than 10 000 tons per year and only a handful of them produce products of international quality. Due to the highly capital-intensive nature of the paper and paperboard production, China needs a significant amount of investments to modernize its pulp and paper industry. A number of international companies have invested in China in recent years, including Indonesia-based Asia Pulp and Paper Co., UPM-Kymmene Co. (Finnish), and Stora Enso (Finnish-Swedish).[4] And at least 43 new projects have been scheduled in China's paper and paperboard industry for the period of 2002–04, adding a new capacity of nearly six million tons per year to the industry in the near future.

Despite the worldwide interest in this burgeoning industry, there is no existing study on the demand for paper and paperboard products in China, although there are a number of studies for other countries. Buongiorno and Kang (1982) investigated short- and long-run elasticities of US demand for paper and paperboard. Hetemäki and Obersteiner (2002) examine the demand for newsprint in the United States for the period 1971–2000. Chas-Amil and Buongiorno (2000) used panel data to estimate paper and paperboard demands for 14 European Union countries. And Simangunsong and Buongiorno (2001) used panel data on 62 countries during the period 1973–97 to estimate the price and income elasticities for nine groups of forest products.

In this chapter, we investigate the demand pattern for paper and paperboard products in China, focusing on the structural changes caused by economic reform and integration into the world market. The total demand for paper and paperboard products consists of two parts: domestic products and imports. The domestically produced paper and paperboard products are generally lower quality products. In particular, over 80 percent of the pulp produced in China is made from wheat straw, rice straw, reed, bamboo and other non-wood sources, which yield lower quality products relative to those produced from wood pulp.[5] Based on the information from China Paper Association, in 2000, 80 percent of China's paper and paperboard products are low-quality and medium-quality grades, requiring China to rely on imports for high quality grades.[6]

Given the quality difference between the domestic product and imports, simply pooling the domestic and import demands imposes restrictions of homogeneous income and price elasticities on the two different demand functions. Thus, we extend our theoretical model on demand to include imports, and estimate the two demand functions separately, that is, the demand for domestic products and the demand for imports. Following the traditional approach to demand estimation, we first estimate demand functions using an instrumental variable estimator and test for a structural change in demand. Second, in order to address the concern for nonstationarity of the variables in the demand function, cointegration analysis and error-correction models are applied to the demand functions.

The chapter is organized as follows. In Section 2, we outline a theoretical framework for the demand structure and develop empirical models. Section 3 briefly describes the data. Section 4 discusses the results based on instrumental estimations; and Section 5 reports the results based on co-integration analysis and error correction models. Section 6 concludes.

2. A SIMPLE DEMAND MODEL

Since paper and paperboard products mostly serve as inputs in many industries, in the classical approaches, the demand is derived from the demand for final products.[7] Paper and paperboard products enter the production function as intermediate goods. To capture the quality differences, we generalized the commonly used production function to treat imported paper and paperboard products as a separate input. This specification will also help to control for the institutional changes caused by economic transition, because international markets play an increasing role in China's domestic demands.

Therefore, as commonly used in other studies (e.g. Chas-Amil and Buongiorno, 2000; Simangunsong and Buongiorno, 2001) and for the simplicity, we assume a Cobb–Douglas production function as below

$$Y_t = a D_t^{*b} \cdot I_t^{*c} \cdot X_t^d \qquad (7.1)$$

where Y_t is the production function of final products, D_t^* is paper and paperboard inputs made domestically, I_t^* is the imported paper and paperboard, X_t is a vector of other inputs, a is an index for the state of technology, and b, c, and d are positive parameters.[8] Total cost C_t is represented by:

$$C_t = D_t^* P_t^D + I_t^* P_t^I + X_t P_t^X \qquad (7.2)$$

where P_t^D, P_t^I, and P_t^X are the paper and paperboard price, imported paper and paperboard price, and the prices of other inputs, respectively. Minimizing cost with regard to D_t^*, I_t^*, and X_t, subject to the production function, we obtain the demand function for domestic paper and paperboard and for imports:

$$D_t^* = F(Y_t, P_t^D, P_t^I, P_t^X) = \delta_0 Y_t^{\delta_1} \left(\frac{P_t^D}{P_t^X}\right)^{\delta_2} \left(\frac{P_t^I}{P_t^X}\right)^{\delta_3} \qquad (7.3)$$

$$I_t^* = F(Y_t, P_t^I, P_t^D, P_t^X) = \delta_0 Y_t^{\tau_1} \left(\frac{P_t^I}{P_t^X}\right)^{\tau_2} \left(\frac{P_t^D}{P_t^X}\right)^{\tau_3} \tag{7.4}$$

where

$\delta_1 = \tau_1 = 1/(b + c + d),$
$\delta_2 = -(c + d)/(b + c + d),$
$\delta_3 = c/(b + c + d),$
$\tau_2 = -(b + d)/(b + c + d)$ and
$\tau_3 = b/(b + c + d).$

Equations (7.1) and (7.2) represent a static demand model assuming that equilibrium is achieved within time period t (one year for this analysis), and D_t^* and I_t^* is the equilibrium consumption for paper and paperboard products. If the adjustment takes a longer time, there will be a dynamic adjustment process. In order to allow for such a possibility, we assume that during time period t, the adjustment process can be represented by the following model:

$$\frac{D_t}{D_{t-1}} = \left(\frac{D_t^*}{D_{t-1}}\right)^{\alpha_1} \quad \text{or} \quad \frac{I_t}{I_{t-1}} = \left(\frac{I_t^*}{I_{t-1}}\right)^{\alpha_2} \tag{7.5}$$

where α is the speed of adjustment, $0 \le \alpha \le 1$, and D_{t-1} or I_{t-1} is consumption in the previous time period. Substituting equation (7.5) in equations (7.3) and (7.4), we obtain a dynamic demand model:

$$D_t = \gamma_0 Y_t^{\beta_1} \left(\frac{P_t^D}{P_t^X}\right)^{\beta_2} \left(\frac{P_t^I}{P_t^X}\right)^{\beta_3} D_{t-1}^{\beta_4} \tag{7.6}$$

$$I_t = \varphi_0 Y_t^{\lambda_1} \left(\frac{P_t^I}{P_t^X}\right)^{\lambda_2} \left(\frac{P_t^D}{P_t^X}\right)^{\lambda_3} I_{t-1}^{\lambda_4} \tag{7.7}$$

where
$\gamma_0 = \delta_0^{\alpha_1}, \beta_1 = \delta_1\alpha_1, \beta_2 = \delta_2\alpha_1, \beta_3 = \delta_3\alpha_1, \beta_4 = 1 - \alpha_1,$
$\varphi_0 = \delta_0^{\alpha_2}, \lambda_1 = \tau_1\alpha_2, \lambda_2 = \tau_2 \alpha_2, \lambda_3 = \tau_3\alpha_2,$ and $\lambda_4 = 1 - \alpha_2.$

Taking logarithms of equation (7.6) and (7.7) yields the following empirical demand functions:

$$\ln D_t = \beta_0 + \beta_1 \ln Y_t + \beta_2 \ln P_t + \beta_3 \ln PA_t + \beta_4 \ln D_{t-1} + u_t \qquad (7.8)$$

$$\ln I_t = \lambda_0 + \lambda_1 \ln Y_t + \lambda_2 \ln PA_t + \lambda_3 \ln P_t + \lambda_4 \ln D_{t-1} + \varepsilon_t \qquad (7.9)$$

where D_t is the domestic demand in year t, I_t is the import demand in year t, Y_t is represented by real gross domestic product (GDP), P_t is the real domestic price index of paper and paperboard, PA_t is the real international price index of paper and paperboard, and both u_t and ε_t are disturbance terms. In the domestic demand function, β_1, β_2, and β_3 represents, respectively, the income elasticity, own price elasticity, and cross price elasticity of domestic demand; in the import demand function, λ_1, λ_2, and λ_3 are the income elasticity, own price elasticity, and cross price elasticity of import demand, respectively.

The above models do not control for possible structural changes caused by China's economic transition. The transition can be characterized by a rising degree of market-oriented mechanisms and an increasing integration into the world market. Such changes will affect the demand structure for paper and paperboard products. For example, state-owned enterprises (SOEs) used to operate under a state planning system, and were not responsible for profits and losses. In this situation, SOEs may not respond to price signals. The reforms have forced most SOEs to enter the market system. In order to survive in competitive markets, SOEs have to be more sensitive to input prices. On the other hand, during the economic transition, non-state-owned enterprises represent an increasing share of the economy. Like other capitalist firms, these enterprises are sensitive to input costs. Therefore, as the economic transition continues, the economy should become more responsive to price changes and the demand should be more price elastic. Similarly, the greater access to international markets may also influence the demand pattern for imported paper and paperboard products.

As a result, these institutional factors must be taken into account. The economic reform in urban area in China started in 1983–85. Prior to 1992, the Chinese economy was still largely a command economy under the old planning system, with the share of state-owned enterprises (SOE) in gross industrial output value above 53 percent. The economic reforms accelerated after 1992, subsequent to Deng Xiaoping's dramatic political campaign visit to south China. Since that time, China has moved quickly towards an open economy market system. For a two-year period from 1992 to 1994, the share of SOE dropped 14 percentage points (from 48.1 percent to 34.1 percent), which is almost half of the total drop of SOE share for a fourteen-year period from 1978 to 1992. The decline of SOE has continued since then, and the SOE share reached 18.1 percent in 2001. Moreover, in 1993, the total number of bankruptcy proceedings of state-owned enterprises was larger than the total number of the previous four years.[9]

Therefore, there seemed to be a structural change in the Chinese economy in 1992–94. In order to capture this structural effect, we chose 1993 as a structural break point. Prior to 1993, state-owned enterprises roughly controlled more than half of the industrial output and then dropped quickly. We define a dummy variable (R_t) that equals 0 prior to 1993 and 1 for 1993 and after.[10]

3. THE DATA

We use annual data from 1979–2001 for this analysis. The demand for domestic paper and paperboard products is measured by total domestic output minus exports and the demand for imports is measured by actual imports. The statistical sources for the analysis included *China Statistical Yearbook 2002*, the *Almanac of the Paper Industry of China 1999*, the World Bank Development Indicator Database, and the US Bureau of Labor Statistics. Following previous studies, China's real GDP is used as a proxy for economic activity. Nominal GDP is converted to real GDP, with 1979 as the base year. We use the ex-factory price indices to measure the domestic real price for paper and paperboard, deflated by the GDP deflators based on 1979 purchasing power.[11]

When we measure the price for imported paper and paperboard products, three factors need to be considered. One is the shipping cost, which has dropped considerably during this 23-year period. The second factor is the exchange rate. The official exchange rate of Chinese yuan varied from 1.55 to 8.28 during the period of this analysis. The variation will significantly affect the cost of imported paper and paperboard. The last factor is the tariff.

In order to control for these factors, we fist calculate the import price based on US dollars. In particular, for all grades of paper and paperboard, the Chinese statistics reported both the imported value in US dollars and the total imported volume in tons. The total value of imported paper and paperboard is calculated on the CIF base (i.e., costs, insurance and shipping costs).[12] Thus the import price is calculated by dividing the value of paper and paperboard imports by the volume of imported paper and paperboard. The import price is converted into Chinese currency by multiplying the calculated import price in US dollars with official exchange rates. The *China Statistical Yearbook* does not contain the values of imports for 1979 and 1980. These two missing observations are extrapolated by regressing

Table 7.1:   *Descriptive Statistics*

Variable	Variable description	
Domestic demand	Paper and paperboard output minus exports, in million metric tons	15.62* (8.88) [4.77] {37.09}
GDP	Real gross domestic product, in 100 million yuan	13432.77 (8131.61) [4038.20] {29718.47}
Domestic price	Real ex-factory price indicies in China	107.04 (11.52) [91.03] {129.13}
Import price	Real prices of paper and paperboard imported	203.53 (40.04) [137.05] {278.39}
Import demand	Imports of paper and paperboard into China, in million metric tons	2.44 (2.11) [0.49] {6.52}
R_t	Dummy = 1 for 1993 and subsequent years, zero otherwise	

Note: *In each data cell the first entry is the mean, the second is the standard deviation, the third is the minimum value and the fourth is the maximum value.

import price on the US producer price index (PPI) for all grades of paper and paperboard products (excluding converted and building paper).[13]

Finally, the calculated import price is converted into a real price using Chinese GDP deflator, with 1979 as the base year. The adjusted import price controls for shipping costs and exchange rate but it may not capture the effect of tariffs. Unfortunately, such information is not available. Since the period covered in this study is mostly before China's joining the WTO, the change in tariff for paper and paperboard product is not expected to be dramatic, and thus we assume that the effect of tariff on import price is relatively small. Descriptive statistics are reported in Table 7.1.

4.   INSTRUMENTAL VARIABLE ESTIMATION

In estimating the demand equation, we first apply the traditional regression analysis based on the structural model discussed in the above section. Since demand and price are jointly determined in the market, price should be endogenous in the demand function. Existing studies of paper demand treat this issue differently. For example, Chas-Amil and Buongiorno (2000) used unit values of imports and/or exports to construct price indices. They argue that such a price index is exogenous because the demand in each country is too small to affect the international price. Hetemäki and Obersteiner (2002) investigated US newsprint demand, and they addressed the possible simultaneity between newsprint consumption and prices using a vector autoregression model (VAR).

In this study, we use instrumental variable (IV) estimation to control for price endogeneity.[14] Given the data limitations, we follow the traditional practice in time series analysis by using the previous price as instrument for the current price. Presumably, the current demand is not determined simultaneously with the previous price. The import price is mainly determined in the international market, and hence it is treated as exogenous because Chinese imports of paper and paperboard products are still relatively small in the world market and do not affect the world price.

4.1.   The Demand for Domestic Paper and Paperboard Products

In preliminary work, we applied ordinary least squares (OLS) to estimate the demand function for domestic paper and paperboard products.[15] We then use instrumental variable estimation to estimate the demand function. The estimation results from two-stage-least-squares (2SLS) are reported in Table 7.2. Given the possibility of serial correlation in the regression error, we tested each model for serial correlation.[16] The test result on the correlation coefficient is also reported in the table, and indicates no evidence of serial correlation. This result is not surprising because we are estimating a dynamic model using annual data. As discussed below, the adjustment of paper and paperboard demand to its equilibrium level appears to be completed in the year (for most models, the lagged dependent variable is not significant). Therefore, the demand models estimated are 'dynamically complete' with one lag of the dependent variable, and thus the regression error should not be serial correlated.

In Table 7.2, Model 1 is the base model and does not control for institutional changes in China caused by the economic transition. In this model, only the lagged demand variable is statistically significant. In order

Table 7.2:   *Demand for Paper and Paperboard in China by IV Estimation*

Variable	Domestic demand		Import demand
	1	2	3
Constant	4.42	−8.11***[a]	−9.30*
	(6.86)	(2.74)	(5.11)
GDP	0.19	1.01***	0.89**
	(0.32)	(0.20)	(0.38)
Domestic price	−1.46	0.35	0.96
	(1.14)	(0.90)	(1.64)
Import price	0.13	−0.07	−0.60*
	(0.19)	(0.25)	(0.30)
Lagged domestic demand	0.98**		
	(0.45)		
R_t * Domestic price		−0.69*	
		(0.39)	
R_t * Import price		0.59*	0.10*
		(0.34)	(0.05)
Test for autocorrelation ρ[b]	0.41	0.52	0.08
	(0.68)	(0.33)	(0.31)

Notes:
[a]   The symbols *, ** and *** denote significant at the 10, 5 and 1 percent levels respectively.
[b] ρ = coefficient of AR(1) serial correlation.

to control for possible structural changes, we interact the economic transition dummy with prices and GDP. In different specifications, the interaction between the dummy and GDP never appears statistically significant. Since the transition dummy mainly captures the progress of moving to a market system, it is likely that the relationship between the demand for paper and paperboard products and GDP has not undergone a significant change in these two periods.[17]

After including structural change terms, the lagged demand variable becomes insignificant. As discussed in the theoretical model, lagged demand controls for the process of demand adjustment toward equilibrium. The result indicates that the demand adjustment is complete within a year. In order to save degrees of freedom, we do not include lagged demand in Model 2. Based on the results, GDP has a significant impact on the demand, with a unitary income elasticity (that is, the demand grows at the same speed as GDP). A unitary income elasticity of demand is higher than that found for developed countries. For example, depending upon the type of paper and paperboard grades, Baudin and Lundberg (1987) reported income elasticities ranging from 0.54 to 0.66 for all major consuming countries for the period 1961–81. Chas-Amil and Buongiorno (2000) found income elasticities ranging from 0.18 to 0.39 for the European Union.[18]

Given that China is still at a relatively low level of economic development, the higher income elasticity of demand found is plausible and consistent with the finding that the demand for paper and paperboard becomes less income elastic as a country's income increases. For instance, Baudin and Lundberg (1987) found that the income elasticity was highest in the low income groups (per capita GDP under $2000). In the study of Buongiorno (1978), in which 43 countries were divided into low-income countries and high-income countries, the author found that, with the exception of printing and writing paper, the income elasticities are higher in low-income countries.

Interestingly, both the domestic price elasticity and the international price elasticity are statistically insignificant before 1993. As discussed in the above section, in the early stage of economic reforms, SOEs still produced a large portion of the product and they were not yet transformed into market oriented enterprises. Therefore, to a large extent, SOEs did not have to meet market criteria for continued operation. As a result, the demand was relatively insensitive to price changes. Thus, we cannot reject the hypothesis that the own-price elasticity of demand is zero.

This situation has changed as China has deepened its economic reforms. Most SOEs have been transformed to a so-called modern enterprise system and are now required to satisfy market criteria for continued operations and, accordingly, implying that demand will be more sensitive to price changes. From the results, the own-price elasticity after 1993 is −0.69 and statistically significant at the 10 percent level. This price elasticity is similar to that found in market economies. For example, Chas-Amil and Buongiorno (2000) reported price elasticity in the European Union from −0.30 to −0.89.[19] Notwithstanding this, demand is price inelastic, suggesting that few substitutes are available.

The response of the demand for domestic paper and paperboard products to international price is positive and significant at about the 10 percent level after 1993. This cross-price elasticity is 0.59, indicating that the demand for domestic paper and paperboard products is affected by the international markets as China becomes more integrated into the world. If the international price is high, the demand for domestic products increases; otherwise, China increases imports and reduces demand for domestically produced products. Therefore, imports appear to be a substitute for domestically made products. Clearly, the international markets can offer almost all types of paper and paperboard products needed in China, and these products can certainly substitute for the products that China produces domestically. As expected, the demand for domestic products is more responsive to own price change than to international price change.

4.2. The Demand for Imported Paper and Paperboard Products

China's imports of paper and paperboard products have increased rapidly. The share of imports in total paper and paperboard consumption, for example, has grown from 9 percent in 1979 to 17 percent in 2000. As China becomes a major player in the international paper and paperboard market, its demand for imports will have an increasing impact on the world market. Therefore, we also estimate the demand function for imports.

Since imports account for almost 20 percent of the total consumption in recent years, it is possible that the domestic price is affected by the amount of total imports, and thus is considered endogenous. Hence, we estimate the demand using IV estimation with lagged domestic price as an instrument. Since it is unlikely that Chinese imports affected the world price for the period studied, we assume that the international price is exogenous.

The results are reported in Table 7.2. We do not include lagged dependent variable because it is insignificant. The demand elasticity with respect to GDP is 0.89 and is significant at the 5 percent level (there is no significant change in the two periods). We cannot reject that the income elasticity is one, suggesting that as the Chinese economy continues to grow, the demand for imports will also grow rapidly and China will be an important potential market for international producers. The income elasticities of demand for both domestic products and imports appear to close to unitary elasticity. This result is somewhat surprising because if imports are mostly high quality products, like luxury goods, the income elasticity should be higher than that for domestic products. A possible explanation is that some trade barriers (especially administrative barriers) may exist and have depressed the demand. Another explanation would be that, as discussed in Section 1, the demand is also affected by increasing the amount of foreign direct investment (FDI) to produce high quality products in China.

Import demands are also sensitive to changes in the international price, with price elasticity equal to −0.60, in the same range of price elasticity for domestic demand. The inelastic response to price changes also suggests that relatively few substitutes are available for imported paper and paperboard products as a whole. This observation is also confirmed by the insignificant cross-price elasticity. The import demand does not seem to be affected by the domestic price, although the demand for domestic products is responsive to international price as discussed above. Therefore, these results are consistent with the notion that imports are a substitute for domestically produced paper and paperboard produces but that domestically produced products are not a substitute for imports. Such a difference can almost certainly be attributed to quality differences, and thus the two demand functions are in fact consistent with each other.

As the economic reforms deepen, the own-price elasticity appears to drop slightly. In other words, the import demand response to own-price becomes even less price elastic in the second period starting from 1993 (the difference of 0.10 is significant at the 10 percent level). One explanation is that as China's ability to produce higher quality products increases (for example, due to FDI), the imports focus increasingly on some specific grades of products. Thus, demand becomes less elastic. If this is the case, we may expect that the income elasticity of imports for high quality imports will increase as the economic transition continues. Yet we cannot discern this effect in our model, probably because the effect has not fully materialized in our period of study.[20]

5.   VECTOR ERROR CORRECTION MODEL ESTIMATION

The above traditional regression analysis provides estimates of various elasticities, and can conveniently test the possible structural change in the demand. One particular concern for the regression analysis using time series data is the possibility of nonstationarity of the variables. Nonstationarity (for example, caused by unit root) may result in spurious regression. To explore this, we analyze the stationarity property of some time series used in the regression and apply cointegration techniques to study the demand.

Although cointegration analysis has advantages in dealing with non-stationary data, it can only identify long-run relationships and it is generally difficult to test structural changes. Moreover, the Chinese economy is evolving as the economic transition continues. It is unclear whether China has reached the long-run equilibrium demand relationship or the stability of such a relationship, given the rapid structural changes in the Chinese economy. In this sense, the results from the regression analysis in the section above and the results based on non-stationary time series in this section should be viewed as complementary.

Although most previous studies on paper and paperboard demand have ignored the stationarity issue, a number of other studies have applied techniques for non-stationary data in studying pulp market and paper imports. Sarker (1996) used cointegration analysis to investigate the effects of price, income and other factors on Canadian softwood lumber exports to the United States. Riis (1996) adopted an error correction model to forecast the Danish timber price. Alavalapati et al. (1997) investigated the determinants of the Canadian pulp price. Laaksonen et al. (1997) estimated short- and long-run export demand for Finnish printing and writing paper in the United Kingdom.

We first employ Augmented Dickey–Fuller (ADF) unit root tests (Dickey and Fuller, 1979) for demand, GDP, and domestic price.[21] The results of the ADF test are presented in Table 7.3 (lags are selected based on Akaike information criterion). These variables appear to be nonstationary in levels; however, the unit root hypothesis is rejected for first differences, implying that they are $I(1)$. Based on the ADF test, we conduct cointegration analysis and estimate a vector-error-correction model (VEC) based on Johansen methodology (Johansen 1988, 1991). For a kth order unrestricted VAR model:

$$X_t = \pi_0 + \pi_1 X_{t-1} + \pi_2 X_{t-2} + \cdots + \pi_k X_{t-k} + \varepsilon_t \qquad (7.10)$$

where X_t is an $(n \times 1)$ vector of $I(1)$ variables, π_i are $(n \times n)$ parameter matrices $(i = 1, \ldots, n)$, k is the lag-length, and $\varepsilon_t \sim \text{iid}(0, \sigma^2)$, an error correction representation is,

$$\Delta X_t = \pi_0 + \Pi X_{t-1} + \sum_{i=1}^{k-1} \Gamma_i \Delta X_{t-i} + \varepsilon_t \qquad (7.11)$$

where Δ is the first difference operator,

$$\Pi = \sum_{i=1}^{k} \pi_i - I, \ \Gamma_i = -\sum_{j=i+1}^{k} \pi_j$$

and I is the identity matrix.

This VEC model is a traditional first difference VAR model plus an error correction term ΠX_{t-1}. The matrix Π contains information on the long-run co-movement of the variables. If r, the rank of Π, is $0 < r < n$, we have r cointegrated vectors. A likelihood ratio (LR) test is used to determine the optimum number of lags (Sims, 1980).[22] The LR statistic is obtained by estimating the unrestricted and restricted VAR, each with different lags. Due to limited sample size, the unrestricted equation started with lag-length k equal to four. The test is then conducted sequentially by reducing k one at a time. The results show that the appropriate lag-length in the VAR model is three, and thus for the VEC model is two.

Johansen's maximum likelihood cointegration tests are applied to find the cointegrated series. Johansen's method tests the restrictions imposed by cointegration on the unrestricted VAR. The method entails two tests for the number of cointegrating vectors r: the trace and the maximum eigenvalue tests (see also Hamilton, 1994, for more discussions). The results are summarized in Table 7.4. The trace test suggests two cointegrating vectors but the maximum eigenvalue test suggests that there is one cointegrating vector. Our estimated cointegration relationship is following:[23]

$$\ln D_t = -7.99 + 1.01 * \ln Y_t - 0.22 * \ln P_t + 0.42 * \ln PA_t \qquad (7.12)$$
$$ (0.03) \qquad (0.23) \qquad (0.09)$$

Table 7.5 lists the elasticities from both the IV estimation (Model 2) and the cointegration analysis. The elasticity estimates based on cointegration analysis is in line with that from the IV estimation. The own-price elasticity based on cointegration is lower than the IV estimates for the period after 1992, and it is statistically insignificant. This is because the cointegration analysis does not control for structural change, and thus it pools the two periods before and after 1993 together. It appears that the demand-price relation prior to 1993 dominates such a relationship, and thus the price effect becomes insignificant overall. This is also the case for the cross-price relationship. As for the income elasticity, the IV results do not show any structural change, and the estimated income elasticities based on both approaches are very close to each other.

Since the cointegration relationship represents a long-run equilibrium, it is desirable to examine the short-run dynamics. Thus, we estimate a VEC model to study the demand adjustment. Based on the results summarized in Table 7.5, the error-correction term in the demand function is −1.13 and significant at the 1 percent level. The negative coefficient of error-correction term ensures that the long-run equilibrium is achieved when there was a deviation in the previous period. More specifically, if there is a 1 percent positive deviation of demand from the long-run equilibrium in last period, the growth rate of demand falls by 1.13 percentage points in current period. Thus the system automatically adjusts to eliminate the positive discrepancy from long-run equilibrium.[24] In addition, to check for the statistical adequacy of the VEC model, various diagnostic tests are conducted; and the test statistics, also presented in Table 7.6, show no clear evidence of serial correlation, heteroskedasticity, and non-normality.

Table 7.3:   Augmented Dickey-Fuller Tests for Individual Variables

Variables	ADF Statistics	LAGS	Trend	Intercept
Level				
Domestic demand	−1.90	8	Yes	Yes
GDP	−3.61	6	Yes	Yes
Domestic price	−2.06	1	No	Yes
Import price	−2.94	0	No	Yes
First Difference				
Domestic demand	−4.10*	3	No	Yes
GDP	−3.26*	6	No	Yes
Domestic price	−4.01*	0	No	No
Import price	−6.58*	0	No	No

Note: *Test significant at the 5 percent level for the null hypothesis that the series has unit root.

Table 7.4:   Johansen's Cointegration Test

Null hypothesis	Alternative hypothesis	Likelihood ratio statistic	5 Percent critical value	1 Percent critical value
λ_{trace} test		λ_{trace} value		
$r = 0$	$r > 0$	93.49	47.21	54.46
$r \leq 1$	$r > 1$	39.28	29.68	35.65
$r \leq 2$	$r > 2$	14.21	15.41	20.04
λ_{max} test		λ_{max} value		
$r = 0$	$r = 1$	54.21	27.07	32.24
$r = 1$	$r = 2$	25.06	20.97	25.52
$r = 2$	$r = 3$	12.33	14.07	18.63

Note: This allows for linear trends in data and intercepts in cointegrating equations. The 5 and 1 percent critical values for the statistics are calculated by Osterwald-Lenum (1992). Maximum eigenvalue test indicates one cointegrating equation at the 1 percent significance level.

Table 7.5:   *The Long-Run Elasticities from IV and Cointegration Test*

| | Long-Run Elasticities | | |
	GDP	Domestic price	Import price
IV Estimates after 1992	1.01***	−0.69*	0.59*
	(0.20)	(0.39)	(0.34)
Johansen's Maximum likelihood	1.01***	−0.22	0.42***
	(0.03)	(0.23)	(0.09)

Note: The symbols *, ** and *** denote significant at the 10, 5 and 1 percent levels respectively.

Table 7.6:   *Estimates of the Vector Error Correction Model*

Dependent Variable: ΔDomestic Demand$_t$

Regressors[a]	Coefficients	Standard Error
Error Correction Term	−1.13***[b]	0.18
ΔDomestic Demand$_{t-1}$	0.92***	0.20
ΔDomestic Demand$_{t-2}$	1.02***	0.21
ΔGDP_{t-1}	−1.61**	0.67
ΔGDP_{t-2}	−0.38	0.80
ΔDomestic Price$_{t-1}$	−0.58**	0.25
ΔDomestic Price$_{t-2}$	0.19	0.26
ΔImport Price$_{t-1}$	−0.12	0.10
ΔImport Price$_{t-2}$	0.10	0.10
Adj. R^2	0.78	
LM(1)	17.39 (0.36)[c]	
White test	184.93 (0.39)	
Jarque-Bera	38.51 (0.96)	

Notes:
[a]   Allows for linear trends in data and intercepts in cointegrating equations.
[b]   The symbols *, **, *** denote significant at the 10, 5 and 1 percent levels respectively.
[c]   Figures in parentheses denote probability value.

6.   CONCLUSIONS

Employing instrumental variable and vector error correction procedures, we analyzed the demand for domestic and imported paper and paperboard products in China. As predicted by economic theory, income and price are important determinants of demand. For domestically made paper and paperboard products, the estimated income elasticity of the demand is about one, indicating that the demand increases at the same speed of the economic growth. However, the demand does not respond to own-price in the early stage of economic reform; and it becomes about −0.7 as the reforms deepen. This result demonstrates that, because of the old centrally controlled planning system, the economy to a large extent was operated based on non-market-oriented criteria and the demand is less sensitive to price. This phenomenal changed with China's economic reforms. The demand response to international price also shows the same pattern: It is only responsive to price in the second stage of economic reform starting from 1993 with the elasticity of approximately 0.6.

The demand for imports is also about unitary elastic with respect to economic growth. As expected, the demand for imported paper and paperboard respond negatively to increase of prices in the world market. The estimated own-price elasticity is −0.6. As economic transition progresses, the response appears to be even more inelastic. This is probably caused by the difference in quality between domestically made and imported products. As the reliance on some specific grade of high quality paper and paperboard increases, the demand becomes less elastic. The relatively high-income elasticity and low-price elasticity of the demand for imports indicate that China has a huge market potential for international producers in this industry.

The demand for domestic product appears to respond to the price in world market with an estimated cross-price elasticity of 0.59. This is not surprising because imports can certainly be used as substitutes for domestically produced products. On the other hand, the demand for imports does not respond to domestic price, indicating that domestically made products may not be used as substitutes for imports.

In order to address the issue of nonstationarity for variables in the demand function, we also estimated an error correction model to study the cointegration relationship and short run dynamics for the demand system for domestic products. The results from cointegration analysis are in line with the IV estimates. In addition, the error-correction term in the VEC model has a negative and statistically significant coefficient, which ensures a return to the long-run equilibrium if there is any deviation in the short-run.

Based on the results, it is clear that, as economic transition progresses, the Chinese economy is becoming an increasingly market-oriented system. This is particularly evident from the increasing response of demand to both domestic price and international price. Although some studies claimed that the Chinese economy becomes increasingly disintegrated internally (e.g. Young, 2000), the results from this study at least do not offer any direct support for the claim. The implication is that, even if some interregional distortions exist during the course of economic transformation, the overall economy is still becoming a more market-oriented system.

Notwithstanding the small number of observations for this analysis, we are able to obtain interesting results, especially related to structural changes in demand. Among the implications of this analysis for future work is the need for a larger sample. With a larger sample, we may be able to discern other structural changes and the effect of joining the WTO. A related limitation deriving from the sample size is an inability to test alternative econometric specifications based upon a richer set of explanatory variables.

NOTES

1. Consumption, import and capacity are defined in metric tons throughout this chapter.
2. The statistics source is FAO Statistical Databases.
3. 'China and Taiwan Lower Import Tariffs for Pulp, Paper and Board', available at: http://www.paperloop.com.
4. In March 1999, Singapore based Asia Pacific Resources International Holdings began operating a 350 000 ton/yr uncoated woodfree paper machine at Changshu, China; and Asia Pulp and Paper Co. started two woodfree paper machines at its Dagang mill in China.
5. Although bamboo can offer comparable quality fibers, technical problems persist with bamboo fibers. For example, the coarseness of bamboo fibers limits their use in coated grades. Other problems include runnability on the paper machine and well as linting and picking problems in the press room.
6. 'The Tenth Five-year Plan of China's Paper and Paperboard Industry' (in Chinese), China Paper Association, 12 April 2001, available at: http://www.cppi.com.cn/zylt/a18.htm.
7. According to 'The Tenth Five-year Plan of China's Paper and Paperboard Industry', well above 80 percent of total paper and paperboard products in China are employed as inputs for other industries such as publishing, package and printing, and less than 20 percent are directly consumed by consumers.
8. It is possible to use a more sophisticated demand function such as AIDS (e.g. Deaton and Muellbauer, 1980). However, this type of functions generally requires additional data information such as cost shares, which is unavailable in our data. More importantly, as one of the first studies on demand for paper/board in China, we adopt the simpler approach in order to focus on the structural changes in demand as a result of economic transition.
9. See Lee, Wong and Mok (1999).
10. To test the sensitivity of the estimation results to alternative definitions of the structural break, we re-estimated the model using 1992 and 1994 as the structural change dummy variable and found no change in the conclusions.

11.   The Chinese State Statistic Bureau gives the following definition: Ex-factory Price Index of Industry Products reflects the change in general ex-factory prices of all industrial products, including sales of industrial products to commercial enterprises, foreign trade sector, materials supplying and distribution sectors as well as sales of production means to industry and other sectors and sales of consumers goods to residents.

12.   The CIF price is the purchaser's price that would be paid by an importer taking delivery of the good at his own frontier, before paying any import duty or other tax levied at the frontier.

13.   Based on US Bureau of Labor Statistic, the Producer Price Index (PPI) measures the average change over time in the selling prices received by domestic producers for their output. The prices included in the PPI are from the first commercial transaction for many products and some services.

14.   Since the consumption for paper product is part of GDP, it is also possible that GDP is endogenous. However, paper and paperboard consumption are generally a very small portion of the GDP, comprising, for example, only 1.78 percent in China in 2000 (*China Statistical Yearbook 2001*). Thus, the endogeneity for GDP is not considered here, but will be addressed in the VAR model estimation in the next section.

15.   The estimated short run income elasticity was 0.52 and statistically significant at the 0.05 level; the estimated price elasticity was 0.39 prior to 1993 and −0.11 after 1993, but was not statistically significant; the short run cross price elasticity had the expected sign (−0.05 prior to 1993, and 0.38 after 1993) but was insignificant. OLS results suggest that there was a structural shift in China's demand for paper and paperboard after 1993.

16.   Because the model included a lagged dependent variable, we follow Durbin (1970) to test for AR(1) error. We first regress consumption on all explanatory variables including lagged consumption by 2SLS, and obtain the residual $\hat{e}$. We then regress the residuals on all explanatory variables and the lagged $\hat{e}$, and test whether the coefficient of lagged $\hat{e}$ is significant.

17.   Studies find that the demand response to GDP has changed for some specific grades of paper products, such as newsprints and printing papers, in some countries due to the development IT technology (Hetemäki and Obersteiner, 2002).

18.   Chas-Amil and Buongiorno (2000) also provided elasticities for the individual countries. The estimated income elasticity ranged from 0.15 in Portugal to 0.64 in Denmark.

19.   The demand seems to be even more price sensitive than that found in some other countries. For example, Baudin and Lundberg (1987) reported price elasticities in the range of −0.48 to −0.31.

20.   It is likely that the import demand structure will change with China's joining the WTO in 2000. With the availability of future data, the WTO effect can be evaluated.

21.   The ADF test for the international price gives an insignificant ADF statistic of −1.7 for the level series, and a highly significant statistic of −5.23 for the first differenced series, indicating that the international price is I(1).

22.   LR $= -2 \, (\ell_k - \ell_{k+1})$, where ℓ_k is the log likelihood of VAR with lags k. The LR statistic is asymptotically distributed with degrees of freedom χ^2 equal to the number of restriction.

23.   We also estimated the two possible cointegration vectors indicated by the trace test. The resulting relationship was not reasonable. For example, the estimated coefficients had the wrong signs and inappropriately large magnitudes. Therefore, based on the maximum eigenvalue test, we chose to estimate one cointegration equation.

24.   Innovation accounting, such as impulse response functions (IRFs) and variance decomposition analysis, is used to obtain information on the dynamic response of endogenous variables to system shocks. Since this chapter focuses on the effect of China's structural shift to a more market-oriented economy, we did not conduct an IRF analysis for this study.

REFERENCES

Alavalapati, J.R.R., W.L. Adamowicz and M.K. Luckert (1997), 'A cointegration analysis of Canadian wood pulp prices', *American Journal of Agriculture Economics*, **79**, 975–86.

Baudin and Lundberg (1987), 'The world model of the demand for paper and paperboard', *Forest Science*, **33**, 185–96.

Buongiorno, J. (1978), 'Income and price elasticities in the world demand for paper and paperboard', *Forest Science*, **24**, 231–46.

Buongiorno, J. and Kang (1982), 'Econometric models of the United States demand for paper and paperboard', *Wood Science*, **15**, 119–26.

Chas-Amil, M.L. and J. Buongiorno (2000), 'The demand for paper and paperboard: Econometric models for the European Union', *Applied Economics*, **32**, 987–99.

China Technical Association of Paper Industry (1999), *The Almanac of the Paper Industry of China*, China Light Industry Publishing House.

Deaton, A. and J. Muellbauer (1980), 'An almost ideal demand system', *The American Economic Review*, **70**, 312–26.

Dickey, D. and W.A. Fuller (1979), 'Distribution of the estimates for autoregressive time series with unit root', *Journal of the American Statistical Association*, **74**, 427–31.

Durbin, J. (1970), 'Testing for serial correlation in least squares regression when some of the regressors are lagged dependent variables', *Econometrica*, **38**, 410–21.

Hamilton, J.D. (1994), *Time Series Analysis*, Princeton University Press.

Hetemäki, L. and M. Obersteiner (2002), 'US newsprint demand forecasts to 2020', Working Paper, http://groups.haas.berkeley.edu/fcsuit/publications.html# publications.

Johansen, S. (1988), 'Statistical analysis of cointegration vectors', *Journal of Economics and Control*, **12**, 231–54.

Johansen, S. (1991), 'Estimation and hypothesis testing of cointegration vectors in Gaussian vector autoregressive models', *Econometrica*, **59**, 1551–80.

Laaksonen, S., A. Toppinen, R. Hanninen, and J. Kunuluvainen (1997), 'Cointegration in Finnish paper exports to the United Kingdom', *Journal of Forest Economics*, **3**, 171–85.

Lee, G.O.M., L. Wong and K.-H. Mok (1999), 'The decline of state-owned enterprises in China: Extent and causes', Working Paper, City University of Hong Kong.

Osterwald-Lenum, M. (1992), 'A note with quartiles of the asymptotic distribution of the maximum likelihood cointegration rank test statistics', *Oxford Bulletin of Economics and Statistics*, **54**, 461–72.

Riis, J. (1996), 'Forecasting Danish timber prices with an error correction model', *Journal of Forest Economics*, **2**(3), 257–71.

Sarker, R. (1996), 'Canadian softwood lumber export to the United States: A cointegrated and error-corrected system', *Journal of Forest Economics*, **2**(3), 205–31.

Simangunsong, B.C.H. and J. Buongiorno (2001), 'International demand equations for forest products: A comparison of methods', *Scandinavian Journal of Forest Research*, **16**, 155–72.

Sims, C.A. (1980), 'Macroeconomics and reality', *Econometrica*, **48**, 683–91.

State Statistical Bureau, People's Republic of China (2001), *China Statistical Yearbook*, China Statistical Publishing House.

Young, A. (2000), 'The razor's edge: Distortions and incremental reform in the People's Republic of China', *Quarterly Journal of Economics*, **115**, 1091–135.

8. Export Composition and Technology Spillovers in China: An Empirical Study Based on the Extended Feder Model

Helian Xu, Qun Bao and Mingyong Lai

1. INTRODUCTION

Technology is an important factor explaining income levels across countries. Recent work has shown, however, that the major sources of technical change leading to productivity growth in OECD countries are not domestic; instead, they come from abroad (Eaton and Kortum, 1999; Keller, 2001). Many authors have studied the mechanisms, or channels, through which international technology diffusion primarily occurs. Generally speaking, international technology spillover channels can be classified into two types. One is the so-called embodied spillovers, which refer to the technology spillovers embodied in the international flows of specific investment goods or trade commodities. The other is disembodied spillovers, which focus on the spillover effects of certain international activities such as academic conferences, publications of journals, communication of information, and also transnational training. Among the embodied technology spillovers, international trade has been recognized as one of the major spillover channels, whose importance can be shown through the following four effects. First, the contagion effect, which was originally advocated by Findlay (1978), suggests that the higher the degree of economic openness one country has, the more chances of learning advanced technology from outside it will have. Second, the learning by doing effect, which mainly applies to exporters who improve the quality and variety of their products due to pressure from competitors in other countries and also based on the information feedback from outside consumers. Third, the demonstration effect, which suggests that by imitating and learning from those exporters and importers, non-export sectors can improve their own productivity and management experience due to the externality effect of trade activities. Fourth, industrial linkages emerge so that once trade sectors set up certain backward or forward linkages with domestic firms they definitely help to enhance the technology levels of domestic partners.

Coe and Helpman (1995) first showed the importance of spillovers from imported international technology by measuring the contribution of research and development (R&D) inputs to the changes in total factor productivity (TFP) in 22 industrialized countries. According to their estimation, foreign R&D plays a more important role in promoting technological progress than domestic R&D. The model introduced by Coe and Helpman (1995) has been widely applied by many other researchers to investigate the importance of international technology spillovers (see Coe et al., 1997; Hakura and Jaumotte, 1999; Xu and Wang, 1999; and Mohnen, 2001). Since the model introduced by Coe and Helpman (1995) is essentially a partial equilibrium model, other authors, such as Eaton and Kortum (1997, 1999) extended the model to study the relationship between the quality improvement of imported intermediate goods and domestic technical change based on a general equilibrium model. A recent paper by Keller (2002) using the OECD countries' economic data from 1983 to 1997, demonstrated that nearly 90 percent of international spillover effects come from the R&D activities of the G-5 countries.

Few researchers have studied the technology spillover effects of exports with most authors instead focusing on the importance of imports in international technology spillover. As a matter of fact, exports should play a more significant role in international technology spillover since not only do they have demonstration effects and contagion effects which are similar to imports, but they also promote domestic firms' technological progress through learning by doing, competition effects and also industrial linkage effects, which will affect the R&D activities of domestic producers and domestic industrial structures to a much larger extent.

Few authors have attempted to investigate the importance of exports in international technology spillover. By establishing a two-sector model, Feder (1982) first studied the spillover effects of exports. Based on two data samples of 19 and 31 countries respectively during the period of 1964–73, Feder (1982) pointed out that exports may promote economic growth through two channels. First, there may be a comparative advantage in the productivity of the export sector relative to the productivity of the non-export sector. Second, the externality effect of exports may benefit the non-export sector due to imitation and learning effects. Therefore, the development of exports actually causes resource reallocation from the lower productivity non-export sector, to the export sector, and hence promotes domestic economic growth. Levin and Raut (1997) further introduce the role of human capital into this analysis. Using data from 30 semi-industrialized countries from 1965 to 1984, the authors find a complementary relationship between trade policy and human capital investment, which is measured as education expenditures. Changes in export structure also have a significant role in economic growth. The authors conclude that the export of primary goods has an insignificant influence on economic growth and that technology spillover effects actually happen in the export of manufacturing goods. Other authors, such as Rheeet al. (1984) and Clerides et al. (1998) also investigate the relationship between exports and technology spillover using different sample data. However, it is hard to reach a clear conclusion that exports truly have technology spillovers for countries in the sample.

The technology spillover of China's exports on its non-export sectors has been studied by few authors. Yang (1998) estimates the technology spillover effect of China's exports based on the Feder (1982) model using data from 29 provinces from 1985 to 1994. However, the author does not find that there is a significant technology spillover effect from exports on China's domestic sectors as found in Feder (1982). Chen (2001) also introduces time-changing variables into Feder's (1982) model, and shows that there is truly a significant technology spillover effect of exports by using Shanghai's economic data from 1969 to 1999. The author also finds that export growth promotes an increase in the employment rate. Bao et al. (2003) use China's panel data for 30 provinces during the period 1989–97, and find that although exports are one of the major technology spillover channels in China, human capital does not play such an important role in promoting spillover effects as other authors have shown.

Based on these findings, this chapter aims to further investigate the technology spillover effect of exports by using an extended three-sector Feder (1982) model. In Feder's original two-sector model it is assumed that the export of both primary goods and manufacturing goods have the same technology spillover effect. However, since different factor combinations have been used to produce these export goods, that is primary goods are more labor-intensive and resource-intensive while manufacturing goods are more technology-intensive and capital-intensive, their technology spillover effects can be expected to vary. Levin and Raut (1997) provide some support for this argument. The authors find that for the sample of semi-industrialized countries, the export of manufacturing goods has a significant influence on economic growth, while the export of primary goods does not. Additionally, great changes have occurred in China's export structure due to reforms and the opening of the economy. The share of primary good exports is decreasing while the share of manufacturing good exports has risen from 49.7 percent in 1980 to 89.78 percent in 2000. Therefore, it is important to investigate the influence of the changes in export structure on the technology spillover of exports, which has been neglected in previous research.

2. THE EXTENDED THREE-SECTOR MODEL

In a much-cited contribution to the growth literature, Feder (1982) proposed a model of growth for developing countries (LDCs) that recognized the importance of dualism – in his case, technology differences between sectors. Feder incorporated a sectoral disequilibrium in the form of a productivity differential, and externality spillovers between two sectors into a neoclassical growth model using an export/non-export distinction. This approach underlies most subsequent investigations of dualistic growth, though an agriculture–manufacturing distinction has more commonly been adopted (see Feder, 1986; Hwa, 1989; Dowrick, 1990; and Dowrick and Gemmell, 1991).

In this chapter we extend the original Feder model into a three-sector model, which specifies an economy composed of a non-export sector, a manufacturing-export sector, and a primary-export sector as follows:

$$Y = N + PX + MX$$
$$N = F(K_n, L_n, PX, MX)$$
$$PX = G(K_{px}, L_{px})$$
$$MX = H(K_{mx}, L_{mx}) \tag{8.1}$$

Where the total output of the economy, Y, is the sum of outputs from the non-export sector (N), the manufacturing-export sector (MX), and the primary-export sector (PX). The production function for the manufacturing-export sector contains K_{px} and L_{px} which represent the capital and labor inputs in this sector, and similarly for the primary export sector, where K_{mx} and L_{mx} are capital and labor inputs in the primary-export sector. However, following Feder's model, the output of the non-export sector is not only a function of its own capital and labor inputs K_n and L_n but also a function of PX and MX, where PX and MX capture the externalities of the export sectors.

Total inputs in the three sectors are given by the following equations:

$$K_n + K_{px} + K_{mx} = K$$
$$L_n + L_{px} + L_{mx} = L$$

The model also assumes that the relative factor productivities in the three sectors are different, such that:

$$\frac{G_k}{F_k} = \frac{G_L}{F_L} = 1 + \delta \ , \ \frac{H_k}{F_k} = \frac{H_L}{F_L} = 1 + \eta \tag{8.2}$$

The lower-case subscripts indicate the partial derivatives of the functions with respect to subscripted inputs. For example, G_k denotes the marginal productivity of capital in the primary export sector. It is obvious from equation (8.2) that the sign of $\delta(\eta)$ indicates which sector has higher marginal factor productivity. Thus a positive $\delta(\eta)$ means that input productivity in the primary export sector (manufacturing export sector) is higher than that in the non-export sector.

It can be derived by differentiating the equation $Y = N + PX + MX$:

$$dY = dN + dPX + dMX$$

$$\begin{aligned} = F_k dK_n + F_L dL_n + F_{PX} dPX + F_{MX} dMX + (1+\delta)F_k dK_{PX} \\ + (1+\delta)F_L dL_{PX} + (1+\eta)F_k dK_{MX} + (1+\eta)F_L dL_{MX} \end{aligned} \tag{8.3}$$

Since investment is always equal to the change of capital stock, we have:

$$I = I_n + I_{Px} + I_{MX} = dK_n + dK_{PX} + dK_{MX}$$

and we also have:

$$dL = dL_n + dL_{PX} + dL_{MX}$$

which indicates:

$$\begin{aligned} dY = F_k I + F_L dL + F_{PX} dPX + F_{MX} dMX \\ + \delta(F_k dK_{PX} + F_L dL_{PX}) + \eta(F_k dK_{MX} + F_L dL_{MX}) \end{aligned} \tag{8.4}$$

From (8.2), it can be derived:

$$F_k dK_{PX} + F_L dL_{PX} = \frac{1}{1+\delta}(G_k dK_{PX} + G_L dL_{PX}) = \frac{1}{1+\delta} * dPX$$

$$F_k dK_{MX} + F_L dL_{MX} = \frac{1}{1+\eta}(H_k dK_{MX} + H_L dL_{MX}) = \frac{1}{1+\eta} * dMX$$

Thus we have:

$$dY = F_k I + F_L dL + \left(\frac{\delta}{1+\delta} + F_{PX}\right) dPX + \left(\frac{\eta}{1+\eta} + F_{MX}\right) dMX \qquad (8.5)$$

The following equation can be derived by dividing (8.5) by:

$$\frac{dY}{Y} = F_k * \frac{I}{Y} + \frac{F_L * L}{Y} * \frac{dL}{L} + \left(\frac{\delta}{1+\delta} + F_{PX}\right) \frac{dPX}{PX} * \frac{PX}{Y}$$

$$+ \left(\frac{\eta}{1+\eta} + F_{MX}\right) \frac{dMX}{MX} * \frac{MX}{Y} \qquad (8.6)$$

According to Bruno (1968), it is assumed that a linear relationship exists between the marginal productivity of labor in certain sector and the average labor output of the whole economy:

$$F_L = \beta * (Y/L)$$

and by setting $F_k = \alpha$, then (8.6) can be written as:

$$\frac{dY}{Y} = \alpha * \frac{I}{Y} + \beta * \frac{dL}{L} + \left(\frac{\delta}{1+\delta} + F_{PX}\right) \frac{dPX}{PX} * \frac{PX}{Y}$$

$$+ \left(\frac{\eta}{1+\eta} + F_{MX}\right) \frac{dMX}{MX} * \frac{MX}{Y} \qquad (8.7)$$

where I/Y is capital–output ratio, and dL/L is the growth rate of total labor. The terms dPX/PX and dMX/MX are the growth rates of export in the primary export sector and manufacturing sector, and $PX/Y (MX/Y)$ is the ratio of output in the primary export sector (manufacturing export sector) to the total output.

$$F_{PX} = \frac{\partial N}{\partial PX} \left(F_{MX} = \frac{\partial N}{\partial MX}\right)$$

measures the inter-sectoral externalities of the primary export sector (manufacturing export sector) on the non-export sector. When $F_{PX} = 0$ and $F_{MX} = 0$, there are no inter-sectoral externalities for the two export sectors, which is the traditional neo-classical production function.

To further specify the externalities of both export sectors on the non-export sector, it is assumed in our model that constant elasticity holds in the production function of the non-export sector:

$$N = F(K_n, L_n, PX, MX) = PX^\vartheta * MX^\varphi * \Phi(K_n, L_n) \tag{8.8}$$

where ϑ, φ are the constant output elasticities of the externality of both the primary-export and the manufacturing sectors.

Thus, we have:

$$\frac{\partial N}{\partial PX} \equiv F_{PX} = \vartheta * PX^{\vartheta-1} * MX^\varphi * \Phi(K_n, L_n) = \vartheta * \frac{N}{PX}$$

$$\frac{\partial N}{\partial MX} \equiv F_{MX} = \varphi * MX^{\varphi-1} * PX^\vartheta * \Phi(K_n, L_n) = \varphi * \frac{N}{MX} \tag{8.9}$$

where the parameters ϑ, φ actually measure the externalities of the two export sectors.

Substituting (8.9) into (8.7), we have:

$$\frac{dY}{Y} = \alpha * \frac{I}{Y} + \beta * \frac{dL}{L} + \left(\frac{\delta}{1+\delta} + \vartheta \frac{N}{PX}\right)\frac{dPX}{PX} * \frac{PX}{Y}$$

$$+ \left(\frac{\eta}{1+\eta} + \varphi \frac{N}{MX}\right)\frac{dMX}{MX} * \frac{MX}{Y} \tag{8.10}$$

On the other hand, since

$$\vartheta \frac{N}{PX} = \vartheta \frac{N/Y}{PX/Y} = \frac{\vartheta}{PX/Y} - \vartheta - \vartheta \frac{MX/Y}{PX/Y}$$

$$\varphi \frac{N}{MX} = \varphi \frac{N/Y}{MX/Y} = \frac{\varphi}{MX/Y} - \varphi - \varphi \frac{PX/Y}{MX/Y} \tag{8.11}$$

Substituting (8.11) into (8.10), it can be derived:

$$\frac{dY}{Y} = \alpha * \frac{I}{Y} + \beta * \frac{dL}{L} + \left(\frac{\delta}{1+\delta} - \vartheta\right)\frac{dPX}{PX} * \frac{PX}{Y}$$

$$+ \left(\frac{\eta}{1+\eta} - \varphi\right)\frac{dMX}{MX} * \frac{MX}{Y} + \vartheta\left(1 - \frac{MX}{Y}\right)\frac{dPX}{PX} + \varphi\left(1 - \frac{PX}{Y}\right)\frac{dMX}{MX} \tag{8.12}$$

It can be seen from (8.11) that the economic growth rate depends not only on capital and labor inputs, but also the development of the export sectors. It can be further shown that exports promote economic growth in two ways. First, the change in productivity of the export sectors may affect the growth rate directly. For the primary-export sector, the productivity is:

$$[(\delta/(1+\delta))]\cdot(dPX/PX)\cdot(PX/Y),$$

while the productivity in the manufacturing-export sector is:

$$[(\eta/(1+\eta))]\cdot(dMX/MX)\cdot(MX/Y).$$

In addition, exports also promote the economic growth rate by their externality effects on the non-export sector, among which the externality of the primary-export sector is

$$\vartheta[1-(MX+PX)/Y]\cdot(dPX/PX),$$

and that of the manufacturing export sector is

$$\varphi[1-(MX+PX)/Y]\cdot(dMX/MX).$$

3. ECONOMETRIC ESTIMATION

This study uses cross-sectional data for 30 provinces in China[1] during the two periods of 1991–95 and 1996–2000. The principal data sources are China's statistical yearbooks from 1992 to 2001. Total output Y is measured as each province's GDP in each year, total investment I is indexed as each province's fixed assets investment, and labor L is each province's number of employed at the end of each year. PX and MX are primary goods export and manufacturing goods export respectively. In our econometric estimation, each variable is measured by the average value during the two periods. The average growth rate of each variable is calculated in the following way:

$$\ln z_t = a + bt$$

Where z_t is the level value, and t is the time variable. We can calculate the value of b based on the above regression equation, and then obtain the average growth rate r:

$$r = e^b - 1$$

Our regression results are listed in Table 8.1. Based on the regression results, we find that during the period 1991–95, the output–capital ratio is 0.294, and the t-statistic is significant at the 1 percent level. At the same time, it can be seen that the role of labor input in China's economic growth is not significant. The estimation results for the period 1996–2000 are very similar. According to our regression results, the output–capital ratio is 0.318 and the t-statistic is significant at the 1 percent level. Similarly, the t-statistic for the labor input variable is still insignificant. As shown in other papers, investment is one of the major sources of China's economic growth. In the period 1991–96, a 1 percent increase in investment leads to 0.294 percent economic growth, and for 1996–2000, a 1 percent increase in

Table 8.1:   *Regression Results*

Independent Variables	Regression Model One[a] 1991–95	Regression Model One[a] 1996–2000	Regression Model Two 1991–95	Regression Model Two 1996–2000
Constant	0.089^{***b}	0.094^{***}	-0.024	0.094^{***}
	(3.37)	(14.19)	(−0.756)	(14.22)
$\dfrac{I}{Y}$	0.294^{***}	0.318^{***}	0.314^{***}	0.398^{***}
	(4.414)	(3.107)	(4.812)	(10.39)
$\dfrac{dL}{L}$	0.659	−0.0921	0.462	−0.302
	(1.002)	(−0.646)	(0.718)	(−0.688)
$\dfrac{dPX}{PX} \cdot \dfrac{PX}{Y}$	−0.0386	−0.0449	0.201	0.160
	(−0.69)	(−0.755)	(0.813)	(0.198)
$\dfrac{dMX}{MX} \cdot \dfrac{MX}{Y}$	0.190^{**}	0.189^{***}	0.086^{**}	0.123^{**}
	(2.646)	(2.807)	(2.385)	(2.325)
$\left(1 - \dfrac{MX}{Y}\right) \cdot \dfrac{dPX}{PX}$			−0.042	−0.036
			(−0.486)	(−0.419)
$\left(1 - \dfrac{PX}{Y}\right) \cdot \dfrac{dMX}{MX}$			0.125^{**}	0.063^{*}
			(2.030)	(1.85)
R^2	0.632	0.706	0.690	0.718
F	10.741^{***}	2.754^{**}	8.549^{***}	2.747^{**}

Notes:
[a]   All regression results are from the econometric software Spss10.0.
[b]   The t-statistics are in parenthesis, among which ***, ** and * stand for 1, 5 and 10 percent significance levels respectively.

investment leads to 0.318 percent economic growth. However, due to the large number of unemployed in China, labor inputs may not play an important role in economic growth.[2] Since 1996, a remarkable reform has been carried out, which aims to improve the operation efficiency of China's SOEs. As a result of these reforms, many laid-off workers have added to the surplus of labor supply in the market. Feder (1982) also points out that the surplus in labor supply possibly leads to an insignificant t-statistic in econometric estimation.

Two major conclusions about the role of exports in China's economic growth since 1991 can be drawn from our estimation results. First, the coefficient of

$$\frac{dPX}{PX} \cdot \frac{PX}{Y}$$

in both models is negative, and the insignificant t-statistics demonstrate that the increase in primary goods exports from China is not a major source of China's economic growth. By comparison, the role of exports of manufacturing goods in China's economic growth is much more significant. The coefficients of $(dMX/MX) \cdot (MX/Y)$ are 0.190 and 0.189 respectively in the two models, and their t-statistics are both significant at the 5 percent level. Since in our model the externality of the export sectors on the non-export sector is taken into account, our estimation results do not find evidence of the externality of the primary goods sector on the domestic sector. On the other hand, exporting manufacturing goods promotes China's economic growth through its spillover effect on the non-export sector. Our estimation results based on China's economic data are similar to that of Levin and Raut (1997). The authors use data from 30 semi-industrialized countries during the period 1965–84 and find that the share of total exports from manufacturing goods export has a significant impact on economic growth, while the share of primary goods export does not play such an important role. This also shows that the externality effect of exports on the non-export sector mainly refers to manufacturing goods export.

Such empirical findings fit the real growth path of China's economy very well for the years we consider. During the period 1991–2000 remarkable changes happened in China's export structure. The share of total exports contributed by primary goods decreased to 10.2 percent in 2000 from 22.5 percent in 1991, while the share of exports in manufacturing goods increased to 89.8 percent in 2000 from 77.5 percent in 1991. Food and edible live animals (SITC0) are the major types of primary goods exported. In 1995, SITC0 comprised 46.3 percent of the total primary goods exports, and the share has increased to 48.2 percent. Since these exports are both resource-intensive and labor-intensive products, both the technology intensity and the added-value are lower for food and edible live animal exports, which mainly explains our findings that there is less of an externality for primary goods export on the non-export sector.

Among manufacturing goods export, machinery and electric goods always play an important role. The share of total manufacturing exports contributed by machinery and electric goods has grown quickly. For instance, in 1995 exports of machinery and electric goods comprised 34.4 percent of the total exports in manufacturing goods, and five years later, it reached 47.0 percent. Another notable fact is the significant growth in the export of high-tech goods. In 2000, 16.5 percent of the total manufacturing goods exports in China were high-tech exports. The value of these exports reached 37 billion US dollars. It is generally acknowledged that machinery and electric goods, especially high-tech goods, are much more technology-intensive and have a higher value-added than primary goods. This produces a greater externality effect on the non-export sectors. In addition, compared with primary goods export, it is more likely for producers who export manufacturing goods to establish industrial linkages with non-export sectors, which is also one of the important technology spillover channels. Finally, when the demonstration effect occurs and non-export producers imitate and learn from the manufacturing goods exporters they can improve their own production efficiency.

Another fact which draws our attention is that foreign-invested firms have played a key role in the export of China's manufacturing goods, which is also one of the important technology spillover sources. During the sample period, there is always a remarkable contribution of foreign firms to the rapid growth in exports of manufacturing goods in China. Foreign firms comprised 47.0 percent of the total manufacturing exports in 1995, and 63.4 percent of the total five years later (see Table 8.2). Moreover, foreign firms dominate China's high-tech exports. In 2000 for example, the value of foreign firms' high-tech exports was 2.98 billion US dollars, or an 80.52 percent share of all high-tech exports. For the two most technology-intensive industries, computers and mobile communication, the shares of foreign firms' export in 2000 were 84.0 percent and 96.4 percent respectively. It is widely acknowledged that compared with China's domestic firms, foreign-invested firms usually have more advanced production technology and management experience, especially for large multinational enterprises. By using the data from the third national industrial survey, Yao (1998) points out that compared with SOEs, the production efficiency of foreign-invested enterprises from other countries is 39 percent higher, and that of foreign-invested enterprises from Hong Kong,

Table 8.2: *Values of Foreign Firms' Machinery and Electric Goods Exports and their Shares*

Year	Machinery and electric goods exports from foreign firms	The share of total exports from foreign firms (percent)	The share of total machinery and electric goods exports (percent)
1992	61.0	35.1	31.2
1993	83.9	33.2	37.0
1994	132.8	38.3	41.5
1995	206.2	44.0	47.0
1996	269.1	43.8	55.8
1997	343.3	45.8	57.9
1998	401.2	49.6	60.3
1999	464.2	52.4	60.3
2000	667.3	55.9	63.4

Source: Jiang (2002).

Taiwan and Macao is 33 percent higher. Therefore, it can be concluded that the larger spillover effect of manufacturing goods export on the non-export sector actually reflects the technology spillover effect of foreign firms on domestic ones.

According to the regression results from model two, we can further estimate the effects of primary goods export and manufacturing goods export on China's economic growth. It can be seen from Table 8.1 that ϑ, which measures the externality effect of the primary goods export, is respectively −0.042 and −0.036 during the two periods we consider, demonstrating that there is no obvious spillover effect from the export of primary goods on non-export sectors. The productivity difference between the export and non-export sectors, δ, is 0.19 and 0.14 during the two periods,[3] which shows that the productivity of primary goods export sector is slightly higher than that of non-export sectors. However, it can also be seen that the relative productivity advantage of the primary goods export sector, compared with non-export sector, has been weakened, which is a sign of technology convergence between the primary goods export sector and the non-export sectors due to the technology spillover effect from exports on non-export producers.

By comparison φ, which measures the degree of externality of manufacturing goods export, is 0.125 and 0.063 during the two periods, and both coefficients are statistically significant at the 5 percent level. Further calculation shows that η, which is also the productivity difference between the manufacturing goods export sector and the non-export sector, is 0.267 and 0.228. It can be concluded from these findings that the export of manufacturing goods promotes economic growth in China through its technology spillover effect on the non-export sector and through its relative productivity advantage. However, similar to the case of primary goods, it can also be seen that there is a productivity convergence between the manufacturing goods export sector and the domestic sectors since η decreases to 0.228 in the second period from 0.267 in the first one. The technology spillover effect from exports of manufacturing goods is much more significant than that of exports of primary goods. In the period 1991–95, a 1 percent increase in manufacturing goods export leads to 0.125 percent growth in the production of non-export sectors via technology spillovers. By comparison, in the period 1996–2000, a 1 percent increase in manufacturing goods export will cause 0.063 percent growth in the production of the non-export sectors. Since the importance of international technology spillover has been greatly emphasized in the literature,[4] this chapter further verifies the role of exports in technology spillover, especially with changes in the export structure.

4.   CONCLUSIONS AND POLICY IMPLICATIONS

According to our estimation results for the two periods we consider, we conclude that technology spillover effects mainly happen through the export of manufacturing goods rather than the export of primary goods. In addition both of these export sectors have a higher relative productivity advantage over the non-export ones. Even though the role of exports in China's economic growth has been widely argued, the estimation results in this chapter indicate that because the export sectors usually have a higher productivity advantage, resource allocation efficiency can be improved by promoting exports. Specifically, more resource flows should be channeled to the export sector from the domestic sector, especially in the area of manufacturing. However, as we have seen in the above analysis, since there is productivity convergence between export sectors and non-export sectors, such resource transfers cannot last forever. Additionally, such productivity convergence occurs due to the technology spillovers from the export to the non-export sectors. However, according to our estimation, it is through the export of manufacturing goods rather than primary goods that improves the productivity of the non-export sector through technology spillovers.

Therefore, in order to keep promoting economic growth, the export structure in China needs to improve by increasing the share of total exports that are manufacturing goods. The optimal export structure for developing countries has been widely debated. According to classic trade theories such as Ricardo's theory of comparative advantage, trade participants are supposed to produce export goods based to their own relative advantage in either productivity or factor endowments. Thus, an obvious inference is that developing countries should export more labor-intensive or resource-intensive goods than technology-intensive or capital-intensive goods according to their own comparative advantages. However, it has also been argued that while developing countries may benefit from this export strategy in the short term, in the long run the export competitiveness and export terms of developing countries will be weakened, and in addition, the benefits of developing countries are actually lower since most labor-intensive goods have lower value-added.

Beyond these two sides, another argument has been provided in this chapter which calls for policy makers to consider the externality effect of exports on the domestic economy more than just export growth itself when they attempt to make export policies. If the externality effect of exports is taken into account, it can be seen that the export of manufacturing goods is the major source of technology spillover rather than primary goods according to our estimation. Therefore, increasing the share of exports in manufacturing goods will not only improve the exporter's own competitiveness, but will also lead to more technology spillovers for domestic producers. What's more, due to such spillover effects, non-export sectors will improve their own productivity and management efficiency, which is one of the important sources of technological progress in an open economy.

In sum, it can be concluded that the relationship between exports and economic growth is actually dynamic, and hence the formulation of trade policy should change with stages of economic development. In brief, at the initial stages of an economic boom, a developing country may trade with others according to its own comparative advantage, by exporting labor-intensive or resource-intensive goods. However, with the increasing growth rate of its economy, the developing country needs to adjust its export and trade structures. At this stage, on one hand, the developing country is supposed to optimize and update its export structure by increasing the share of manufacturing goods exported, especially high-tech goods export, and also using more technology in the production of export goods. On the other hand, more attention should be paid to strengthening the industrial linkage between the export sectors and the non-export sectors to promote the technical progress of domestic producers. Non-export producers also need to improve their own absorptive capability in order to efficiently imitate and learn from the export sectors. Compared with the static benefits from comparative advantages emphasized by classic trade theories, the dynamic benefits from externality and technological progress highlighted in this chapter undoubtedly are much more crucial to economic growth.

NOTES

1. Chongqing city is considered as a part of Sichuan Province.
2. However, if we note the difference between China's actual employment and its potential employment, the role of labor inputs on China's economic growth should be re-evaluated.
3. The parameter δ can be identified as follows. First, it is easy to know that ϑ is actually the coefficient of

$$\left(1 - \frac{MX}{Y}\right) \cdot \frac{dPX}{PX}$$

in model two, and we can further calculate the value of δ since the coefficient of

$$\frac{dPX}{PX} \cdot \frac{PX}{Y}$$

in model two is just equal to

$$\frac{1+\delta}{\delta} - \vartheta$$

and we have the known values of ϑ.
4. For a research review see Keller (2000).

REFERENCES

Bao, Q., X. Helian and L. Mingyong (2003), 'How does export promote China's economic growth? An empirical research on its total factor productivity changes', *Shanghai Economic Review*, **3**, 1–8.

Bruno, M. (1968), 'Estimation of factors contribution to growth under structural disequilibrium', *International Economic Review*, **9**(1), 49–62.

Chen, Z. (2001), 'Empirical research on the relationship between trade and economic growth in China', *World Economic Review*, **5**, 46–51.

Clerides, S., S. Lach and J. Tybout (1998), 'Is learning by exporting important? Micro-dynamic evidence from Colombia, Mexico, and Morocco', *Quarterly Journal of Economics*, **113**, 903–47.

Coe, D.T. and E. Helpman (1995), 'International R&D spillovers', *European Economic Review*, **39**, 859–87.

Coe, D.T., E. Helpman and Hoffmaister (1997), 'North–South R&D spillovers', *Economic Journal*, **107**, 134–49.

Dowrick, S. (1990), 'Sectoral change, catching up and slowing down: OECD post-war economic growth revisited', *Economics Letters*, **31**, 331–5.

Dowrick, S. and N. Gemmell (1991), 'Industrialization, catching-up and economic growth: A comparative study across the world's capitalist economies', *Economic Journal*, **101**, 263–75.

Eaton, J. and S. Kortum (1997), 'Engines of growth: Domestic and foreign sources of innovation', *Japan and the World Economy*, **40**, 235–59.

Eaton, J. and S. Kortum (1999), 'International patenting and technology diffusion: Theory and measurement', *International Economic Review*, **40**, 537–70.

Feder, G. (1982), 'On exports and economic growth', *Journal of Development Economics*, **12**, 59–73.

Findlay, R. (1978), 'Relative backwardness, direct foreign investment and the transfer of technology: A simple dynamic model', *Quarterly Journal of Economics*, **92**, 1–16.

Hakura, D. and F. Jaumotte (1999), 'The role of inter- and intra-industry trade in technology diffusion', IMF Working Paper No.WP 99/58.

Hwa, E-C. (1989), 'The contribution of agriculture to economic growth: Some empirical evidence', in J. Williamson and V. Panchamurtchi (eds), *The Balance between Industry and Agriculture in Economic Development, Vol. 2*, New York: The World Bank.

Jiang, X. (2002), 'The contribution of foreign firms on China's export growth and export structure', *Nankai Economic Review*, **2**, 30–34.

Keller, W. (2001), 'Knowledge spillovers at the world's technology frontier', CEPR Working Paper, No. 2815.

Keller, W. (2002), 'Trade and the transmission of technology', *Journal of Economic Growth*, **7**, 5–24.

Levin, A. and L.K. Raut (1997), 'Complementarities between export and human capital in economic growth: Evidence from the semi-industrialized countries', *Economic Development and Cultural Change*, **46**, 155–74.

Mohnen, P. (2001), 'International R&D spillovers and economic growth', in M. Pohjola (ed.), *Information Technology, Productivity, and Economic Growth: International Evidence*, UNU/WIDER and Sitra, Oxford: Oxford University Press.

Rhee, Y., B. Ross-Larson and G. Pursell (1984), *Korea's Competitive Edge: Managing the Entry into World Markets*, Baltimore, MD: Johns Hopkins University Press for the World Bank.

Xu, B. and J. Wang (1999), 'Capital goods trade and R&D spillovers in the OECD', *Canada Journal of Economics*, **32**, 1258–74.

Yang, Q. (1998), 'The output effect of China's export: An empirical research', *Economic Research*, **7**, 22–6.

Yao, Y. (1998), 'The influence of non-state own enterprisers on China's industrial efficiency', *Economic Research*, **12**.

9. Technology Spillovers, Absorptive Capacity and Economic Growth

Mingyong Lai, Shuijun Peng and Qun Bao

---

1. INTRODUCTION

Endogenous growth theory differs from neoclassical growth theory in the explicit introduction of research and development (R&D) activities that can affect the long-run growth rate. Human capital formation and/or R&D activities are usually modeled as being subject to increasing returns, or, more accurately, a lower bound on diminishing returns to capital. Endogenous growth models can be broadly classified into two groups according to the underlying 'engines of growth'. In the first, growth is generated through the positive externalities that are associated with accumulation of either physical or human capital. These models are typically referred to as investment-based growth models. Examples include Romer (1986, 1987), Lucas (1988), Barro (1990), and Rebelo (1991). The second group emphasizes the role of technological progress, which is created as an economic good in a separate research and development sector. Models here are known as R&D-based growth models. The prototypical R&D-based models are Romer (1990), Grossman and Helpman (1991), and Aghion and Howitt (1992, 1998).

Although endogenous growth theory has increased our general understanding of the importance of technological investment by exploring the implications of the properties of technology as knowledge, international technology spillovers are seldom modeled in the endogenous growth literature. As some of the empirical research shows (e.g., Coe and Helpman, 1995; Eaton and Kortum, 1996; Keller, 2001), international technology spillovers have been a major source of technological progress for both developed countries and less developed countries (LDCs). Some exceptions in the theoretical literature are Grossman and Helpman (1991), Rivera-Batiz and Romer (1991), and Aghion and Howitt (1998), who modeled the effects of trade liberalization and economic integration on domestic technological change. However, since the authors generally assume non-rival technology

(Romer, 1986, 1990), which implies that technology imitation or spillovers are costless, these models have achieved few robust policy implications for less developed countries. Furthermore, these models predict a 'catch-up' effect, which implies LDCs may catch up with developed countries by technology imitation and learning in the long run, but have not obtained empirical support (Barro, 1991; Williamson, 1991).

Borensztein et al. (1998) first confirmed the importance of the host country's absorptive capability, measured by human capital accumulation in the host country, in absorbing the spillovers of foreign firms' technology.[1] In other words, even though less developed countries may attempt technology imitation by importing intermediate goods and/or attracting multinational enterprises, the learning effect is crucially limited by technology absorptive capability. By utilizing data on Foreign Direct Investment (FDI) flows from industrial countries to 69 developing countries over the period of 1970–89, the authors find that the higher productivity of FDI holds only when the host country has a minimum threshold stock of human capital. Thus, FDI contributes to economic growth only when a sufficient absorptive capability of the advanced technologies is available in the host countries. According to the authors' estimates, the minimum threshold stock of human capital in the host country, measured by the initial-year level of average number of years of male secondary schooling constructed by Barro and Lee (1993), is 0.52. By comparison, cross-section regressions in Xu (2000), estimate the minimum threshold stock of human capital at 2.4 years of secondary school attainment. Apart from the host country's human capital investment, its degree of openness is also another key variable of absorptive capability. To summarize, the effects of openness on technology absorption can be classified into two types. The first is the 'pull effect'. As pointed out by Grossman and Helpman (1991), the higher a country's degree of openness, the more chances it will have of imitating and learning from outside. The other is the 'push effect', where competitive pressure from foreign firms pushes the indigenous firms to increase their R&D expenditures and adapt themselves to the intense competition in the international market (Holmes and Schmitz, 2001). Some researchers have found empirical support for the positive effects of openness on technology spillovers, such as Boer et al. (2001) and Comin and Hobijn (2004).[2] Other variables, such as the host country's financial market efficiency (Alfaro et al., 2004) and domestic firms' R&D activities (Griffith et al., 2000; Kinoshita, 2000; Keller, 2001) are also widely used to measure absorptive capability in other studies.

Using an R&D-based model introduced by Romer (1990), the main purpose of this chapter is to analyze the connections between international technology spillovers, domestic technology absorptive capability, endogenous technological change and the steady-state economic growth rate. Three economic sectors are included in the model: a final goods sector, an intermediate goods sector and a R&D sector. Our model differs from Romer (1990) in that domestic final goods producers can buy intermediate goods from both domestic and foreign producers. Furthermore, the knowledge output of the R&D sector depends on international technology spillovers in addition to human capital investment in the R&D sector and its own knowledge stock. However, technology spillover effects are limited by domestic technology absorptive capability, which is the key variable determining the steady-state economic growth rate in our model. The model is applied to Chinese data; therefore the empirical approach is constrained to available series. For instance, it is very hard to find the implicit relationship between China's financial system and FDI's technology spillover due to the special function of China's financial system. Therefore, the host country's human capital stock and degree of openness are used as measures of its absorptive capability.[3]

In our model, we show that at the steady-state equilibrium, long-run growth arises from the improvement of absorptive capability and higher human capital stock, while the relationships between openness, the technology gap, and the steady-state growth rate are uncertain, which is the key finding of our theoretical model. Compared with previous theoretical findings, the predictions in this chapter explain the real world well: A higher degree of openness has truly led certain countries like Singapore and South Korea to experience successful growth in the past decades. However, we do not always observe a positive correlation between openness and economic growth for Latin American and African countries. It has also been pointed out that there is a non-linear and uncertain relationship between the technology gap and economic growth in this chapter, which has seldom been highlighted in previous analyses. There is an optimal level of imported technology that must be predetermined by developing countries and the optimal technology gap is a function of such variables as consumer preferences, production conditions, and factor endowments, as shown in our theoretical model. Estimation using provincial Chinese data from 1996 to 2002 demonstrates that technology spillovers essentially depend on the host country's human capital investment and degree of openness. Furthermore, FDI is a more significant spillover channel than imports. To our knowledge, few empirical studies have estimated the influences of absorptive capability on China's economic growth, and few authors have compared the technology spillover effects of FDI and imports, which have been considered the two major spillover channels.

We proceed as follows: Section 2 sets out our theoretical model and characterizes its steady state. In Section 3, we specify our estimation model and use China's panel data to analyze the effects of technology spillover and absorptive capability on China's economic growth. Section 4 summarizes the major findings and discusses policy implications.

2. THE MODEL

The model is based on Romer's (1990) knowledge-driven R&D model. Production occurs using many, imperfectly substitutable inputs, so that technological progress arises from the invention of new input varieties through R&D activity. Consider two countries, home and foreign. In the home country, the economy consists of three sectors. First, there is a final-goods sector where a single, homogeneous good, Y is produced under perfect competition. The production function[4] is:

$$Y = AH_Y^\alpha \left[\int_0^N x_i^\beta di + \int_0^{N^*} x_{i^*}^{*\beta} di^* \right] \quad \alpha, \beta > 0, \ \alpha + \beta = 1 \qquad (9.1)$$

Where $A > 0$ is the general level of productivity, which is a function of institutional factors such as government behavior, the maintenance of law and order, and property rights. H_Y is the amount of human capital employed in the final-good sector,[5] and x_i (resp. $x_{i^*}^*$) are the quantities of the N (resp. N^*) domestic (resp. imported) intermediate inputs (specialized capital goods), indexed by i (resp. i^*).

The intermediate goods are developed or 'invented' in the R&D sector. Production in the R&D sector depends on international R&D spillovers through trade in addition to human capital investment in this sector and its own technology knowledge stock.[6] Since the technology knowledge stock is identified with the available variety of capital goods, the output of designs for new varieties in the home country can be written as:

$$\dot{N} = \delta H_N \left[N + G(D,H)N^* \right] \qquad (9.2)$$

where δ is a constant productivity parameter, H_N is the amount of human capital employed in research, and the total quantity of human capital H, represents the fixed available stock of knowledge and skill in the economy, $H = H_Y + H_N$. $G(D,H)$ represents absorptive capability which is determined by the domestic human capital stock, and openness, D, where $D \in (0, +\infty)$. In a perfectly integrated economy $D = 0$, while $D \to +\infty$ in autarky. Furthermore, $0 \le G(\cdot, \cdot) \le 1$, $G(+\infty, \cdot) = 0$, $G(\cdot, 0) = 0$ and $\partial g / \partial D < 0, \partial g / \partial H < 0$.

Finally, there is an intermediate-goods sector. After a design has been developed, an intermediate-goods firm can purchase it and manufacture the input under imperfect competition.[7] For simplicity, we suppose that once invented, intermediate inputs of type i cost one unit of Y to produce.

2.1. Market Equilibrium

The price of the good Y is normalized to one. W_{H_Y} and W_{H_N} refer to the wages paid to human capital in the final-output and R&D sectors, P_{x_i} and $P_{x_{i^*}}$ are the price of domestic and foreign intermediates, respectively, and r is the interest rate on a perfect financial market. We assume that the markets for Y and H are competitive for the firms which produce Y. For the intermediate goods, we make two standard assumptions. First, we assume that there is free entry into the business of being an inventor. Second, once invented, each intermediate good is produced by a monopoly.

Given (9.1), the maximization problem for final goods producers can be represented as:

$$\max_{H_y, x_i, x_{i^*}} \pi = Y\left\{H_Y, x_i, x_{i^*}\right\} - W_{H_Y} H_Y - \int_0^N P_{x_i} x_i di - \int_0^{N^*} P_{x_{i^*}} x_{i^*} di^* \quad (9.3)$$

Derived from first order necessary conditions for the above maximization problem, we have:

$$W_{H_Y} = \frac{\alpha Y}{H_Y} \quad (9.4)$$

$$x_i = H_Y\left[A\beta/P_{x_i}\right]^{\frac{1}{\alpha}} \quad \text{i.e.} \quad P_x = A\beta H_Y^\alpha x^{-\alpha} \quad (9.5)$$

$$x_{i^*}^{\cdot} = H_Y\left[A\beta/P_{x_{i^*}}\right]^{\frac{1}{\alpha}} \quad \text{i.e.} \quad P_{x^{\cdot}} = A\beta H_Y^\alpha x^{\cdot -\alpha} \quad (9.6)$$

From the above condition it is clear that all intermediate goods are used symmetrically in final-good production and, therefore, share the same demand function. Hence, we drop the subscript i in the last part of equations (9.5) and (9.6).

Producers in the intermediate inputs sector set the price P_x at each date to maximize current profits:

$$V(t) = \int_t^\infty \left(P_x \cdot x - 1 \cdot x\right) e^{-\bar{r}(s,t)(s-t)} ds$$

where x is the total quantity produced at each date and is given by the demand function (9.5), and

$$\overline{r}(s,t) = \left[1/(s-t)\right]\int_t^s r(v)dv$$

represents the average interest rate between data t and s.

Therefore, with the assumption of constant r (it is easy to prove that the interest rate r must be constant in the steady-state equilibrium),[8] the intermediate firm's problem becomes:

$$\max_{P_x} \pi_m = P_x \cdot x - 1 \cdot x \qquad (9.7)$$

The solution for the monopoly price:

$$P_{x_i} = P_x = \frac{1}{\beta} \qquad (9.8)$$

An analogous procedure yields the pricing equation for the foreign intermediate input:

$$P_{x_{i^*}} = P_{x^*}$$

Since the real economic world is imperfectly integrated, we consider the effect of the degree of the economy's openness 'D', following from a similar index in the approach of Samuelson (1954); delivering x units of a foreign intermediate to the home country requires sending xe^D units. Then, one can show that optimal pricing of the foreign monopolists implies:

$$P_{x_{i^*}} = P_{x^*} = \frac{e^D}{\beta} \qquad (9.9)$$

Substituting (9.8) and (9.9) into (9.5) and (9.6) for the expressions of x_i and x_i^*, we can determine the equilibrium quantities of x_i and x_i^* as:

$$x_i = \overline{x} = A^{\frac{1}{a}}\beta^{\frac{2}{a}}H_Y \qquad (9.10)$$

$$x_{i^*}^* = \overline{x}^* = A^{\frac{1}{a}}\beta^{\frac{2}{a}}H_Y e^{-\frac{D}{a}} \qquad (9.11)$$

Then, using (9.1), (9.10) and (9.11), the equilibrium level of output is determined as:

$$Y = AH_Y^\alpha \left(N\bar{x}^{-\beta} + N^* \bar{x}^{*\beta} \right)$$

$$= A^{\frac{1}{\alpha}} H_Y \beta^{\frac{2\beta}{\alpha}} \left(N + N^* e^{-\frac{D\beta}{\alpha}} \right) \qquad (9.12)$$

$$= A^{\frac{1}{\alpha}} H_Y \beta^{\frac{2\beta}{\alpha}} \left[N + F(D)N^* \right]$$

where

$$F(D) = e^{-\frac{D\beta}{\alpha}}$$
$$F(0) = 1$$
$$F(+\infty) = 0$$
$$\partial F / \partial D < 0$$

Equation (9.12) states that output increases with openness.

Define the patent price of intermediate goods as P_N. Free entry into the intermediate sector ensures that the discounted value of profit equals the patent price:

$$P_N = V(t) = \int_t^\infty \pi_m(s) e^{-\bar{r}(s,t)(s-t)} ds \qquad (9.13)$$

With the assumption of constant r, we seek a solution characterized by a constant value for P_N, in which case the arbitrage equation reduces to:

$$Y = AH_Y^\alpha \left(N\bar{x}^{-\beta} + N^* \bar{x}^{*\beta} \right)$$

$$= A^{\frac{1}{\alpha}} H_Y \beta^{\frac{2\beta}{\alpha}} \left(N + N^* e^{-\frac{D\beta}{\alpha}} \right)$$

$$= A^{\frac{1}{\alpha}} H_Y \beta^{\frac{2\beta}{\alpha}} \left[N + F(D)N^* \right] \qquad (9.14)$$

In the R&D sector, the total returns of R&D activities are:

$$TR = P_N \dot{N} = P_N \delta H_N \left[N + G(D,H)N^* \right]$$

and the total costs are:

$$TC = W_{H_N} \cdot H_N$$

Therefore, free entry into the R&D sector ensures that the wage paid to human capital inputs in R&D sector is:

$$W_{H_N} = \delta P_N \left[N + G(D,H)N^* \right] \tag{9.15}$$

Following Romer (1990), it is assumed that human capital can move costlessly between sectors of employment. As a result, the equilibrium condition determining the allocation of human capital between the final-output and R&D sectors says that the wages paid to human capital in each sector must be the same, that is:

$$W_{H_Y} = W_{H_N} \tag{9.16}$$

From (9.16) in combination with (9.4), (9.12), (9.14), and (9.15), we obtain:

$$\alpha A^{\frac{1}{\alpha}} \beta^{\frac{2\beta}{\alpha}} \left[N + F(D)N^* \right] = \delta \left(\frac{\alpha}{r\beta} \bar{x} \right) \left[N + G(D,H)N^* \right]$$

Substituting (9.10) for $\bar{x}$ into above equation

$$H_Y \frac{\delta}{r} \left[N + G(D,H)N^* \right] = \frac{1}{\beta} \left[N + F(D)N^* \right]$$

Hence,

$$H_Y = \frac{r[N + F(D)N^*]}{\delta \beta [N + G(D,H)N^*]} \tag{9.17}$$

To solve H_Y, for the simplicity of computation, we suppose:

$$N^{world} = N + N^* \quad \text{and} \quad \frac{N^*}{N} = u \tag{9.18}$$

where $u \geq 0$ represents the technology gap between domestic and foreign firms. A larger u indicates that a larger technology gap exists. In the special case when $u = 0$, our model is very similar to Romer (1990) by implying that domestic R&D output only depends on self-innovation. Thus

$$N = \frac{1}{1+u}N^{world} \quad \text{and} \quad N^* = \frac{u}{1+u}N^{world} \tag{9.19}$$

Substituting (9.19) into (9.17), we have:

$$H_Y = \frac{r[1+uF(D)]}{\delta\beta[1+uG(D,H)]} \tag{9.20}$$

Next, as $H_N = H - H_Y$, equations (9.2) and (9.19) can be used to obtain the rate of growth of technology as

$$g_N = \frac{\dot{N}}{N} = \delta H_N[1+uG(D,H)]$$

$$= \delta(H - H_Y)[1+uG(D,H)]$$

Substituting (9.18) for N^* into (9.12) yields

$$Y = A^{\frac{1}{a}}H_Y\beta^{\frac{2\beta}{a}}[1+uF(D)]N \tag{9.21}$$

With a constant interest rate in the steady state, equation (9.20) implies that H_Y is constant. Given that, (9.10) reveals that $\bar{x}$ is also constant. Then, in this economy total output, total usage of capital, and aggregate consumption, must grow at the same rate as N in steady state. The common growth rate g for all these variables is therefore

$$g = g_Y = g_C = g_N = \delta H_N[1+uG(D,H)]$$

$$= \delta(H - H_Y)[1+uG(D,H)] \tag{9.22}$$

The main message of (9.22) is that there is a positive correlation between the steady-state equilibrium economic growth rate, g, and human capital investment in R&D, H_N, and absorptive capability, $G(D, H)$. More accurately, increases in human capital investment in R&D and improvement of domestic absorptive capability will lead to a higher steady-state economic growth rate. Specifically, there is no long-term economic growth $(g = 0)$ if $H_N = 0$.

Specification of household behavior completes the model. As usual, the representative consumer tries to maximize their total discounted utility over an infinite time horizon while satisfying given income and wealth constraints.

$$U(C) = \begin{cases} \int_0^\infty \dfrac{C^{1-\sigma}-1}{1-\sigma} e^{-\rho t} dt, & \sigma, \rho > 0, \sigma \neq 1 \\ \int_0^\infty \ln C\, e^{-\rho t} dt, & \rho > 0, \sigma = 1 \end{cases} \quad (9.23)$$

where ρ is the pure rate of time preference, and $1/\sigma$ is the intertemporal elasticity of substitution.

The only way in which these preferences enter the computation of the balanced growth equilibrium is through the relationship that they imply between the rate of growth of consumption and the market interest rate:

$$g_C = \frac{\dot{C}}{C} = \frac{1}{\sigma}(r - \rho) \quad (9.24)$$

Finally, it can be concluded from (9.20), (9.22), and (9.24)

Proposition 1: *The economy's steady-state growth rate, g , is*

$$g = \frac{\delta H[1 + uG(D,H)] - (\rho/\beta)[1 + uF(D)]}{1 + (\sigma/\beta)[1 + uF(D)]} \quad (9.25)$$

2.2. Comparative Statics

To see clearly the effects of human capital investment, openness, and various parameters on the steady-state growth rate, we can obtain the derivatives of the steady-state growth rate with respect to these variables. Thus we have:

Proposition 2: $\partial g / \partial G > 0$; $\partial g / \partial H > 0$.

There are two positive effects of absorptive capability G on the steady-state growth rate. First, it can be seen from (9.2) that an improvement in technology absorptive capability will directly improve the knowledge output growth rate in the domestic R&D sector. Second, according to (9.15), an increase in G will shift human capital from the final goods sector to the R&D sector since the return to human capital investment, W_{H_N} is actually an increasing function of G.

The same goes for human capital investment: An increase in H improves the steady-state growth rate H_N directly since increases with H. Additionally, it can be seen from (9.20) that

$$\partial\left(\tfrac{H_N}{H_Y}\right)\big/\partial H > 0 \,,$$

which means the higher stock of human capital one economy has, the higher the share of human capital investment in the R&D sector. This result sheds some light on the reason why countries with higher human capital stocks usually have higher economic growth rates. Finally, a larger H also implies a higher technology absorptive capability and therefore a higher steady state growth rate.

Proposition 3: $\partial g/\partial D \underset{<}{\overset{>}{=}} 0$

Since Adam Smith (1776), the relationship between openness and economic growth has been widely debated. Although it has been universally supported by theorists that higher a degree of openness surely promotes economic growth, the empirical results are less supportive.[9] Proposition 3 shows that an uncertain relationship truly exists between openness and the steady-state growth rate. On the one hand, a larger degree of openness improves domestic absorptive capability and therefore the knowledge stock available in the domestic R&D sector. This results in more human capital investment in the R&D sector than in the final-goods sector. On the other hand, the larger degree of openness implies that intermediate goods inputs increase in the final-goods sector due to technology imports, and domestic dependence on foreign technology increases. This results in an inverse human capital shift from the R&D sector to the final goods sector due to the higher productivity of human capital in the final-goods sector.

Such uncertainty between openness and the growth rate has been well documented by the growth history of many countries. Although the successful growth experience of new industrial countries (NIEs) such as Singapore and South Korea has demonstrated the importance of openness in economic growth, the evidence which supports the 'openness-led growth' hypothesis is not so strong for certain countries' economic development experience in other regions like southeast Asia, Africa and Latin America.[10] It is generally acknowledged that the correlation between openness and economic growth varies greatly for different countries and different development stages. In our model, even though a larger degree of openness means more chances for technology learning, it may also weaken domestic innovation and invention ability due to higher dependence on foreign technology. Especially in the short run, by increasing the wage rate in the final-goods sector, openness causes a human capital shift from the R&D sector to the final goods sector, and hence hinders the long-run growth rate.

Proposition 4: $\partial g / \partial u \gtrless 0$

It is shown from Proposition 4 that the correlation between the technology gap, u, and the economic growth rate is also ambiguous. As demonstrated by Romer (1990), a larger initial technology gap means there are more advanced technologies to be imitated by followers and imitation cost is significantly smaller than innovation cost, which is defined as the 'advantage of backwardness'. Proposition 4 provides some insight into the question regarding why this advantage of backwardness is not fully utilized by most developing countries, which denies the findings of Romer (1990). As is shown in our model, if technology absorptive capability is taken into account, a larger technology gap actually means that indigenous firms lack enough technology capability to effectively learn and absorb foreign advanced technology even though they have more chances of learning. Again, although the successful experience of NIEs shows that an advantage of backwardness truly exists, more LDCs' experience reminds us that the lack of technology absorptive capability is the key factor that limits technology imitation.

3.   ECONOMETRIC ESTIMATION OF CHINA'S GROWTH

Since the conclusions in our theoretical model only hold true for the economy which has been on its steady-state equilibrium growth path, the major problem with the empirical test of our theoretical model lies in the fact that most economies are not actually on their steady-state growth path, especially for such transition economies as China, as pointed out by Lucas (1988). Therefore, we focus on testing the key hypothesis in our model that technology spillovers are essentially dependent on the host country's absorptive capability. Meanwhile, in order to compare the technology spillover effect of imports with that of foreign direct investment (FDI), both spillover channels are taken into account in our empirical research.[11] Two indicators are chosen to measure absorptive capability, the host country's degree of openness and human capital, which are based on our theoretical model and the availability of the original data. For instance, although the technology gap is highlighted as one of the key variables in our theoretical model, it is not considered in the empirical test since it is hard for us to accurately calculate the technology gap between the host country and abroad or indigenous firms and foreign ones for our data set. Panel data are used in our estimation since the combined information of both cross-section and time series data can remarkably alleviate the problem of omitted variables,[12] as well as the spurious regression due to unit roots of time series data.

3.1. Specification of the Econometric Model and Data Source

According to our theoretical model, there are three potential regression models:

Equation I: $g_{it} = c_i + \gamma_t + \alpha H_{it} + \beta FRD_{it} + \varphi DRD_{it} + \varepsilon_{it}$

Where, g_{it}, DRD_{it}, H_{it} are respectively the economic growth rate, domestic R&D input, and human capital investment for the i province in year t, and c_i and γ_t are cross-section -specific and time -specific effects respectively. FRD_{it} measures the technology spillover effect of foreign R&D input through two channels, imports and (FDI). Based on Coe and Helpman (1995), two methods of constructing FRD_{it} are given here, which construct the weighted foreign R&D input (RD_t^f) as FDI and import shares of each province are respectively chosen as the weights:[13]

1) FDI as the technology spillover channel: $FRD_{it} = \dfrac{FDI_{it}}{\sum FDI_t} \cdot RD_t^f$

2) Import as the technology spillover channel: $FRD_{it} = \dfrac{IM_{it}}{\sum IM_t} \cdot RD_t^f$

Equation II: $g_{it} = c_i + \gamma_t + \alpha H_{it} + \beta OPEN_{it} * FRD_{it} + \varphi DRD_{it} + \varepsilon_{it}$

Equation II further investigates the influence of the host country's absorptive capability, which is measured by the host country's degree of openness, on the technology spillover effect. Here $OPEN_{it}$ represents the openness for the i province in year t, and c_i and γ_t are cross-section-specific and time-specific effects respectively.

Equation III: $g_{it} = c_i + \gamma_t + \alpha H_{it} + \beta H_{it} * FRD_{it} + \varphi DRD_{it} + \varepsilon_{it}$

Equation III is similar to Equation II; however, in this equation, the host country's human capital stock is chosen to measure the host country's absorptive capability.

As usual, the economic growth rate (g_{it}) is measured as the real GDP growth rate. We choose two indicators to measure China's domestic R&D inputs by regions. The first indicator is the total domestic R&D expenditures (DRD_{it}), including R&D expenditures of independent research institutions, large and medium-sized enterprises as well as higher education.[14] The second one is government expenditures on science and technology activities in various levels (Government S&T). We choose different measures of domestic R&D expenditures to see whether research and development supported by the government is more or less efficient. As shown in many previous papers (e.g., Barro and Lee, 2000), human capital (H_{it}) can be measured as the average educational attainment, which is the ratio of total educational attainment to the total population.[15] Based on Wang (2000), the education attainment is specified as 6 years for primary school graduates, and 9, 12, and 16 years for junior middle school graduates, senior middle school graduates, and university graduates respectively. Since it is impossible for us to measure the degree of openness for each province by such indicators as trade barriers and black market premiums, the usual method is used here to construct the degree of openness for each province:

$$OPEN_{it} = Trade_{it} / GDP_{it}$$

which is the ratio of trade volumes ($Trade_{it}$) to real GDP. As pointed out by Wacziarg (1998), the main problem with this method is the endogeneity that exists since trade volumes are usually determined by other economic variables. Therefore, we follow the method introduced by Low et al. (1998) to avoid the endogeneity problem.[16]

We choose the total R&D expenditures of G-7 countries as the measure of foreign R&D inputs RD_t^f for two reasons. First, it is assumed in our theoretical model that technology spillovers usually come from developed countries, which accords with other findings such as Eaton and Kortum (1996) and Keller (2001). Second, the G-7 countries have the major share of R&D inputs for both the whole world and the developed countries according to statistics from the UN and other institutes such as OECD and NSF. For example, in 1998 nearly 85 percent of the total R&D input in the 30 OECD countries comes from the G-7 countries, with the US share at 44 percent of the total. In 2002, for the total foreign R&D input of 672 billion US dollars (except China), the share of G-7 countries is nearly 81 percent.

Most of our original data are available and calculated from the yearly issues of the *China Statistical Yearbook* from 1997 to 2003. The variables include the real GDP growth rate, the governments' R&D expenditures, foreign direct investment, degree of openness, and human capital investment. We choose the sample period from 1996 to 2002 due to the fact that average educational attainment in each province is only available since 1996. Thirty provinces are included in our sample, excluding Tibet since the time series data for FDI in Tibet are unavailable. Domestic expenditures of R&D by region are collected from the *China Statistical Yearbook on Science and Technology* (reported in billions of RMB in current year price). The original data of the R&D expenditures of G-7 countries are RD_t^f available from the OECD, Main Science and Technology Indicators database 2003, which includes the R&D inputs of government, firms, scientific and research institutes and foreign organizations. The original RD_t^f is calculated based on PPP with 1995 as the base year.

For our panel data estimation, there are three alternative models we can choose: pooled OLS, fixed effects or random effects.[17] Due to significant differences in regional development between coastal areas and non-coastal areas, it is not suitable to use the pooled OLS method to estimate our empirical model due to this provincial-specific effect. Therefore, we only employ the fixed effects (FE) and random effects models (RE) and perform Hausman tests to justify the two models. If the value of the Hausman test statistic is larger than the critical value, this means that the null hypothesis can be rejected and that fixed effects are to be preferred to random effects.

3.2. Empirical Results and Analysis

3.2.1. FDI as a technology spillover channel

First, we investigate the spillover effect of foreign R&D expenditures with FDI as the spillover variable. Summary statistics for the data are presented in Table 9.1. Data for 30 provinces from 1996 to 2002 are used to regress estimate equations I, II, and III respectively, and the results are shown in Table 9.2. For our fixed effect model estimation, by adding cross-section weights we estimate a feasible GLS specification allowing for the presence of cross-section heteroskedasticity, which means that each pooled equation is down weighted by an estimate of the cross-section residual standard deviation. As emphasized before, the specification of our empirical model is made based on a Hausman test to justify whether fixed effect model or random effect model is preferred. It can be seen from Table 9.2 that our

Table 9.1:   Descriptive Statistics

	Growth rate of GDP	Avg. educ.	Degree open	FRD[1] a	FRD[2] b	Gov. S&T	DRD
Mean	9.28	7.29	0.27	14.65	14.59	2.51	0.34
Med.	9.45	7.25	0.09	4.96	2.53	1.18	0.22
Max	18.10	10.26	1.66	130.5	164.0	21.95	3.77
Min	4.10	4.69	0.03	0.01	0.03	0.07	0.01
Std. Dev.[c]	1.82	0.96	0.38	24.16	31.29	3.43	0.42

Notes:
[a]   FRD[1] is the foreign R&D expenditure weighted by each province's FDI share.
[b]   FRD[2] is the foreign R&D expenditure weighted by each province's import share.
[c]   Each regression contains 30 cross sections and 210 observations.

Source: *China Statistical Yearbook on Science and Technology, China Statistical Yearbook.*

Hausman tests show that the fixed effect model is preferred over the RE model for the estimation of all three equations in each specification. We estimate each model twice since two measurement methods of China's domestic R&D expenditures are chosen in this chapter. Table 9.2 also shows that there is a positive relationship between human capital investment H_{it} and economic growth. According to our regression results, a one year increase in educational attainment will increase China's economic growth rate by 0.151–0.176 percentage points.

There is no statistically significant relationship between government S&T expenditures and growth. By comparison, DRD_{it}, domestic expenditures for R&D by independent research institutions, large and medium-sized enterprises, as well as higher education, have a positive and statistically significant effect on China's economic growth. According to our estimation result, the marginal effects of an increase in DRD_{it} on domestic economic growth range from 0.019 to 0.028. These results may be explained by the indirect impact of government's S&T inputs on technological progress, compared with direct impact of firms' micro R&D activities due to the reason that the S&T activities of governments are not usually profit-maximization oriented. Furthermore, it is usually more costly for the government to evaluate and monitor those publicly funded R&D projects compared with individual R&D activities.

The regression results also remind us of the fact that there is a trade-off relationship between self-innovation and technology imitation and

Table 9.2:   *Regression Results*

	1 [a]	2	3	4	5	6
H	0.18*[b]	0.17*	0.12*	0.16*	0.15**	0.11*
	(2.51)	(2.38)	(2.39)	(2.43)	(2.71)	(2.19)
FRD	0.24**	-	-	0.24**	-	-
	(4.61)			(4.78)		
Open * *FRD*	-	0.18**	-	-	0.18**	-
		(3.78)			(4.03)	
*H*FRD*	-	-	0.11**	-	-	0.11**
			(3.10)			(3.37)
Gov. S&T	−0.04	0.03	0.05	-	-	-
	(1.25)	(0.88)	(1.18)			
DRD	-	-	-	0.03*	0.02*	0.02*
				(2.32)	(2.20)	(2.04)
Adj. R^2	0.90	0.92	0.90	0.91	0.84	0.88
Hausman Test	15.96	18.41	19.58	21.46	19.62	23.16

Notes:

[a]   Industry fixed effects are included for all regressions and each contains 210 observations.

[b]   Standard errors are in parentheses. * and ** denote significance at the 5 and 1 percent levels respectively.

absorption. It has been generally argued that due to resource constraints and the high costs of self-innovation, it is obviously less efficient to make redundant investment in old and outdated technologies. Therefore, technology policy in developing countries should focus on technology imports and imitation from outside instead of self-innovation. Such a viewpoint is highlighted in Table 9.2 since the coefficient on foreign R&D expenditures FRD_{it} is 0.236 in fixed effects model estimation, which shows that a positive relationship exists between foreign R&D expenditures and domestic technological progress and hence economic growth. Note that in Table 9.1 FRD_{it} is actually constructed with each province's share of FDI as the weights, therefore, such regression results confirm the technology spillover effects of foreign firms. As discussed in our theoretical model, FDI has been one of the major technology spillover channels. In general, the results suggest that both domestic and foreign R&D are important forces for domestic technological progress and economic growth, which is very similar to the results of other authors.[18] In their seminal paper, Coe and Helpman (1995) also find that both domestic R&D and foreign R&D are driving forces of domestic TFP growth. According to Coe and Helpman

Table 9.3:   Educational Attainment in OECD Countries: 1971–98

	OECD countries	G-7 countries	US	Japan
Average educational attainment (in years)	10.81	10.95	12.32	10.73

Source: Bassanini and Scarpetta (2001).

(1995), while both domestic R&D and foreign R&D play a positive role in TFP growth for 22 countries, domestic R&D is more important for larger countries and foreign R&D is more important for smaller ones.

It can be seen from Table 9.2 that once China's technology absorptive capability is taken into account, the technology spillover effect of foreign R&D expenditures changes. In the results for regression equation II, the coefficient of $OPEN_{it} * FRD_{it}$ decreases to 0.175 (0.183) from 0.236 (0.241). Meanwhile, the coefficient of $H_{it} * FRD_{it}$ decreases to 0.114 (0.107) in regression III. The results suggest that it is the host country's absorptive capability that determines the technology imitation and absorption effects. Our results are very similar to those of Borensztein et al. (1998), which find that indigenous firms effectively absorb and learn from foreign firms only when the host country's average human capital stock is higher than the threshold value. To see the reason why there is a relative shortage of human capital investment in China, we can compare China's average educational attainment with those of developed countries, that is, the source countries of technology spillover.

It can be seen from Table 9.3 that average educational attainment in OECD countries is greater than ten years. By comparison, the average educational attainment in China is much lower; only 7.289 years during the period 1996–2002. Therefore, according to our findings the reason why the technology level of imitation cannot catch up with that of innovators lies in the shortage of their absorptive capability more so than the existence of technology barriers.

3.2.2.   Imports as a technology spillover channel
In this section, we consider the spillover effects of foreign R&D expenditures with imports serving as the spillover channel. We also use feasible GLS to eliminate between-group heteroskedasticity in the fixed effects model, and Hausman tests to show that for all three equations, fixed effect estimation is preferred to random effects. The results are shown in Table 9.4, which further demonstrates that there is a positive relationship between human capital investment, domestic R&D and China's economic

growth, while the relationship between government S&T and economic growth in China is still insignificant. Even though less developed countries may attempt to imitate technology by importing intermediate goods, the learning effect is crucially limited by their own technology absorptive capability, which is measured by the host country's degree of openness and human capital stock. In fact, these results partly resemble those obtained in Table 9.2, but here we also find noticeable differences that raise new questions.

First of all, our estimation sheds some new light on how to evaluate the role of imports in economic growth. According to the traditional SNA analysis framework, importing is only regarded as a leakage in total national demand. Meanwhile, it is traditionally emphasized by trade protectionists that import restrictions can protect domestic markets and thus promote the development of domestic infant firms and industries, and therefore economic growth. However, as shown in our theoretical model, with a greater role of technological progress in economic growth, imports improve the productivity of domestic firms and the variety and quality of their products through technology spillovers such as demonstration effects. Therefore, imports have been one of the key international spillover channels in an open economy, through which one country can share the research and development outcomes of others. Some earlier research has also verified the growth effect of China's imports. For instance, Liu (2001), and Xu and Jiang (2002) find a positive relationship between imports and China's economic growth using China's aggregate economic data. However, since this research focuses on analyzing the simple statistical relationship between the two variables, it does not explain how imports promote China's economic growth. One of the contributions in this chapter is the use of panel data. We find that imports actually promote China's economic growth by producing spillover effects on domestic sectors.[19]

Given the existing literature, the presence of spillover effects from imports is inconclusive: Some authors such as Coe et al. (1997), Sjoholm (1996), and Keller (1997, 2000) support the conclusion that imports are an important channel in international technology spillover, while little evidence has been found by others such as Eaton and Kortum (1996), Lumenga-Neso et al. (2001) and Keller (2002). Most studies emphasize the importance of the methods of constructing foreign R&D stock by using different weights, which is the major reason why their estimation results vary greatly. However, apart from the differences in weights and data sources used, this chapter highlights that importers' absorptive capability is the key factor determining technology spillover effects. By comparing the estimation results of equations I, II and III, we can find that once absorptive

Table 9.4:   *Regression Results*

	1[a]	2	3	4	5	6
H	0.14^{**b}	0.18^{**}	0.13^{*}	0.16^{**}	0.17^{**}	0.10^{*}
	(2.75)	(2.88)	(2.10)	(3.02)	(2.91)	(2.24)
FRD	0.06^{**}	-	-	0.07^{**}	-	-
	(4.82)			(3.28)		
Open*FRD	-	0.02^{**}	-	-	0.04^{**}	-
		(3.99)			(3.33)	
H*FRD	-	-	0.01^{*}	-	-	0.01^{**}
			(2.19)			(2.92)
Gov. S&T	0.09	0.02	0.05	-	-	-
	(1.75)	(0.61)	(1.18)			
DRD	-	-	-	0.02^{**}	0.01^{*}	0.02^{*}
				(2.58)	(2.18)	(2.33)
Adj. R^2	0.86	0.88	0.91	0.86	0.83	0.88
Hausman Test	18.09	20.17	22.53	24.02	26.91	22.67

Notes:
[a] Industry fixed effects are included for all regressions and each contains 210 observations.
[b] Standard errors are in parentheses. * and ** denote significance at the 5 and 1 percent levels respectively.

capability is taken into account, technology spillover effects vary greatly. For equation I where we do not consider the role of absorptive capability, the coefficient of foreign R&D stock is 0.057 (0.072) in the fixed effect estimation. However, for equations II and III, where we actually consider the role of the host country's human capital investment and degree of openness, the technology spillover effect significantly decreases to 0.0091 (0.012) and 0.021 (0.038). Such findings remind us of the fact that technology spillover effects also depend on the indicators we have chosen to measure absorptive capability.

Finally, the technology spillover effects of imports and FDI can be compared according to the results shown in Table 9.2 and Table 9.4. A general conclusion is that the technology spillover effects of FDI are more significant than those of imports, even when taking the host country's absorptive capability into account. How can such findings be explained? Compared with imports, which mainly reflect the purchase of advanced intermediate goods such as machinery and software, FDI may promote domestic firms' technological progress in various ways. Foreign firms do not only provide imitation and learning chances for indigenous ones by demonstration effects, but also indirectly improve the product quality and variety of its backward or forward firms by industrial linkages. Furthermore, the entry of foreign firms undoubtedly helps to intensify the competition in domestic markets, which propels domestic firms to increase their R&D inputs and to increase their innovation speed, which therefore improves resource allocation efficiency in the host country. Finally, foreign firms may help to promote human capital investment in the host country by providing employment training. Other researchers such as Barrell and Pain (1997) and Hood et al. (1999) make similar conclusions in their empirical work, while the importance of industrial linkages between foreign firms and domestic ones are especially emphasized by Hood et al. (1999). One of the notable facts which should draw our attention is that even though we make a distinction between the different roles of imports and FDI in different regression models, foreign firms actually play a key role in China's imports in the period we consider, especially for high-tech goods import. In 2002, the share of total imports contributed by foreign firms has been as high as 53.6 percent, while for the sample period of 1996–2002, the average share is 53.16 percent.[20] Such results highlight the fact that on the one hand, there is a complementary relationship between imports and FDI in terms of technology spillover; and on the other hand, the technology spillover effects of imports greatly depend on the import behavior of foreign firms.

4. CONCLUSION AND POLICY IMPLICATIONS

By introducing technology absorptive capability and the technology gap into an endogenous growth model, this chapter focuses on how technology spillovers and domestic absorptive capability affect the long-run growth rate. As mentioned above, a powerful explanation is maintained in our model to compare the different growth paths among LDCs and NIEs, and therefore robust policy generalizations are achieved in our model.

As emphasized in many previous studies, especially in human-capital-based endogenous growth models, human capital investments are crucial to achieving sustainable economic growth. Two important roles of human capital investments are also highlighted in this chapter. On the one hand, human capital investment directly improves output levels by improving the education and skill level of the labor force. On the other hand, human capital investment also indirectly promotes economic growth by enhancing the host country's absorptive capability and R&D efficiency. However, the problem is that while the direct output effect of human capital investment will be reflected in rising wages, the indirect effect of human capital investment is not likely to be reflected in wages. Since an individual's human capital investment basically depends on the investment return rate, it is crucial to enhance the rate of return to human capital investment in China in order to encourage investment in education or training. The rate of return on human capital in China is widely debated (Heckman, 2003). According to the estimation result of Chow, the return rate to education in China was 20 percent for human capital investment and only 4 percent for physical capital investment in the early 1990s. Young (2003) has compared the relative wage rates in China with those in newly industrialized countries in Asia in terms of educational levels, and the results are shown in Table 9.5. It can be seen from Table 9.5 that for both middle and high school graduates, the relative wage rates in China are much lower than those in such NIEs as Hong Kong and Singapore. What should draw our attention is that even though human capital is assumed to move between the final goods sector and the R&D sector in our theoretical model, in the real world the R&D sector is much more human-capital-intensive than the final goods sector. An implicit conclusion shown in Table 9.5 is since at present, enough incentives have not been provided to encourage individuals to receive higher levels of education and training, the current wage structure may hinder knowledge production in the R&D sector and therefore China's long-run economic growth.

The following policy suggestions may help to promote individual human capital investment. As shown by other authors, it is necessary to provide subsidies for individuals' human capital investment, especially for those investments in higher levels of human capital. One important reason for doing so lies in the fact that due to the externality effect of human capital investment, the individual return rate of human capital investment is definitely lower than the social return rate. Subsidies are also required to provide financing convenience for individuals' human capital investment due to rising education costs in China. Last but not least, it is crucial to develop a competitive and more liquid labor market in China to provide valid incentives and signals for individuals.

One related topic with human capital investment is the influence of imports and FDI on the host country's labor market. The impacts of imports/FDI on labor markets and wage rates can be reflected in the following two ways in our theoretical model. First, in the final goods sector, imports/FDI directly improve the marginal output level and hence wage rates due to more varieties of intermediate goods. Second, as shown in (9.15), imports/FDI indirectly enhance the knowledge output level of human capital in the R&D sector and therefore their wage rates by spillover effects. In conclusion, either by expanding the variety of intermediate goods or by technology spillover effects on domestic producers, imports/FDI finally improve wage rates in the host country, which also encourages

Table 9.5: *Relative Wage Rates in Terms of Education Levels in China and NIEs*

	China	Hong Kong	Singapore	South Korea	Taiwan
Wage for middle school education	1.16^*	1.42	1.94	1.44	1.22
Wage for higher education	1.25	2.09	2.60	1.99	1.51

Note: *The data are the wage rates for workers of various education levels relative to those who only receive primary school education.

Source: The data for China are cited from Young (2003), whose calculations are based on two Chinese Household Surveys in 1988 and 1995 by China's Social Science Academy, and the data for NIEs are cited from Young (1995).

individuals to invest more in human capital accumulation. Therefore, both imports and entry of foreign firms help to promote investment in and accumulation of human capital in the host country.

It has been generally argued that due to the constraint of limited resources in most developing countries and high costs of self-innovation, it is obviously inefficient to make redundant investments in old and outdated technologies. Therefore, technology policy in developing countries should focus on technology imports and imitation from outside instead of self-innovation. However, such arguments definitely neglect the domestic absorptive capabilities for LDCs. As is shown in our model, pure technology import and imitation is not equal to technological progress, since the final international technology spillover effect is essentially determined by technology absorptive capability. Hence, it is economically appropriate for developing countries to develop absorption capabilities in order to make better use of imported technology. Furthermore, as a result of the increase in technology absorptive capability for both domestic enterprises and the R&D sector, more adaptive invention is needed in order for developing countries to catch up.

Our model also reveals that an optimal technology gap exists for developing countries. It reminds us of the fact that it is not advisable for developing countries to import the most advanced technologies since it is hard to absorb them. On the contrary, the optimal technology gap implies that only when the domestic technology level is appropriate to the imported technology, can the largest benefits can be shared.

An optimal degree of openness also holds true for developing countries. The relationship between openness and China's economic growth since

1978 has been widely debated, and empirical results differ greatly. It is also revealed in our model that trade policy should focus on how to choose an optimal degree of openness by combining the short-term output-enhancement effect and the long-term growth effect of openness.

NOTES

1. In a much-cited contribution to the growth literature, Abramowitz (1986) also proposes the concept of social capability, which states that an economy must have some fundamental capabilities in order to benefit from foreign technology absorption. However, it is Boreinsztein et al. (1998) who show empirical evidence for the importance of the host country's absorptive capability using cross-section regressions.

2. However, few authors have taken the causality question into account. Comin and Hobijn (2004) argue that by having a micro measure of technology as the dependent variable, they are inclined to interpret the identified correlations with aggregate explanatory variables as causal relations. The endogeneity problem of openness has been emphasized by many others such as the Frankel and Romer (1999) study on the openness-growth relationship, which argues that the instrumental variable method (IV) should be preferred to the OLS method. In this chapter, we follow the method of Patrick et al. (1998) by using GDP and population as the instrumental variables for openness.

3. Other studies use the host country's financial market efficiency and government regulation as measures of absorptive capability. However, it is easy to extend our theoretical model by including more variables in our theoretical framework without changing our major conclusions.

4. Spence (1976), and Dixit and Stiglitz (1977) used a form similar to (9.1) to express consumer preferences over a variety of goods. This representation was first used to describe production with a variety of intermediate goods by Ethier (1982).

5. In the original Romer (1990) model, both labor input (L) and human capital (H) are used in the final goods production. The key difference between them lies in the assumption that human capital is used as inputs in both final goods sector and R&D sector, while labor is only used in the former. We can also endogenize human capital investment by following Lucas (1988). However, for model simplicity we assume the total human capital stock is given as in Romer (1990).

6. For simplicity only intermediate goods imports are examined. However, the fact is that other factors, such as FDI and communication links, also have remarkable spillover effects on the domestic R&D sector. For our econometric estimation, both FDI and imports are chosen as the two major technology spillover channels.

7. In order to motivate research, successful innovators have to be compensated in some manner. So, it is assumed in this model that inventor of the good j retains a perpetual monopoly right over the production and sale of good x_j, that uses his or her design. The flow of monopoly rents will then provide the incentive for invention. For further discussion, see the analysis of the behavior of a monopolist in inventing new varieties of products in Barro and Sala-i-Martin (1995, Ch. 6).

8. We assume that the interest rate r is constant since we only study equilibrium at the steady-state, and similar studies (e.g., Barro and Sala-i-Martin, 1995) show that the interest rate must be constant in this case.

9. While some authors, such as Edwards (1992), Sachs and Warner (1995), and Stiglitz (1998), show empirical support for the positive effects of openness on economic growth, others deny such a conclusion or find it only holds true under certain conditions. For instance, a significantly negative relationship between openness and economic growth is revealed in Lee (1993). Seven indicators are chosen by Harrison (1996) to investigate the relationship between openness and economic growth, however the author finds that only three indicators show positive influences on economic growth.

10.   Here we should note the fact that most of countries in Africa and Latin America have not followed an openness-led strategy until recently, and degrees of openness among those countries vary greatly. For example, Botswana has a higher degree of openness due to its dependence on diamond exports (Harvey, 1992). However, although significant differences in terms of economic development strategy exist among those countries, it can be generalized that the role of openness on economic growth essentially depends on other variables. For example, by studying the economic development experience of countries in Latin America and Africa, Rodrik (2000) emphasizes that it is domestic openness and macroeconomic stability that make openness work.

11.   To our knowledge, few researchers have attempted to do the same work that we do in this chapter. For example, by using China's provincial data from 1995 to 2000, Cheung and Lin (2004) find positive effects of FDI on the number of domestic patent applications in China. However, the key role of absorptive capability has been neglected in these papers.

12.   As demonstrated in our theoretical model, key variables in neoclassical growth models such as physical capital and labor are omitted, which may lead to an omitted variables bias in our results.

13.   Another way to measure technology spillover is to normalize the amount of FDI in a certain province to the total stock capital or output in that province. The key question is whether the absolute amount of FDI or the relative importance of FDI makes sense in producing technology spillover. Here we prefer the former.

14.   We gratefully acknowledge here that our chapter's referee reminds us of different R&D expenditure measurements, especially the original data sources of China's domestic R&D expenditure.

15.   There is a problem that the mere change of population may affect the estimated coefficient of human capital since our measure of human capital here is defined as average educational attainment, that is educational attainment per capita. However, as is well known, China has paid much attention to human capital investments during our sample years, and taking into account the fact that China's provincial population remained stable during the period 1996–2002, it can be expected that the estimated coefficient reflects the role of China's human capital investment on economic growth to a large degree.

16.   The revised model by Low et al. (1998) is as follows:

$$\ln\left(Trade_{it}\right) = \beta_i + \beta_t + \beta_1 \ln\left(GDP_{it}\right) + \beta_2 \ln\left(GDP_{it}\right)^2 + \beta_3 \ln\left(POP_{it}\right) + \beta_4 \ln\left(POP_{it}\right)^2$$
$$+ \beta_5 \ln(GDP_{it} / POP_{it}) + \beta_6 \ln(GDP_{it} / POP_{it})^2 + \varepsilon_{it}$$

$Trade_{it}$, and GDP_{it} have the same definition as above, and POP_{it} is the total population for province i in year t. Therefore, the revised degree of openness is:

$$ADJTrade_{it} = \exp\left[\ln\left(Trade_{it}\right) - \varepsilon_{it}\right].$$

Our original data are from each issue of the *China Statistical Yearbook*.

17.   Certainly, it is also possible to allow the slopes to vary across *i*; however, due to the limitation of our sample data, we do not consider varied-slope estimation in this chapter.

18.   It is hard to say whether technology imitation and absorption are a more effective way of improving productivity than self-innovation according to our estimation result since we do not consider the complementarity or substitution relationship between technology absorption and self-innovation. It can be seen from Table 9.1 that both technology spillovers and domestic R&D efforts are important driving forces of technological change. However, the major challenge that governments in developing countries usually face is how to allocate limited resources between technology absorption and self-innovation. Some other authors have studied the impact of technology imports on China's indigenous technological capability. By using time series data from 1960 to 1991, Zhao (1995) finds that imported technology complemented the enhancement of

indigenous technological capability in China. However, the impact of international technology spillovers on domestic self-innovation is a more complicated issue than technology imports.

19. To our knowledge, even though some theorists such as Romer (1993) and Rodrik (2000) have emphasized the technology effect of imports, few have studied the indirect effect of imports on China's economic growth through spillover effects.

20. Calculated from the *China Statistical Yearbook*, each issue from 1997 to 2003.

REFERENCES

Abramovitz, M. (1986), 'Catching up, forging ahead and falling behind', *Journal of Economic History*, **46**, 385–406.

Aghion, P. and P. Howitt (1992), 'A model of growth through creative destruction', *Econometrica*, **60**, 323–51.

Aghion, P. and P. Howitt (1998), *Endogenous Growth Theory*, Cambridge, MA: MIT Press.

Alfaro, L., A. Chanda, S. Kalemli-Ozan and S. Sayek (2004), 'FDI and economic growth: The role of local financial markets', *Journal of International Economics*, **64**, 89–112.

Barrell, R. and N. Pain (1997), 'Foreign direct investment, technological change, and economic growth within Europe', *Economic Journal*, **107**(445), 1770–86.

Barro, R.J. (1990), 'Government spending in a simple model of endogenous growth', *Journal of Political Economy*, **98**, S500–S521.

Barro R.J. (1991), 'Economic growth in a cross section of countries', NBER Working Papers no. 3120.

Barro, R.J. and J.-W. Lee (1993), 'International comparisons of educational attainment', *Journal of Monetary Economics*, **32**(3), 363–94.

Barro, R. and X. Sala-i-Martin (1995), *Economic Growth*, New York: McGraw Hill.

Bassanini, A. and S. Scarpetta (2001), 'Does human capital matter for growth in OECD countries? Evidence from pooled mean-group estimates', OECD Economics Department Working Papers no. 282.

Boer, P., A. Bayar, C. Martinez, T. Pamukçu and B. Hobijn (2001), 'Did trade liberalization induce a structural break in imports of manufactures in Turkey? Modeling of economic transition phenomena', in R. Kulikowski, Z. Nahorski, and J.W. Owsinski (eds), Warsaw: University of Information Technology and Management Press, pp. 198–219.

Borensztein, E., J.D. Gregorio and J.-W. Lee (1998), 'How does foreign direct investment affect economic growth?', *Journal of International Economics*, **45**, 115–35.

Cheung, K.Y. and P. Lin (2004), 'Spillover effects of FDI on innovations in China: Evidence from the provincial data', *China Economic Review*, **15**, 25–44.

Coe, D. and E. Helpman (1995), 'International R&D spillovers', *European Economic Review*, **39**, 859–87.

Coe, D.T., E. Helpman and A.W. Hoffmaister (1997), 'North–South R&D spillovers', *Economic Journal*, **107**(440), 134–49.

Comin, D. and B. Hobijn (2004), 'Cross-country technology adoption: Making the theories face the facts', *Journal of Monetary Economics*, **51**(1), 39–83.

Dixit, A.K. and J.E. Stiglitz (1977), 'Monopolistic competition and optimum product diversity', *American Economic Review*, **67**, 297–308.

Eaton, J. and S. Kortum (1996), 'Trade in ideas: Patenting and productivity in the OECD', *Journal of International Economics*, **40**, 251–78.

Edwards, S. (1992), 'Trade orientation, distortions, and growth in developing countries', *Journal of Development Economics*, **39**, 31–57.

Ethier, W. J. (1982), 'National and International returns to scale in the modern theory of international trade', *American Economic Review*, **73**, 389–405.

Frankel, J. and D. Romer (1999), 'Does trade cause growth?', *American Economic Review*, **89**(3), 379–99.

Griffith, R., S. Redding and J. Van Reenen (2000), 'Mapping the two faces of R&D: Productivity growth in a panel of OECD industries', CEPR Discussion Paper no. 2457.

Grossman, G. and E. Helpman (1991), *Innovation and Growth in the Global Economy*, Cambridge, MA: MIT Press.

Harrison, A. (1996), 'Openness and growth: A time-series, cross-country analysis for developing countries', *Journal of Development Economics*, **48**, 419–47.

Harvey, C. (1992), 'Botswana: Is the economic miracle over?', *Journal of African Economies*, **1**(3), 335–468.

Heckman J. (2003), 'China's investment in human capital', *Economic Development and Cultural Change*, 795–804.

Holmes, T.J. and J.A. Schmitz (2001), 'Competition at work: Railroads vs. monopoly in the U.S. shipping industry', *Quarterly Review*, 3–29.

Hood, N., J. Taggart and S. Young (1999), 'German manufacturing investment in the UK: Survey result and the economic impact', in R. Barrell and N. Pain (eds), *Innovation, Investment and the Diffusion of Technology in Europe: German Direct Investment and Economic Growth in Postwar Europe*, Cambridge: Cambridge University Press.

Keller, W. (1997), 'Are international R&D spillovers trade-related? Analyzing spillovers among randomly matched trade partners', NBER Working Paper no. 6065.

Keller, W. (2000), 'Do trade patterns and technology flows affect productivity growth', *World Bank Economic Review*, **14**, 17–47.

Keller W. (2001), 'International technology diffusion', NBER Working Paper no. 8573.

Keller W. (2002), 'Trade and the transmission of technology', *Journal of Economic Growth*, **7**, 5–24.

Kinoshita, Y. (2000), 'R&D and technology spillovers via FDI: Innovation and absorptive capacity', CERGE-EI, mimeo.

Lee, J.-W. (1993), 'International trade, distortion and long-run economic growth', *International Monetary Fund staff papers*, **40**(2), 299–328.

Liu X. (2001), 'An empirical research on the relationship between trade and China's economic growth', *Nankai Economic Review*, **5**, 21–7.

Low, P. Olarreaga, M. and Suarez, J. (1998), 'Does globalization cause a higher concentration of international trade and investment flows', WTO Working Papers series, ERAD–98–08.

Lucas, R.E. (1988), 'On the mechanics of economic development', *Journal of Monetary Economics*, **22**, 3–42.

Lumenga-Neso, O., M. Olarreaga and M. Schiff (2001), 'On indirect trade-related research and development spillovers', World Bank Policy Research Working Paper no. 2580.

Patrick, L., O. Marcelo and S. Javier (1998), 'Does globalization cause a higher concentration of international trade and investment flow?', WTO Working Paper, August.

Rebelo, S. (1991), 'Long-run policy analysis and long-run growth', *Journal of Political Economy*, **99**, 500–521.

Rivera-Batiz, L.A. and P.M. Romer (1991), 'Economic integration and endogenous growth', *Quarterly Journal of Economics*, **106**, 531–55.

Rodrik, D. (2000), 'The New Global Economy: Making Openness Work', Washington, DC: Overseas Development Council, Policy Essay.

Romer, P.M. (1986), 'Increasing returns and long-run growth', *Journal of Political Economy*, **94**, 1002–37.

Romer, P.M. (1987), 'Growth based on increasing returns due to specialization', *American Economic Review*, **77**(2), 56–62.

Romer P.M. (1990), 'Endogenous technological change', *Journal of Political Economy*, **98**, 71–102.

Romer, P.M. (1993), 'Idea gaps and object gaps in economic development', *Journal of Monetary Economics*, **32**(3), 543–73.

Sachs, J.D. and A.M. Warner (1995), 'Economic reform and the process of global integration', *Brookings Papers on Economic Activity*, 1–118.

Samuleson, P. (1954), 'The transfer problem and transport cost: Analysis of effects of trade impediments', *Economic Journal*, **64**, 264–89.

Sjoholm, F. (1996), 'International transfer of knowledge: The role of international trade and geographic proximity', *Weltwirschaftliches Archiv*, **132**(1), 97–115.

Smith, A. (1776), '*An Inquiry into the Nature and Causes of the Wealth of Nations*', London: W. Strahan and T. Cadell.

Spence, M. (1976), 'Product selection, fixed costs, and monopolistic competition, *Review of Economic Studies*, **43**(2), 217–35.

Stiglitz, J. (1998), 'Towards a new paradigm for development: Strategies, policies, and processes', Prebisch Lecture at UNCTAD (Geneva, October 19).

Wacziarg, R. (1998), 'Measuring the dynamic gains from trade', World Bank Working Paper no. 2001.

Wang, X. (2000), 'Sustainability of China's economic growth and institutional change', *Economic Research*, 7, 1–14 (in Chinese).

Williamson, J.G. (1991), 'Inequality, Poverty, and History: The Kuznets Memorial Lectures of the Economic Growth Center', Yale University, New York: Basil Blackwell.

Xu, B. (2000), 'Multinational enterprises, technology diffusion, and host country productivity growth', *Journal of Development Economics*, **62**, 477–93.

Xu, Q. and C. Jiang (2002), 'An empirical study on the correlation between trade and economic growth in China', *The Journal of Forecasting*, **2**, 14–9.

Young, A. (1995), 'The tyranny of numbers: Confronting the statistical realities of the East Asian growth experience', *The Quarterly Journal of Economics*, **110** (3), 641–80.

Young, A. (2003), 'Gold into base metals: Productivity growth in the People's Republic of China during the reform period', *Journal of Political Economy*, **111**, 1220–61.

Zhao, H. (1995), 'Technology imports and their impacts on the enhancement of China's indigenous technological capability', *Journal of Development Studies*, **31**, 585–602.

10. Productivity Spillovers from FDI: Detrimental or Beneficial? A Study of Chinese Manufacturing

Sarah Y. Tong and Youxin Hu

1. INTRODUCTION

Attracting foreign direct investment (FDI)[1] has become an important element of development strategies. FDI, especially in manufacturing, is considered a combination of capital and technology, as well as managerial and marketing skills. Technology flows from advanced nations to developing economies linked with FDI are essential as developing countries often lack the knowledge, the capacity, and the resources to develop new technologies. Cross-border investment provides important channels to reduce the technology gap between the developing and advanced world through both direct technology transfer and indirect spillovers.

While there is little controversy from a theoretical prospective, empirical studies have found mixed results on whether FDI carries positive spillover effects. Many studies find that FDI generates significant positive spillovers while others find either no or statistically insignificant evidence of technology spillover. Using firm-level data on Chinese manufacturing, this chapter attempts to help reconcile the divergence in the empirical outcomes. Our first goal is to identify and study the different effects of FDI due to different modes of technology spillover from foreign affiliates to indigenous Chinese firms. More specifically, we examine FDI's spillover effects from both the within-industry and the across-industry perspectives. Our second goal is to identify any association between spillover effects and the source country characteristics. We examine whether FDI from newly industrialized economies (NIEs) has a different impact compared to FDI from more advanced countries.

China's recent success in attracting foreign investment and economic growth has provided a unique opportunity to study the impact of FDI on development. First, China has become the largest FDI recipient among developing countries in recent years. Large FDI inflow has been associated with rapid trade expansion and economic growth. It is an important policy issue for China, as well as for other developing countries, to evaluate the relations between FDI inflow and domestic economic growth. Second, the source of FDI in China is diverse and has undertaken a great transformation. During the 1980s and early 1990s, FDI originated mainly from Hong Kong and other neighboring economies. Since the mid-1990s, FDI is increasingly committed by multinational corporations from the industrial world. This enables an investigation of whether FDI's spillover effects are affected by the sources of the investment.

The remainder of the chapter proceeds as follows. In Section 2, we present a brief literature review on the studies of FDI spillovers and on China's FDI. We also develop a theoretical framework in Section 2. In Section 3, we construct our empirical specification and introduce the data. Descriptions and discussions of the main variables are also included. In Section 4, regression results are presented and evaluated. We conclude with Section 5.

2.   LITERATURE REVIEW AND ANALYTICAL FRAMEWORK

It is widely established that FDI contributes significantly to a host country's economic growth. FDI may affect the host economies both directly and indirectly. As foreign joint ventures or wholly-owned subsidiaries are established, FDI influences an economy directly through capital inflow, increased employment, and the use of advanced equipment and technology. FDI could also generate a significant indirect impact on local economies through various channels. One channel is to facilitate technological innovation through intensified competition in the host market. Another is to generate technology spillover from foreign invested firms to indigenous firms in the host countries. FDI's spillover effects are the main focus of this study. Discussion on the impact of intensified competition will also be included.

The existing literature contains extensive studies on FDI's spillover effects from both theoretical and empirical perspectives. First, it is generally recognized that multinational corporations (MNCs) possess more advanced technology. When MNCs choose to penetrate a foreign market through direct investment, they are likely to take with them more sophisticated technology and superior managerial practices. These give them a competitive edge over indigenous firms who tend to be more familiar with the consumer preferences, business practices, and government policies in the host market (Blomstrom and Sjoholm, 1999). It is realistic to assume that at least a portion of the technologies transported by MNCs will inevitably be diffused to the indigenous establishments in the host economy. Secondly, business associations with MNCs provide important learning opportunities for domestic firms. They could reduce the costs of innovation and imitation for local firms, which will in turn speed up productivity improvement (Helpman, 1999). Thirdly, workers and managers employed and trained by the MNCs may later either move to the local firms or establish their own businesses. In both cases, the number of people with technical know-how in domestic industries is greatly expanded.

The technology spillovers described above apply mainly to firms within the same industry, which we hereafter refer to as intra-industry spillovers. Spillovers may also occur through backward and forward linkages between firms in different industries. Foreign-invested firms may provide technical assistance to local suppliers in order to secure quality inputs. They may also provide training and other technical support to their customers. Knowledge diffusions across firms in different industries are hereafter referred to as inter-industry spillovers.

Foreign participation in the host market will inevitably intensify competition. This forces the local indigenous firms to improve efficiency and to adopt new technologies to stay competitive (Kokko, 1996). FDI's impact on host country efficiency through intensified competition sometimes is viewed as a form of spillover effect. This type of spillover works mainly for firms within the same industry.

There are a growing number of empirical studies examining FDI's impact on host economies. The results have been mixed. Some find evidence of positive spillovers. Examples include studies by Caves (1974) on Australian manufacturing, Globerman (1979) on Canadian manufacturing, and Blomstrom and Persson (1983) on Mexican manufacturing industries. Three recent studies on the Indonesian manufacturing industry (Blomstrom and Sjoholm, 1999; Sjoholm, 1999; and Takii, 2005) also find evidence of positive spillovers from FDIs. In contrast, some studies conclude that no significant spillover effects are present. Some find domestic productivity is negatively associated with the intensity of foreign presence. These include studies by Kokko et al. (1996) on the Uruguayan manufacturing sector, Aslanoglu (2000) on Turkish manufacturing, Haddad and Harrison (1993) on Moroccan manufacturing industries, and Aitken and Harrison (1999) on Venezuelan industries.

The empirical disparity arises from various sources. One reason is that the data used are at different degrees of aggregation. Some employ firm data while others examine industry data. It may be difficult to distinguish between the inter-industry effects and the intra-industry effects of FDI for studies using industry data. If intra-industry and inter-industry spillovers are different in direction and magnitude, empirical results may be the combined outcome of the two, which could be either positive or negative.

Another reason is that some studies look at cross-industry variations in efficiency levels while others examine the difference in efficiency growth. The size of the technology gap between foreign firms and domestic firms may also affect the empirical outcome. Studies suggest that the host economies that have a smaller technology gap (such as investment in more developed countries) tend to benefit more from spillover effects. Finally, empirical results are also affected by whether the studies take into account the increased competition due to FDI inflows.

Several studies have examined FDI's spillover effects on Chinese industries. A study by Zhu and Lu (1998) suggests that higher FDI intensity leads to higher domestic productivity. Another by Liu (2002), however, found no evidence of spillovers within industries. Both studies use industry level data. A recent study by Cheung and Lin (2004) found that FDI facilitates patent activities in a region. One study (Jefferson et al., 2003) utilizing firm data found that ownership diversification of large and medium size firms improves efficiency.

This study investigates the impact of foreign participation on both the level and the increase of domestic productivity in China. Following others in the literature, we hypothesize that higher productivity and higher productivity increases are associated with a higher FDI presence in the economy due to technology spillovers. The relations are expressed by the following:

$$Y_i = f(FS_i, \mathbf{X}_i) \quad \text{where} \quad \frac{\partial Y_i}{\partial FS_i} > 0 \qquad (10.1)$$

$$\Delta Y_i = g(Y_{i0}, FS_i, \mathbf{X}_i) \quad \text{where} \quad \frac{\partial \Delta Y_i}{\partial FS_i} > 0 \text{ and } \frac{\partial \Delta Y_i}{\partial Y_{i0}} < 0 \qquad (10.2)$$

Where Y_i measures domestic productivity in industry i, ΔY_i measures domestic productivity increase of industry i, and Y_{i0} measures the initial level of domestic productivity in industry i. FS_i stands for the intensity of foreign presence in industry i, and $\mathbf{X}_i$ denotes other factors important to domestic productivity and domestic productivity increases.

FDI's spillover effects may be influenced by the size of the technology gap between domestic and foreign firms. The direction could be either positive or negative. A larger gap means there is greater potential for domestic firms to benefit through 'catch-up' effects. It may also indicate the low technology capacity of domestic firms which leads to limited spillovers. In other words, domestic firms with low technology capability may benefit more from modest foreign technology. Because of this conceptual ambiguity, we will not be able to attach a sign to the direction in which the technology gap affects FDI spillovers. As a developing country, China lags relatively far behind in most technology areas. We then assume that investment from industrial countries carries technologies that are much more advanced than those in China, while investment from the NIEs in Asia carries technologies that are only modestly advanced.

Hypothesis 1: The magnitude and (possibly) the direction of FDI's spillover effects differ depending on the technology gap between foreign and domestic firms.

In our empirical analysis, we divide FDIs into two groups. The first includes investment from Hong Kong, Macao and Taiwan (HMT)[2] assuming that they resemble investment with moderate technology advancement. We consider the assumption reasonable for two reasons. First, the three economies have only been industrialized quite recently. Second, the entry barrier for HMT-investment in China should be lower as these three economies enjoy proximity in culture, language, and historical heritage with mainland China. All non-HMT investments are included in the second group, used to represent investment with more advanced technology.

In the current study, we identify and estimate FDI's spillovers from both intra-industry and inter-industry perspectives. Intra-industry spillovers refer to the impact of foreign participation within a narrowly defined industry on domestic productivity in the same industry, while inter-industry spillovers refer to the impact of foreign presence on domestic productivity in related industries. We assume that inter-industry spillovers are the strongest in a locality.

Hypothesis 2: There are both intra-industry and inter-industry spillovers from FDI.

We expect that foreign invested firms and domestic firms in the same industry will produce the same or very similar goods. While domestic firms could potentially gain from technology spillovers from foreign invested firms, they will also face tougher competition for market share, for skilled labor, and for other scarce inputs. In contrast, there is much less competition between foreign-invested firms and domestic firms in related industries.

Therefore, foreign participation may present higher potential benefits to domestic suppliers and customers than to competing domestic firms.

To recapitulate, we identify four modes of technology spillovers: intra-industry and inter-industry spillovers from HMT-invested firms and from non-HMT-invested firms. The following is our analytical framework:

$$Y_{ij} = f(FSintra\_HMT_i, FSinter\_HMT_{ij}, \\ FSintra\_FIE_i, FSinter\_FIE_{ij}, \mathbf{X}_{ij}) \tag{10.3}$$

$$\Delta Y_{ij} = g(FSintra\_HMT_i, FSinter\_HMT_{ij}, \\ FSintra\_FIE_i, FSinter\_FIE_{ij}, Y_{ij0}, \mathbf{X}_{ij}) \tag{10.4}$$

where Y_{ij} and ΔY_{ij} are the level and increase of domestic productivity of industry i in region j. Y_{ij0} is the initial domestic productivity of industry i in region j. $FSintra\_HMT_i$ is the employment share of HMT-invested firms in 4-digit industry i, while $FSintra\_FIE_i$ is the employment share of other foreign-invested firms[3] in 4-digit industry i. Similarly, $FSinter\_HMT_i$ and $FSinter\_FIE_i$ are the employment shares of the two types of foreign firms in a 2-digit industry, to which industry i belongs, in region j, respectively. And X_{ij} represents other factors influencing the level and the change of productivity.

3.   EMPIRICAL SPECIFICATION AND DATA

3.1.   Empirical Specification and Key Variables

We use the simple model laid out in the previous section to estimate FDI spillover effects in the Chinese manufacturing sector. In Equation (10.3), the dependent variable is the productivity level of industry i in region j[4] in 1995. In Equation (10.4), the dependent variable is the productivity increase of industry i in region j between 1995 and 1997. Four key variables are used to estimate the effects of foreign presence on the level and change of domestic productivity. In addition, a number of other variables important to industrial productivity are also included.

3.1.1.   Foreign share variables

$FSintra\_HTM_i$ is the employment share of HMT-invested firms in a 4-digit industry i. Investment from Hong Kong, Macau, and Taiwan is used to represent foreign investment with modest technology advancement. $FSintra\_FIE_i$ is the employment share of other foreign invested firms. It is used to approximate investment with more advanced technology. Similarly, *FSinter_HMT$_{ij}$* and *FSinter_FIE$_{ij}$* are the employment shares of HMT invested firms and other foreign invested firms within the 2-digit industry, to which industry *i* belongs, in region *j*.

3.1.2.   Other explanatory variables

Industrial concentration: An industry's productivity is associated with its degree of production concentration. The reason is that firms in highly concentrated industries enjoy a certain degree of monopoly and are in more advantageous positions to set prices. As a result, they tend to have higher productivities (Blomstrom and Persson, 1983). Industrial concentration may also affect the speed of an industry's productivity increase, though the direction is not clear. On one hand, high concentration and higher profitability indicate that the firms are financially more capable to conduct R&D to improve technology. On the other hand, firms in monopolistic positions are less motivated to improve efficiency. The Herfindahl index (*HER$_i$*) is used to measure the concentration level of an industry.

Scale economy: Economy of scale will also affect an industry's productivity. In industries with increasing returns to scale, more sophisticated machinery is used with greater division of labor which leads to higher productivity. Similarly, scale economy may also affect the rate of productivity increase in industries. The importance of scale economy of an industry is measured as the average deviation from the optimal scale of all firms in that industry. We assume that the firm with the highest annual sales in the 4-digit industry has achieved the optimal scale.[5]

Labor quality: Domestic productivity and its growth may be related to the technology capacity of the industry. We include a measure of an industry's labor quality as a proxy for its technology capacity. Higher labor quality will lead to higher productivity and faster productivity increase. It is measured as the share of engineers and managerial staff in an industry's employment.

Share of state-owned enterprises (SOEs): SOEs account for a significant portion of China's industrial employment. Numerous reforms have been implemented to improve the efficiency of the state sector but the SOEs remain one of the least efficient sectors in the economy. As a result, industries with higher share of SOE employment would exhibit lower productivity and slower productivity growth.

Government policies and the degree of openness: Government policies have had a considerable impact on FDI inflow in China. Liberalization policies were first enacted in certain chosen regions before they were implemented across the country. Firms in special economic zones, for example, enjoy more freedom and have more opportunities to establish business linkages with foreign firms than firms in other regions. Domestic firms are exposed to different degrees of foreign technology and foreign competition as a result of policy disparities. Firms in relatively more open regions tend to have higher productivity and more rapid productivity progress. In the empirical analysis, the 30 regions are divided into four groups regarding their relative openness.

Market growth: Productivity increase is affected by the overall business climate. During economic expansion, demand rises and productivity grows faster.[6] We include a measure of economic growth in a region to account for its effect on firms' productivity increase in a region.

Initial level of productivity: An industry's initial level of productivity will affect its productivity growth. Industries with lower initial productivity have greater potential for efficiency improvement relative to those with higher initial productivity. Analysis of productivity growth between 1995 and 1997 takes productivity in 1995 as the initial level.

Other industry specific factors: We discussed a number of industry specific measures such as labor quality and industry concentration. However, there might be other industry specific factors important to productivity. We also include dummy variables for each 2-digit industry to account for the effects of such omitted variables.

We define the following specifications for empirical analysis:

$$
\begin{aligned}
Y_{ij} = {} & \alpha_0 + \alpha_1 FSintra\_HMT_i + \alpha_2 FSinter\_HMT_{ij} \\
& + \alpha_3 FSintra\_FIE_i + \alpha_4 FSinter\_FIE_{ij} \\
& + \alpha_5 HER_i + \alpha_6 SCALE_i + \alpha_7 LQ_i + \alpha_8 SOE_{ij} + \alpha_9 OPEN_j \\
& + \alpha_{10} \mathbf{X}_{ij} + e_{ij}
\end{aligned} \tag{10.5}
$$

$$
\begin{aligned}
\Delta Y_{ij} = {} & \beta_0 + \beta_1 FSintra\_HMT_i + b_2 FSinter\_HMT_{ij} \\
& + \beta_3 FSintra\_FIE_i + \beta_4 FSinter\_FIE_{ij} \\
& + \beta_5 HER_i + \beta_6 SCALE_i + \beta_7 LQ_i + \beta_8 SOE_{ij} + \beta_9 OPEN_j \\
& + \boldsymbol{\beta}_{10} \mathbf{X}_{ij} + \boldsymbol{\beta}_{11} Y_{ij0} + e_{ij}
\end{aligned} \tag{10.6}
$$

Where i denotes a 4-digit industry and j a region. HER is the concentration level measured by the Herfindahl Index. SCALE is a measure of scale economy. LQ measures the labor quality. SOE is SOE's employment share. OPEN is a set of dummy variables indicating the relative degree of openness of a region. And X includes other factors, such as the average starting years of firms.

3.2. Data Introduction

Two datasets are the main source for our empirical analysis. The first is the China Industrial Census of 1995[7] which includes nearly 500 000 industrial firms. Basic characteristic information is provided such as industry, location, and ownership type. The dataset also includes the firms' employment, the original value of fixed assets, and the amount of annual sales. The second dataset provides the same firm-level information for the three years from 1995 to 1997 but only has data for around 100 000 firms. It includes only large and medium-sized firms and small firms with total annual sales above RMB 2 million. Moreover, firms in six administrative regions are excluded in the second dataset.

We obtain the values of the key variables using the two datasets. For the measure on labor quality, we use the printed version of 1995 Industrial census. For real GDP growth, we use the *China Statistical Yearbook*. The definitions of the variables are summarized in Table 10.1.

3.3. Descriptive Statistics

The top panel of Table 10.2 gives the average employment shares of foreign-invested firms across industries. For HMT-invested firms, the average employment shares for 4-digit industries and for 2-digit industries of different regions are 5.6 percent and 4.4 percent, respectively.[8] The figures for other foreign invested firms are 4.8 percent and 3.6 percent, respectively. There are large variations across industries and regions. Across 4-digit industries, employment shares of HMT-invested firms range from zero percent to more than 40 percent, while those of other foreign invested firms range from zero percent to 78 percent. Across 2-digit industries in different regions, employment shares of HMT-invested firms range from zero percent to 63 percent while those of other foreign invested firms range from zero percent to 38 percent. While foreign firms are becoming increasingly important in many sectors and regions, SOEs still account for a large portion of industrial employment, more than 40 percent on average. Engineers and managerial staff make up 10 percent to one third of total employees across industries and the average is 18 percent.

Table 10.1:   Definition of Variables

Name	Definition	Year
Y_{ii}	Productivity of industry i in region j	1995
ΔY_{ij}	Productivity increase of Industry i in region j	1995–97
$FSintra\_HMT_i$	Employment share of HMT-invested firms in industry i	1995
$FSintra\_FIE_i$	Employment share of other foregin-invested firms in industry i	1995
$FSintera\_FIE_{ij}$	Employment shares of HMT-invested firms within the 2-digit industry, which industry i belongs to, in region j	1995
$FSinter\_FIE_{ij}$	Employment shares of other foreign-invested firms within the 2-digit industry, which industry i belongs to, in region j	1995
HER_i	Herfindahl index of industry i $$HER_i = \sum_{l=1,\ldots,ni} (SALE_{il} / \sum_{l=1,\ldots,ni} SALE_{il})^2$$	1995
$SCALE_i$	The average deviation from the optimal scale of all firms in industry i, assume that the firm with the highest annual sales in the industry has achieved optimal scale	1995
LQ_i	The shares of engineers and managerial staff in total employment. The measure is available at the 3-digit level	1995
SOE_{ij}	Employment share of SOEs in industry i region j	1995
$OPEN_j$	Three dummy variables, $OPEN\_X_j$, $OPEN\_Y_j$, $OPEN\_Z_j$, for regions most, second and third open regions	1995
$DATE_{ij}$	The average of the years when firms in industry i in region j started their businesses	
GDP_j	Real GDP growth between 1995 and 1997 in region j	1995–97

The mean for HER is 0.04 and the median is 0.02, indicating that the degree of concentration for most industries is quite low while a small number of industries are highly concentrated. The same distribution bias exists for the measure on scale economy. In many industries, most of the firms are quite small relative to the industry's leader. An average firm's annual sales are less than 4 percent of that of the largest in the industry.

Table 10.2:   *Mean Values of Key Variables (in percent)*

	Mean	Median	Maximum	Minimum	Standard deviation
Foreign shares					
FSintra_HMT	5.63	3.46	40.54	0.00	6.20
FSintra_FIE	4.79	2.96	77.57	0.00	5.58
FSinter_HMT	4.41	1.93	63.02	0.00	7.57
FSinter_FIE	3.64	2.16	37.74	0.00	4.45
LQ	18.28	18.27	33.95	10.19	3.74
RD	0.038	0.027	0.628	0.00	0.04
HER	4.48	2.08	83.70	0.02	7.29
SCALE	3.83	2.69	30.03	0.18	3.63
SOE	40.66	36.36	100.00	0.00	34.30
GDP	23.69	24.32	32.13	3.48	3.48

4.   REGRESSION RESULTS

We now present and discuss our estimation results for the two empirical specifications.

4.1.   What Explains the Differences in Productivity Levels?

The dependent variable for Equation 10.5 is the level of domestic productivity of industry i in region j. The estimation includes more than 10 000 observations[9] and the result (Table 10.3) indicates that 23 percent of the total cross-industry, cross-region variance in productivity is accounted for by the model.

4.1.1.   The effect of foreign investment
We first note that the coefficient for *FSintra_HMT* is significantly negative while that for *FSintra_FIE* is significantly positive (Table 10.3). The average productivity of domestic firms in industries with a higher presence of HMT investment is significantly lower and in industries with a higher presence of other foreign investment is significantly higher, other things equal. This result is consistent with the hypothesis which states that a 'larger technology gap provides larger potential gains to domestic industries through spillovers'. However, it does not explain why the coefficient for employment shares of HMT-invested firms is significantly negative.

One possible explanation is that HMT-invested firms are in direct competition with domestic firms since they have little technological advantage. As a result, market conditions for domestic firms deteriorate which leads to the decline of domestic productivity. Alternatively, it is possible that foreign investment is directed by domestic productivity. HMT investment may be drawn to lower productivity industries while other foreign investments are concentrated in high productivity industries.[10]

We found that domestic productivity is also positively affected by the presence of non-HMT foreign-invested firms in related industries in the region. The coefficient for *FSinter_FIE* is significantly positive, while that for *FSinter_HMT* is negative but insignificant. More specifically, a one percentage point increase in *FSinter_FIE* corresponds to a 1.6 percent increase in the average domestic productivity in the corresponding sector and region. This is again consistent with the hypothesis that a larger technology gap brings positive benefits through both intra- and inter-industry spillovers.

4.1.2.   The effects of other factors

Domestic productivity of industries is affected by the degree of openness of their locality. Coefficients for *OPEN_X* and *OPEN_Z* are both significantly positive. Industries in the most and the third most open regions are 36

Table 10.3:   Estimation Results for Equation (10.5)

Independent Variables[ab]	Coefficient	T-stat
FSintra_HMT	−0.676	−4.387***[c]
FSintra_FIE	0.616	3.648***
FSinter_HMT	−0.003	−0.020
FSinter_FIE	1.591	7.275***
OPEN_X	0.355	10.84***
OPEN_Y	0.017	0.854
OPEN_Z	0.070	2.711***
LQ	2.587	7.275***
HER	1.217	10.51***
SCALE	4.362	20.01***
DATE	0.017	16.46***
SOE	−0.735	−28.07***
Number of observations	10 343	
R^2	0.2291	
R^2 adjusted	0.2263	

Notes:
[a]   The dependent variable is domestic productivity of industry *i* in region *j* in 1995.
[b]   2-digit industry dummies are included.
[c]   *** denotes significant at the 1 percent level.

percent and 7 percent more productive than those in the least open regions.[11] It shows that a more liberal business environment benefits domestic productivity.

The coefficient for *LQ* is positive[12] and that for *SOE* is negative. Both are highly significant. Industries with higher average labor qualities and lower SOE presence have high productivity, as expected. A one percentage point reduction in SOEs' employment share corresponds to a 0.74 percent improvement in average productivity of an industry in a region. The coefficients for *HER* and *SCALE* are both significantly positive. Firms in industries where there is less competition and economy of scale have higher productivity. Finally, industries dominated by new firms are more productive.

4.2.   What Explains the Differences in Productivity Increase?

The dependent variable for Equation (10.6) is the increase in domestic productivity of industry *i* in region *j* between 1995 and 1997. The estimation includes more than 5700 observations and the result (Table 10.4) indicated that 36 percent of the total cross-industry, cross-region variance in productivity increases is explained by the model.

4.2.1.   The effect of foreign investment
The coefficients for both *FSintra_HMT* and *FSinter_HMT* are significantly negative (Table 10.4). More HMT investments are negatively related to domestic productivity increase in their own and other related industries. Coefficients for *FSintra_FIE* and *FSinter_FIE* are also negative but insignificant. We find no evidence that foreign participation facilitates productivity increases and we are not able to rule out the possibility that non-HMT foreign investment is attracted into highly productive industries but does little to improve domestic efficiency.

There are a number of explanations that are worth mentioning. First, spillover effects from foreign participation may take time to materialize and three years may not be a sufficient length of time. Second, the positive effect of foreign presence may be taken up by other variables such as a region's openness and real GDP growth. Third, it is noted that we use total sales and not value-added to estimate the production function. Our measure of productivity increase is closely related to market conditions. Foreign participation, especially HMT-invested firms, is likely to worsen market demand for domestic firms which leads to lower productivity. Finally, even when market efficiency is improved, our measure of productivity increase may not be able to show that improvement. The reason is that higher efficiency leads to lower prices and therefore lower sales.[13]

Table 10.4:   Estimation Results for Equation (10.6)

Independent Variables[ab]	Coefficient	T-stat
FSintra_HMT	−0.648	−3.577***[c]
FSintra_FIE	−0.025	−0.113
FSinter_HMT	−0.332	−1.946**
FSinter_FIE	−0.334	−1.291
OPEN_X	0.123	3.309***
OPEN_Y	0.105	5.069***
OPEN_Z	0.004	0.117
LQ	0.178	0.471
HER	−0.017	−0.099
SCALE	−1.052	−3.537***
DATE	0.007	9.342***
SOE	−0.379	−15.10***
Y_0	−0.367	−24.63***
ΔGDP	2.337	9.616***
Number of Observations	5755	
R^2	0.3656	
R^2 adjusted	0.3613	

Notes:
[a]   The dependent variable is the domestic productivity increase for industry i in region j from 1995–97.
[b]   2-digit industry dummies are included.
[c]   *** denotes significant at the 1 percent level; and ** significant at the 5 percent level.

4.2.2.   The effects of other factors

The coefficient on Yij_0 is significantly negative, indicating that higher initial productivity leads to slower productivity increase. A 1 percent increase in initial productivity corresponds to a 0.4 percent slower productivity increase. The coefficient on real GDP growth in a region is significantly positive. A one percent increase in a region's real GDP growth corresponds to a two percent higher productivity increase. Increasing demand leads to higher capital utilization rate and therefore higher productivity.

The coefficient for *LQ* is positive and that for *HER* is negative, but neither is significant. The coefficient for *SCALE* is significantly negative. This might be important for a number of reasons. For industries dominated by large firms, productivity is high and therefore efficiency improvement is slow. The coefficient on *DATE* is positive while that for *SOE* is negative, both are significant. Industries with more new firms are more productive and have achieved faster productivity increase. Industries with more SOEs, however, are less productive and slow in efficiency improvement.

The relative openness of a region is important for domestic productivity increase of a region. The coefficients for the two most open regions, *OPEN_X* and *OPEN_Y*, are both positive and significant. The coefficient for *OPEN_Z* is positive but not significant. As we know that more open regions have attracted more foreign investment, the results may also indicate that more foreign participation facilitates domestic efficiency improvement.

5.   CONCLUDING REMARKS

This study investigates the spillover effects associated with foreign investment in the Chinese manufacturing sector. Using firm level datasets, we estimate FDI's spillover effects from both within-industry and across-industry separately. By dividing FDI into groups with different technology advancement, we also evaluate the importance of the technology gap on the intensity and direction of spillovers.

First, we compute two measures for the intensity of foreign presence, one for Hong Kong–Macao–Taiwan (HMT)-invested firms and one for other foreign-invested firms. The assumption is that HMT investment has relatively smaller technological advantages over domestic firms compared to other foreign investment. By incorporating such division, we examine the impact of the technology gap on FDI spillovers. Second, for investment from each of the two sources, we compute two measures for the intensity of foreign presence, within-industry and across-industry. Foreign employment share within a 4-digit industry measures the first, while foreign employment share within a 2-digit industry in a location measures the second.

The empirical results lend some support for positive spillovers. Non-HMT investments are shown to benefit domestic productivity within industries when we analyze the level of domestic productivity. This could be through various mechanisms such as knowledge outflow from foreign businesses, labor training and labor movement between domestic and foreign businesses. There are also cross-industry spillovers from non-HMT investment. Domestic firms have higher productivity when there are more non-HMT-invested firms in related industries in the region. However, such spillovers are not present for HMT investment. As we assume that HMT investments are only modestly more advanced than indigenous firms, the results suggest that a larger technology gap presents more benefits for Chinese firms.

In addition to analyze variations in productivity levels, we also evaluate the factors important to domestic productivity increase across industries and regions. Empirical outcomes on the role of foreign investment, however, are much less assuring. One certain result is that higher employment shares of HMT-invested firms are associated with slower productivity increase of domestic firms within the same industry and in related industries. It is likely that HMT-invested firms, with little technology advantage, have become fierce competitors for domestic firms. The coefficients on the measures of other-foreign invested firms are also negative but insignificant.

While we find no direct evidence that a foreign presence leads to a higher domestic productivity increase, foreign investment may indeed be important. It is shown that in more open regions where there is more FDI, domestic productivity increases faster. Moreover, a region's overall economic condition, measured by real GDP growth, is also correlated with higher productivity increase. In contrast, industries with more state linkages have suffered from not only low productivity but also slower productivity increase.

NOTES

1. In the context of this study, foreign direct investment refers to all inward investment originated from outside mainland China.
2. We would prefer to separate the investment originating from developing economies from the investment originating from industrial countries. However, this is not achievable because the Chinese authority only distinguishes foreign invested firms with investment from Hong Kong, Macao, and Taiwan from the rest.
3. Other foreign investments include all investments in China except for those from Hong Kong, Macao, and Taiwan.
4. Each firm has a 4-digit code for industry identification. Aggregate productivity measures for each 4-digit industry at each location are used for the empirical analysis. Firms are located across 30 administrative regions.
5. We think the assumption is reasonable though it may not be true for all industries. Due to past experience in central planning, there has been a high similarity in industrial structure across administrative regions. The result is that in most industries, there are a large number of relatively small firms where few reach economy of scale.
6. This is especially true when productivity and its growth are measured using sale, instead of value-added.
7. More details on the two datasets are provided in the Appendix.
8. The figures are simple averages across industries and are different from the FIEs' overall employment shares.
9. In theory, there should be around 18 000 observations for analysis (590 industries, 30 regions). The actual number is much less as some industries are not present in some regions. Industries with no foreign investments are also excluded.
10. The evidence is not strong as we found that *FSintra_HMT* and *FSintra_FIE* are positively correlated with a correlation coefficient of 55 percent.
11. It is interesting to note that the coefficient for *OPEN_Y*, the second most open region is positive but insignificant. These location dummies may have incorporated other factors such as geographic advantages.
12. Similar results are obtained when an alternative measure, average industry wage, is used.
13. We thank Sadayuki Takii for suggesting this point.

REFERENCES

Aitken, B. and A. Harrison (1999), 'Do domestic firms benefit from direct foreign investment? Evidence from Venezuela', *American Economic Review*, **89**(3), 605–18.

Aslanoglu, E. (2000), 'Spillover effects of foreign direct investments on Turkish manufacturing industry', *Journal of International Development*, **12**, 1111–30.

Blomstrom, M. and H. Persson (1983), 'Foreign direct investment and spillover efficiency in an underdeveloped economy: Evidence from the Mexican manufacturing industry', *World Development*, **11**(6), 493–501.

Blomstrom, M. and F. Sjoholm (1999), 'Technology transfer and spillovers: Does local participation with multinationals matter?', *European Economic Review*, **43**, 915–23.

Caves, R. (1974), 'Multinational firms, competition, and productivity in host country markets', *Economica*, **41**(162), 176–93.

Cheung, K. and P. Lin (2004), 'Spillover effects of FDI on innovation in China: Evidence from the provincial data', *China Economic Review*, **15**, 25–44.

Globerman, S. (1979), 'Foreign direct investment and "spillover" efficiency benefits in Canadian manufacturing industries', *Canadian Journal of Economics*, **12**, 42–56.

Haddad, M. and A. Harrison (1993), 'Are there positive spillovers from direct foreign investment? Evidence from Panel data for Morocco', *Journal of Development Economics*, **42**, 51–74.

Helpman, E. (1999), 'R&D and Productivity: The International Connection', in A. Razin and E. Sadka (eds), *The Economics of Globalization: Policy Perspectives from Public Economics*, Cambridge: Cambridge University Press pp. 17–30.

Jefferson, G, A. Hu, X. Guan and X. Yu (2003), 'Ownership, performance, and innovation in China's large- and medium-size industrial enterprise sector', *China Economic Review*, **14**, 89–113.

Kokko, A. (1996), 'Productivity spillovers from competition between local firms and foreign affiliates', *Journal of International Development*, **8**, 517–30.

Kokko, A., R. Tansini and M.C. Zejan (1996), 'Local technological capability and productivity spillovers from FDI in the Uruguayan manufacturing sector', *Journal of Development Studies*, **32**, 602–11.

Liu, Z. (2002), 'Foreign direct investment and technology spillover: Evidence from China', *Journal of Comparative Economics*, **30**(3), 579–602.

Sjoholm, F. (1999), 'Technology gap, competition and spillovers from direct foreign investment: Evidence from establishment data', *The Journal of Development Studies*, **36**, 53–73.

Takii, S. (2005), 'Productivity spillovers and characteristics of foreign multinational plants in Indonesian manufacturing 1990–1995', *Journal of Development Economics*, **76** (2), 521–42.

Zhu, G. and D. Lu (1998), 'Evidence of spill-over efficiency: Implication on industrial policies towards foreign direct investment in China', *Singapore Economic Review*, **43**(1), 57–73.

APPENDIX

Introduction to the Data and the Main Variables

Two main datasets are used in the study. The first (Dataset A) comes from China's Industrial Census of 1995, conducted by China's Statistics Bureau. It includes close to 500 000 industrial firms. The basic information on firms' characteristics provided in the data includes industry codes, geographic location, size groups, and ownership type. Nearly 600 4-digit industries are represented. The firms are located in thirty administrative regions in the mainland.

There are eight ownership types, including state-owned, collectives, private firms, shareholding companies, domestic joint ventures, Hong Kong, Macao, and Taiwan (HMT)-invested firms, and other foreign-invested firms. Firms belong to various size groups such as super large, large, medium, and small. The data also report the firms' total employment, original and net values of fixed assets, and the amount of annual sales.

The second dataset (Dataset B) provides the same firm-level information for the years 1995–97 but includes only around 100 000 firms. The main reason is that Dataset B includes only large and medium-sized firms and small firms with total annual sale above RMB 2 million. The other reason is that firms in six administrative regions, including the provinces of Anhui, Hainan and Jiangxi, the Autonomous Regions of Inner Mongolia and Tibet, and Bejing Municipal, are also missing from Dataset B.

The key variables used are obtained from the two datasets are summarized hereafter.

Y_{ij} is the productivity level of a 4-digit industry i in region j in 1995. We use information from Dataset A to estimate 28 log equations for each 2-digit industry to obtain the measure. In each equation, the dependent variable is the total sales of all domestic firms in industry i in region j. The independent variables are the total employment and the total value of fixed net assets. Y_{ij} is the residual of the equation.

ΔY_{ij} is the productivity increase between 1995 and 1997 of industry i at region j. Dataset B is used to obtain the measure. We use Dataset B to estimate 28 equations for each 2-digit industry to obtain the productivity levels for both 1995 and 1997. Productivity for 1995 is used as the initial productivity Y_{ij0} and the difference is used to measure productivity increase.

$FSintra\_HMT_i$ is the employment share of HMT-invested firms in industry i in 1995.

$FSintra\_FIE_i$ is the employment share of other foreign firms in industry i in 1995.

FSinter_HMT$_{ij}$ is the employment share of HMT-invested firms in a 2-digit industry to which industry i belongs in region j in 1995. Employment of HMT-invested firms in industry i in region j is excluded.

FSinter_FIE$_{ij}$ is the employment share of other foreign firms in the 2-digit industry to which industry i belongs in region j in 1995. Employment of foreign invested firms in industry i, region j is excluded.

HER$_i$ is industry I's Herfindahl index in 1995, measured as

$$HER_i = \sum_{l=1,\dots,n_i} (SALE_{il} / \sum_{l=1,\dots,n_i} SALE_{il})^2,$$

where *SALE$_{il}$* is the annual sale of the lth firm and n_i is the number of firms in industry i.

SCALE$_i$ is the average deviation of all domestic firms from the optimal scale in industry i, in 1995. We assume that in each industry, the firm with the highest annual sale has achieved the optimal economy of scale. The average ratio of each firm's sale to that of the optimal one is used to measure the degree of scale economy in the industry.

LQ$_i$ measures the labor quality of industry i, calculated as the share of engineers and managerial staff in the industry. The number of engineers and managerial staff are obtained from the Third National Industrial Census of China in 1995 (published version). The report provides information only for the 168 3-digit manufacturing industries.

SOE$_{ij}$ is the employment share of state-owned enterprises in industry i in region j.

OPEN_X$_j$, *OPEN_Y$_j$*, and *OPEN_Z$_j$* are three binary variables measuring the degree of openness of region j in descending order. The least open region is used as default group.

DATE$_{ij}$ is the simple average of the years when firms in industry i in region j started.

ΔGDP$_j$ is the real GDP growth in region j between 1995 and 1997. Information is obtained using data from the *China Statistical Yearbook*.

11. Rural–Urban Migration and Wage Determination: The Case of Tianjin, China

Zhigang Lu and Shunfeng Song

1. INTRODUCTION

The economic reform in China that started in 1978 has created a 'floating population' as over 100 million people have left their villages and streamed into cities where manufacturing and businesses boom. The migration of labor from agricultural to non-agricultural industries has increased the average income of rural people as migrant workers send a significant portion of their income back home. At the same time, rural migrant laborers have made great contributions to economic growth by complementing the labor force of cities and providing low-cost work. However, the benefits from economic growth have not been fairly shared between urban and migrant workers, and clear disparities exist in China's urban and rural labor markets. It is estimated that between 12 and 15 million non-farm jobs will be required annually just to absorb this surplus labor (Johnson, 2002).

Rural migrants generally make less money, receive far fewer benefits, and have no health insurance. Most live in precarious dormitories provided by their employers if they have any housing. Rural surplus laborers who moved to urban areas are called *mingong* to mark their difference from the city-dwelling workers. Rural migrants are treated as strangers and outsiders in cities. They are denied formal urban membership and substantive rights and their children are largely prohibited from attending city schools.

The urban–rural disparities in China's labor market may be categorized into two types. The first difference relates to productivity characteristics, such as education and job training, and the second relates to non-productivity-related characteristics, such as race, gender, or in our case, *hukou* status, which also could affect labor status. Discrimination is present if equally productive individuals within the same enterprise are treated differently simply because of their *hukou* status.

In order to promote labor mobility and efficiency and to improve equality and social stability, it is important to first understand the motivations for migration and then examine the conditions that migrants encounter. Why do farmers migrate to cities? What are the characteristics of migrants? What factors determine wages? Are migrant workers discriminated against in China's urban labor market? To answer these questions, a survey of employees was conducted from October to December 2003 in Tianjin, one of the four central government municipalities in China. We found that in addition to economic and social-demographic factors such as ownership of business, education, experience, and age, the restrictive *hukou* system has negatively influenced migrants' income. This chapter limits its discussions to migrant and non-migrant workers with migrant workers defined as those not having Tianjin *hukou*.

This chapter is structured as follows. Section 2 reviews related literature on rural–urban migration. Section 3 describes the data and presents the basic statistics. The empirical study is in Section 4. Conclusion and discussions are in Section 5.

2. RURAL–URBAN MIGRATION AND WAGE DETERMINANTS: A LITERATURE REVIEW

Millions of people in the rural populations of the developing world confront the decision of migrating to urban areas and every year, many find it worthwhile to leave their villages for cities. The 2000 population census data show that 144.39 million rural residents in China, or 11.6 percent of the total population, moved into cities and towns (*chengzhen*), in 2000 (NBSC, 2002).

The massive rural–urban migration since 1980 can be broadly attributed to the huge surplus of rural labor, widening income and consumption disparities between rural and urban residents, and heavy taxation on the agricultural sector. The rapid expansion of China's rural labor force, improvement in production efficiency, and the continuing reduction of cultivated land have caused a larger portion of rural laborers to be underemployed or unemployed. In the early 1980s the surplus of rural laborers was 70 million, or 18 percent of the entire rural labor force and this surplus grew to about 130 million, or 28 percent ten years later (Zhang, 2004).

The widening income and consumption disparity between rural and urban residents is clearly a factor contributing to increasing migration. In 1978, annual per capita disposable income was 2.6 times higher for urban residents than for rural peasants, and by 2001 that ratio increased to 2.9.

Over the same time period the ratio of urban to rural consumption per capita increased from 2.9 to 3.5, demonstrating widening income and consumption disparities (NBSC, various years, 1994–2003). In addition, urban residents also enjoy various state subsidies on food, education, employment, and medical services.

The heavy tax burden on farmers also influences rural migration. Although the central government emphasized the importance of alleviating this burden, according to Zhang (2004), local governments still tax a significant portion of farmers' income. Even worse, the agricultural taxation is regressive. For example, in 1996, the tax rate was 16.7 percent for rural families with an annual income between 400 and 500 yuan, but only 2.8 percent for those with incomes of 2500 to 5000 (Zhang, 2004). The high tax on farmers' income discourages investment in agricultural production, which also contributes to city migration.

Table 11.1 lists major reasons why the rural laborers surveyed wanted to migrate to the city of Tianjin. As expected rural people migrate to seek higher income, better opportunities, a better quality of life, and a better education for themselves and their children. Interestingly, more than 20 percent of migrants cited loss of land in the countryside as a factor.

The impact of education on rural–urban migration has been examined in the literature with some studies concluding that education is critical in driving rural laborers away from their land (Zhang et al., 1995; Zhao, 1997; Xia, 2004); while others suggest that education is not important in determining migration choice (Meng, 2002; Hare and Zhao, 1996).

Previous studies have argued that non-market factors are more important than market forces in driving the rural population to non-agricultural migrating jobs (Parish et al., 1995; Cook, 1998; Sato, 1998). Wu et al. (1990) and Wu (1994) found that many Chinese rural workers had been securing non-agricultural jobs through their friends or relatives and Hare and Zhao (1996) showed that networks of information and assistance are important for rural workers to get jobs in cities.

The return of education on earnings is extremely low in China. The OLS estimates of the increase in earnings from an additional year of schooling range from 1.4 percent to 5.4 percent (see for example, Byron and Manaloto, 1990; Meng and Kidd, 1997; Johnson and Chow, 1997; Li, 2003). Another study by Li and Luo (2004) uses generalized method of moments estimation for young workers in China, and concludes that the estimated returns to schooling are about 15 percent overall and 16.9 percent for women. Zhao (1997) uses rural school education to show that OLS estimation underestimates the returns to education in China by ignoring the segregation of rural and urban labor markets. She found that the expected

Table 11.1:   Reasons for Rural–Urban Migration

Reasons	Number of responses[*]	Percentage of responses
Higher income in cities	187	41.1
Better opportunities in cities	203	44.6
Better quality of life in cities	143	31.4
Burden of taxes and fees	117	25.7
Better education	170	37.3
Better education for children	123	27.0
Loss of land in the countryside	98	21.5
Other	41	9.0

Note: The total number of respondents is 455. Responses are not mutually exclusive.

Source: Survey conducted by the authors in Tianjin, 2003.

rate of return for a rural senior high school education is rather high because it improves access to urban employment where greater earnings are possible. Scholars have suggested various government policies to address migration issues (see for example De Haan, 2000; Cai and Wang, 2003; and Zhai and Wang, 2003).

While wage and gender discrimination are common in many countries, they are particularly strong in China because of its unique ownership structure and *hukou* system. Meng (1998) found that overall wage discrimination was more prevalent in the state-owned sector. There is some disagreement about the relative level of gender discrimination in the state-owned sector (see Maurer-Fazio and Hughes, 2000; Rozelle et al., 2000), but Dong and Bowles (2002) found that wage discrimination against women and migrant workers exists across ownership types. Significant sorting of rural labor migrants exist by occupation, sector, gender, age, marital status, education and, especially, region of origin (see Roberts, 2001).

3.   DESCRIPTION OF THE DATA AND BASIC STATISTICS

The data used in this study are from a survey conducted in Tianjin from October to December 2003. Tianjin, a coastal city located less than 100 miles southeast of Beijing, is one of the four central government municipalities (the other three being Beijing, Shanghai, and Chongqing). The metropolitan city had a total population of 9.35 million as of 2000.

Surveys were administered by the School of Business, Tianjin University of Finance and Economics, and distributed by students and instructors to both migrant and urban workers. The survey was conducted onsite in a combination of interviews and questionnaires. Of the 2000 forms distributed to randomly selected respondents, 1600 were completed. The responses of 455 migrant workers and 1145 urban workers form the two subgroups in the sample. All respondents were asked general questions relating to employment, income, demographics, and residency status. In addition, migrant workers were asked some special questions about their household composition, place of origin, income sent back to hometowns, life in Tianjin, and future migration decisions. For this study migrants are defined as those who live and work in Tianjin but do not have permanent Tianjin urban *hukou*.

The survey covers 30 different enterprises and organizations, including state-owned enterprises (SOEs), township and village enterprises (TVEs), joint ventures (JVs), foreign-invested firms (FIFs), one school, and one hospital. To focus on a rather homogenous group of employed individuals, employers, the self-employed, retirees, students, and homemakers are not included. In this data monthly income includes wages, bonuses, and subsidies, as well as other income, and social welfare includes medical care, retirement pension, and unemployment insurance.

Data are collected on economic and demographic variables for both migrants and city residents. In the sample, 69 percent of migrant workers are younger than 25 years old and less than 10 percent are older than 40. More than 70 percent of migrants are single, and about 60 percent of rural migrants work in private enterprises. Monthly per capita earning average 671 yuan for female workers and 805 yuan for male workers.

The contrast of educational levels between migrant and urban workers is particularly sharp. Table 11.2 shows that migrant workers are far less educated than urban workers. In the survey, 73.6 percent of migrant workers have an education of middle school or less, while for urban workers that number is only 21.1 percent. About 50 percent of all urban workers graduated from vocational schools and colleges, compared with only 12.5 percent for migrant workers.

In terms of their job longevity and security, migrant workers exhibit the characteristics of the so-called 'floating people', who change jobs and residences more often than do urban laborers. In this survey, 38.7 percent of migrant workers had been employed more than once in a city before their current job and more than half (52.7 percent) of migrant workers have been in their current workplace for less than one year with an average duration of only 2.17 years. Table 11.3 shows much less job security for migrant

Table 11.2:   Education Levels of Migrant and Urban Workers (Percent)

	Rural migrants	Urban laborers
Below Elementary	5.7	2.7
Elementary School	10.3	1.5
Middle School	57.6	16.9
High School	13.8	28.4
Vocational School	9.0	25.8
College or above	3.5	24.5

Source: Survey conducted by the authors in Tianjin, 2003.

Table 11.3:   Comparison of Employment Contracts

Contract Type	Rural migrants (percentage)	Urban laborers (percentage)
Permanent	7.3	31.8
Longer than three years	5.3	19.6
Between one and three years	10.8	17.2
One year	15.9	9.4
Temporary (no contract)	53.4	14.4
Other	6.7	7.6

Source: Survey conducted by the authors in Tianjin, 2003.

Table 11.4:   Income Distribution of Rural Migrants and Urban Residents

Category	Rural migrants (%)	Urban residents (%)
<500 yuan	19	6
500–799 yuan	47	21
800–1000 yuan	16	14
1000–1200 yuan	10	13
1200–1500 yuan	3	14
>1500 yuan	5	32

Source: Survey conducted by the authors in Tianjin, 2003.

workers, with only 7.3 percent having permanent jobs versus 31.8 percent of urban workers. Over half of migrant workers have no contract compared to 14.4 percent of urban workers.

Given the vast differences in education and job tenure, income disparities between migrant and urban workers are not surprising. The survey results show an average monthly income of 762 yuan for migrant workers, which is roughly half the average of 1468 yuan for their urban counterparts. Table 11.4 presents the percentage of each worker type within six income ranges. Migrants are relatively concentrated in lower ranges and urban workers are more concentrated in higher ranges. In addition, the migrants in this sample work 18 more hours per week than their urban equivalents so that when incomes are measured by an hourly rate, urban wages are 2.7 times greater.

Migrant workers also receive far less social protection than do urban workers. Few migrant workers have medical (14.3 percent), retirement (8.6 percent) or unemployment insurance (7.3 percent) in contrast to urban workers with corresponding rates of 68.2 percent, 63.8 percent, and 51.8 percent, respectively. Such disparities reflect a wide coverage gap in China's social protection system and suggest that most rural migrants are still left out of the welfare system.

4. WAGE DETERMINANTS AND DISCRIMINATION: SOME EMPIRICAL EVIDENCE

Using data from the above survey, this chapter analyzes wage determinants for both migrant and urban workers. We expect that various factors – such as individual characteristics, education levels, and types of enterprises – would cause a wage gap between migrants and non-migrants.

Estimation is conducted using a semi-logarithmic wage equation with the natural logarithm of hourly wages as the dependent variable. This variable is used because most migrants tend to work more hours than city workers in our sample. The hourly wages are calculated based on answers to the following two questions: 'What is your monthly income?' and 'How many hours do you work per week?'

The wage equation includes the independent variables: age, duration on current job, years of schooling, length of contract, *hukou* status, gender, training experience, and ownership of the workplace, where Age is the age of an employee, Duration is the number of months on the current job, and Schooling is the number of years of education. Length of contract is divided into five groups: permanent contract (10 years), contract over three years (5 years), contract within one to three years (2 years), contract in one year (1 year), and no contract (0 years). *Hukou*, gender, and training are dummy variables with 1 representing urban residency, male, and having training experience before the current job. The enterprise ownership dummy variables include those for JVs, FIFs, urban collectives, and privately owned enterprises. The SOE dummy variable is left out as a reference to make comparisons.

Regressions were run on both the migrant and the non-migrant sub-samples, and also the pooled sample. Table 11.5 summarizes the results of estimated coefficients and t-statistics for the three separate regressions. There are several interesting differences.

First, the return to education is much higher for urban workers than for migrant workers even though both are statistically significant. This could be due to the poor education quality in rural areas, which means having more years of schooling in rural areas does not necessarily raise the real education level.

Second, age is not a significant wage factor for urban workers, while it is for migrant workers. This could be partly due to a correlation for urban workers between age and the duration on their current job. Thus, the influence of age on wage is partly captured by the variable of duration on the current job. Migrant workers in the sample have only worked at their current job for an average of 2.17 years. Hence, age is not related to the duration of their current job; it reflects experiences.

Third, female workers earn significantly less than their male counterparts in the urban sample, but not in the migrant sample. We do not have a good explanation for this finding, but it certainly may indicate the existence of wage discrimination in China's urban labor market.

Fourth, there is no difference in wage for migrant workers in SOEs or in private- or foreign-owned enterprises, but urban workers receive lower pay in SOEs. This result is not surprising considering that urban workers receive many fringe benefits, including pension and medical insurance in the SEOs. When they move to the private sector, they demand higher pay to compensate for decreases in fringe benefits. Migrant workers receive few fringe benefits no matter where they work, giving them little bargaining power in the labor market.

For the regression of migrants (Model I), a justification was made for the dummy variable, *hukou*, which now assumes 1 for migrants who have either Tianjin rural *hukou* or Tianjin temporary urban *hukou* and 0 for all other migrant workers. The positive and significant estimate indicates that migrants without local rural *hukou* or temporary urban *hukou* receive lower pay. There are two possible explanations. First, local farmers have more choices regarding jobs and pay, enjoy better personal connections to urban enterprises, and are likely to work fewer hours in factories for the same pay. Second, people with temporary *hukou* tend to be better educated and trained workers. The table also shows that as expected older, more experienced, better educated, and better trained migrants receive higher pay.

The significant and positive signs of the variables of urban collectives and jointventures indicate that urban collectives and jointventures tend to

Table 11.5:   *Regression Results of Income Function (Dependent variable: Logarithmic income)*

Variables	Migrants regression (Model I)	Non-migrants regression (Model II)	Migrants and non-migrants regression (Model III)
ln(Age)	0.411***	0.0057	0.1371**
	(4.47)[b]	(0.07)	(2.17)
ln(Duration on current job)	0.0849***	0.0187***	0.0645***
	(4.00)	(5.06)	(4.52)
ln(Years of schooling)	0.187***	0.8024***	0.5882***
	(2.67)	(14.33)	(13.12)
Length of contract	0.0491***	0.0081***	0.0306***
	(4.58)	(4.85)	(6.01)
Hukou[a]	0.126**	–	0.3763***
	(2.44)		(8.66)
Gender	−0.0024	0.1615***	0.1480***
	(−0.04)	(4.53)	(4.83)
Training experience	0.0846*	0.0901**	0.0897***
	(1.65)	(2.50)	(2.97)
Urban collective	0.151	−0.0640	0.0107
	(1.56)	(−0.99)	(0.20)
Private-owned	−0.0684	0.1286**	0.0453
	(−1.06)	(2.43)	(1.10)
Foreign-owned	0.128	0.2212***	0.2339***
	(0.71)	(3.14)	(3.60)
Jointventure	0.416***	0.2061***	0.2473***
	(3.05)	(2.65)	(3.61)
Constant	−0.942***	−0.8808***	−1.0973***
	(−2.83)	(−2.95)	(−4.94)
R^2 (adj)	24.3%	23.2%	38.9%
Number of observations	455	1145	1600

Notes:
[a]   There are no Tianjin Rural *hukou*.
[b]   The t-values are presented in parentheses and *** indicates coefficient significant at 0.01 level; ** indicates coefficient significant at 0.05 level; * indicates coefficient significant at 0.1 level.

pay migrants higher salaries relative to SOEs. Length of contract also has a positive effect, suggesting that a longer contract brings in not only better job security but also higher pay. Interestingly, gender is not significant in this regression even though the previous section shows that the average income of men is higher than that of women. This is probably because gender is correlated with other variables such as education and ownership of workplace. In our sample, average schooling for females (9.36 years) is slightly less than for males (9.49 years), and females are more likely to work in SOEs (23.9 versus 8.2 percent).

In the regression on non-migrant workers (Model II), age is not significant, but job duration, education, and contract length are positive and significant. These results suggest that seniority, or experience, and education contribute to higher pay, and that higher pay and better job security go hand-in-hand. The coefficient of gender is significant and positive, which means males make more money than females even holding other factors constant. Similar to the result for migrant workers, training helps workers receive a higher pay. Working in a private firm, FIF, or JV has a positive effect on income, indicating that these companies pay more to their employees, ceteris paribus. Higher pay may imply that these enterprises either have better economic efficiency or they offer fewer fringe benefits, such as medical care, housing, and pension. If the former is the case, higher pay reflects higher productivity, if the latter is the case, higher pay becomes necessary in order to attract and retain workers, but higher pay does not translate into a higher real income.

In the last regression, which pools all workers in the sample (Model III), the estimates are qualitatively the same as the regression on the non-migrant sample. The pooled sample regression also examines the impact of *hukou* on wages. Since *hukou* itself is a non-productive factor, the positive and significant estimate of this variable may indicate the existence of wage discrimination against migrant workers. This implies that the wage gap between migrant and urban workers is partly due to the *hukou* system because migrant workers receive lower pay because they do not have a city *hukou*. The significance of the gender variable reflects the fact that gender discrimination against women exists in China's urban sector. Holding other things constant, female workers receive lower pay than their male counterparts. Since both *hukou* and gender are thought to be non-productive factors, these findings show the existence of both *hukou* and gender discrimination in China's urban labor market.

5.   DISCUSSION AND CONCLUSIONS

Rural–urban migration has become a socio-economic phenomenon in China since the late 1980s. This study examines factors of rural–urban migration, migrant characteristics, and the determinants of wages. Since the late 1980s, the labor surplus, heavy tax burden, and loss of lands in rural areas, combined with higher income, more opportunities, and better education in cities, have driven farmers to leave their homelands for cities. Past institutions, especially the *hukou* system, however, make rural–urban migration difficult. The government finds itself in a dilemma trying to balance the benefits brought by migrants and limit their inflow at the same time.

A wage regression model is developed to study the determinants of the wage gap between rural and urban workers. Wages for both groups are sensitive to standard worker characteristics in the expected direction. The results also show that urban workers make more than migrant workers, holding all other things constant, which suggests wage discrimination. In this sample, *hukou* does have a significant impact on the wage gap between migrant and non-migrant workers. After accounting for human capital characteristics, female workers earn significantly lower wages than male workers in the urban sample, but not in the migrant sample. The ownership of the enterprise plays an important role in determining a worker's earnings, with workers in SOEs receiving lower pay than those in other enterprises.

The empirical results give the following policy implications. First, the *hukou* system not only hinders rural–urban migration but also contributes to a wage gap between migrant and urban workers. Abolishment of the *hukou* system will thus improve labor mobility, efficiency, and fairness. Second, given the positive influence of education and training on wages for both migrant and non-migrant workers, it is important to invest in human capital in order to increase the productivity of both rural and urban laborers. Strategies to alleviate poverty should place more emphasis on raising the educational level of the rural population than on restricting migration to cities. Third, female workers may face wage discrimination in the urban labor market. Much needs to be done to better protect female workers so that women are not pushed into low-status, low-wage jobs in the service sector.

REFERENCES

Byron, Raymond P. and Evelyn Q. Manaloto (1990), 'Returns to education in China', *Economic Development and Culture Change*, **18**, 783–96

Cai, Fang and Dewen Wang (2003), 'Migration as marketization: What can we learn from China's 2000 census data?', *Institute of Population and Labor Economics, Chinese Academy of Social Sciences*, Beijing.

Cook, Sarah (1998), 'Who gets what jobs in China's countryside? A multinomial logit analysis', *Oxford Development Studies*, **26**(2), 171–90.

Dong, Xiao-yuan and Paul Bowles (2002), 'Segmentation and discrimination in China's emerging industrial labour market', *Chinese Economic Review*, **13**, 170–96.

De Haan, Arjan (2000), 'Migrants, livelihoods, and rights: the relevance of migration in development policies', Working Paper, Social Development Department, World Bank.

Hare, Denise and Shukai Zhao (1996), 'Workers migration as a rural development strategy: a view from the migration origin', presented at the International Conference on the Flow of Rural Workers in China, Beijing, June 25–27, 1996.

Johnson, D. Gale (2002), 'Can agricultural labour adjustment occur primarily through creation of rural non-farm jobs in China', *Urban Studies*, **39**(12), 2163–74.

Johnson, Emily N. and Gregory Chow (1997), 'Rates of return to schooling in China', *Pacific Economic Review*, **2**, 101–13.

Li, Haizheng (2003), 'Economic transition and returns to education in China', *Economic Education Review*, **22**(3), 317–28.

Li, Haizheng and Yi Luo (2004), 'Reporting errors, ability heterogeneity, and returns to schooling in China', *Pacific Economic Review*, **9**, 191–207.

Maurer-Fazio, M. and J. Hughes (2000), 'The effect of institutional change on the relative earnings of Chinese women: Traditional values vs market forces', Working Paper, Department of Economics, Bates College, Maine.

Meng, Xin (1998), 'Male–Female wage determination and gender wage discrimination in China's rural industrial sector', *Labour Economics*, **5**, 67–89.

Meng, Xin (2002), 'Profit sharing and the earnings gap between urban and rural-migrant workers in Chinese enterprises', Australian National University, Mimeo.

Meng, Xin and M. Kidd (1997), 'Labor market reforms across and the changing structure of wage determination in China's state sector during the 1980s', *Journal of Comparative Economics*, **25**(3), 403–21.

National Bureau of Statistics of China (NBSC) (1994–2003), *China Statistical Yearbook*, Beijing: China Statistical Press.

National Bureau of Statistics of China (NBSC) (2002), *Tabulation on the 2000 Population Census of the People's Republic of China*, Beijing: China Statistical Press.

Parish, William L., Xiaoye Zhe and Fand Li (1995), 'Non-farm work and marketization of the Chinese countryside', *China Quarterly*, **153**, 697–730.

Roberts, Kenneth (2001), 'The determinants of occupational choice of labor migrants to Shanghai', *China Economic Review*, **12**(1), 15–39.

Rozelle, Scott, Xiao-Yuan Dong, Linxin Zhang and Andrew Mason (2000), 'Opportunities and barriers in reform China: Gender, work, and wages in the rural economy', presented at the 2000 ASSA Meetings, Boston, January.

Sato, Hiroshi (1998), 'Income generation and access to economic opportunities in a transitional economy: A comparative analysis of five Chinese villages, Hitotsubashi', *Journal of Economics*, **39**, 127–44.

Wu, Harry X. (1994), 'The industrial enterprise workforce', in Christopher Findlay, Andrew Watson and Hurry X. Wu (eds), *Rural Enterprises in China*, London: Macmillan, pp. 117–47.

Wu, Quhui, Hanshang Wang and Xinxin Xu (1990), 'Non-economic determinants of workers' incomes', in William A. Byrd and Lin Qingsong (eds), *China's Rural Industry: Structure, Development and Reform*, New York: Oxford University Press, pp. 323–37.

Xia, Qingjie (2004), 'How the Chinese rural workers choose occupation: A case study on nine villages in Northeast China', Department of Economics, University of Bath, UK.

Zhai, Fan and Zhi Wang (2003), 'Labor market distortions, rural–urban inequality and the opening of China's economy', GTAP Working Paper No. 27.

Zhang, Hong (2004), 'Mitigating farmers' burden and protecting their rights', in Bing Liu, Zhaogang Zhang and Gong Huo (eds), *China Farming Countryside and Peasantry Issue Report*, Beijing: China Development Press, pp. 401–25.

Zhang, Xiao Hui, Zhao Changbao and Liangbiao Chen (1995), '1994: A real description of rural labor's cross-regional flow', *Strategy and Management*, 6, 30–35.

Zhao, Yaohui (1997), 'Labor migration and returns to rural education in China', *American Journal of Agricultural Economics*, **79**, 1278–87.

12. The Role of Home-Market Effects on China's Domestic Production

Fan Zhang and Zuohong Pan

1. INTRODUCTION

Two principal theories have been developed to explain why countries or regions trade. The theory of comparative advantage suggests that trade arises to take advantage of differences in resource endowments, while the theory of increasing returns maintains that trade arises to take advantage of specialization and economies of scale. The recent increasing-returns models, labeled 'economic geography' by Krugman, allow researchers to distinguish comparative advantage from increasing returns by testing the impact of home market demand on a country's or region's production and trade. As Davis and Weinstein (1999) put it, in a world of comparative advantage, a country or region with strong demand for a good will import that good. In a world with increasing returns, when trade costs exist, a country or region with strong demand for a good makes that country or region the site of production and the exporter of the good. In other words, the extra demand in the home market leads to large-scale production and high efficiency, and creates exports. This core concept of new economic geography is labeled by Krugman (1980) as 'home-market effects'.

China has become a major world production site and exporter for many manufactured products. The prevailing explanation of China's role in world trade is its comparative advantage in labor-intensive industries because it is relatively endowed with labor. If comparative advantage is the sole reason for China's role in world trade, China will lose its current position as soon as its labor costs rise to a certain level, like what has happened or will happen in some small-sized East Asian countries. If other reasons like increasing returns exist, China may keep its current position as a world major manufacturer for a longer time due to the demand from its own market. Moreover, cheap labor can only explain the development of China's labor-intensive sectors; it cannot explain the development of its high-tech sectors. In this chapter, we try to find the role of increasing returns in

Table 12.1:   Percentage Share of Total Urban Employment, State-Owned Enterprises

Year	Share	Year	Share	Year	Share
1990	62.27	1994	60.90	1998	41.90
1991	62.70	1995	58.98	1999	38.25
1992	63.16	1996	56.74	2000	35.00
1993	62.08	1997	54.65	2001	31.91

Explaining the reasons for regional trade in China as a first step of the studies on China's role in international trade.

The Chinese economy was mostly a command economy until very recently, with a relatively high degree of government control at the central, provincial and local levels. The output share of the state-owned sector accounted for 31.6 percent of the total industrial output in 1997. This non-market nature of the Chinese economy must be incorporated in the analysis. Over time, the Chinese economy is rapidly transforming from a command economy to a market economy. The output share of state-owned enterprises (SOE) dropped from 77.6 percent in 1978, to 54.6 percent in 1990 and to 28.2 percent in 1998. The SOE's share of total urban employment decreased from 62.3 percent in 1990 to 31.9 percent in 2001 (Table 12.1). The share of the state budgetary appropriation in total investment in fixed assets dropped from 28.1 percent in 1981 to 6.7 percent in 2001. Domestic loans are another source of fixed asset investments, on which the government also has influence. The sum of state budgetary appropriation and domestic loans accounted for 40.8 percent of total investment in fixed assets in 1981, which dropped to 25.8 percent in 2001 (Table 12.2). Data also show the changes in the distribution of output for all above-designated-size industrial enterprises. The SOE's share of output dropped dramatically in the most developed east region from 51.3 percent in 1990 to 39.8 percent in 2001, while the less developed central and west maintain high output shares of SOE (Table 12.3). We use an index of government control in the models to capture this effect of non-market nature of the Chinese economy.

The increasing-returns theory has been used in different fields of economics since Dixit and Stiglitz (1977) developed a formalized CES model of Chamberlinian monopolistic competition. In the late 1970s and early 1980s, a number of economists applied the tools to international trade (e.g., Helpman and Krugman 1985) and economic growth (e.g., Grossman and Helpman 1991). The theory of 'new economic geography' is considered as a new wave of the increasing-returns revolution. Krugman's (1980)

Table 12.2:　Total Investment in Fixed Assets by Source of Fund, %

| Year | Grouped by Source of Funds | | | |
	State budgetary appropriation	Domestic loans	Foreign investment	Fundraising and others
1981	28.1	12.7	3.8	55.4
1982	22.7	14.3	4.9	58.1
1983	23.8	12.3	4.7	59.2
1984	23.0	14.1	3.9	59.0
1985	16.0	20.1	3.6	60.3
1986	14.6	21.1	4.4	59.9
1987	13.1	23.0	4.8	59.1
1988	9.3	21.0	5.9	63.8
1989	8.3	17.3	6.6	67.8
1990	8.7	19.6	6.3	65.4
1991	6.8	23.5	5.7	64.0
1992	4.3	27.4	5.8	62.5
1993	3.7	23.5	7.3	65.5
1994	3.0	22.4	9.9	64.7
1995	3.0	20.5	11.2	65.3
1996	2.7	19.6	11.8	66.0
1997	2.8	18.9	10.6	67.7
1998	4.2	19.3	9.1	67.4
1999	6.2	19.2	6.7	67.8
2000	6.4	20.3	5.1	68.2
2001	6.7	19.1	4.6	69.6

Source:　China Statistical Yearbook 2002.

Table 12.3:　Percentage of Gross Output, State-Owned Enterprises by Region

	1990	1997	2001
East	51.31*	44.86	39.75
Central	60.04	46.99	58.59
West	70.52	63.77	71.22

Note: *Percent of all state-owned and non-state-owned above designated size industrial enterprises.

model of the 'home-market effect' argues that countries will tend to export those kinds of products for which they have relatively large domestic demand. Krugman shows that if high demand leads the good to be exported, production must rise by more than demand in two equal-sized economies. Weder (1995) extends this result to the unequal-sized case. Krugman's theory was extended in a series of papers and a book by Fujita, Krugman and Venables (2000).

While theoretical economic geography has made significant progress, only a few empirical works have been done to test the home-market effects. Most of the empirical work focuses on the relationship between local supply and demand and the Linder (1961) hypothesis (demand deviations cause more-than-proportional supply responses). Justman (1994) calculates sector correlations between supply and demand across regions and finds strong correlations between local demand and supply. Using Japanese data, Davis and Weinstein (1999) find support for the existence of economic geography effects in eight of nineteen manufacturing sectors in Japan. This contrasts with the result of Davis and Weinstein (1996), which found scant economic significance of economic geography for OECD countries using international data.

Feenstra et al. (1998) find home-market effects by using a free entry, imperfect competition, homogeneous good model. More recently, Head and Ries (2001) develop two alternative models of trade in differentiated products between Canada and the US; increasing returns and national product differentiation models, and finds the preponderance of the evidence supports national product differentiation. Brülhart and Trionfetti (2001) develop a discriminating criterion which relies on the assumption that demand is home biased. They test the hypothesis in 29 industries, covering 22 OECD countries for 1970–85 and find that 17 industries can be associated with the increasing returns to scale paradigm.

There is an increasing literature on China's industrial growth from a geographic perspective. Bao et al. (2002) examine the geographic effects on regional economic growth in China, using a regional growth model characterized by foreign direct investment and mobilization of rural surplus labor. Brun, Combes and Renard (2002), and Batisse (2002) study the spillover effects on economic development from a geographic and from a sectoral perspective, respectively.

2. THEORETICAL FRAMEWORK AND THE MODEL

2.1. Theoretical Framework

The empirical work of this chapter is based on the theory developed by Krugman (1980) and Fujita, Krugman and Venables (2000) (hereafter

FKV). With minor revisions, we derived the model used in this chapter directly from FKV. With that, we identified the relation between FKV's theory and the empirical testing model in Davis and Weinstein (1996 and 1999). FKV (2000) gives a formal version of Krugman's model, and derives the home-market effect in the following steps.

The consumer's problem is to maximize representative consumer's utility function for manufactured goods M and agricultural good A:

$$U = M^\mu A^{1-\mu} = \left[\int_0^n m(i)^\rho \, di\right]^{\mu/\rho} A^{1-\mu}$$

subject to a budget constraint. Where m is the consumption of each variety, μ is the expenditure share of manufactured goods, ρ is the intensity of the preference for variety in manufactured goods, and n is the number of varieties. The elasticity of substitution between varieties is $\sigma = 1/(1 - \rho)$. The consumer problem is solved in two steps. First, m is chosen to minimize the cost of attaining M to solve the demand for m. The second step on the upper-level of the consumer's problem is to choose A and M to maximize utility.

FKV then assumes an 'iceberg' form of transportation cost, which means if a good is shipped from location r to s, only a fraction $1/T_{rs}$ arrives. Then the price index becomes a function of price and transport cost in all locations.

Given a fixed input of F, marginal input requirement for manufactured goods c^M, price of manufactured goods at location r, p_r^M, and quantity of manufactured goods at r, q_r^M, a firm producing a specific variety at location r choose its price to maximizes profit, taking price indices G and wage rate w_r^M as given:

$$\pi_r = p_r^M q_r^M - w_r^M (F + c^M q_r^M)$$

Assuming there is free entry and exit, the zero-profit condition implies the equilibrium output of any firm q^*, equilibrium labor input of any firm l^*, and the number of the varieties produced at r, n_r. FKV then derived the price and wage equations for a firm located at r. After making some normalizations, FKV writes the price and wage equations in a more convenient form. The two-location version of these equations is:

$$G_1^{1-\sigma} = \frac{1}{\mu}\left[L_1 w_1^{1-\sigma} + L_2 (w_2 T)^{1-\sigma}\right],$$

$$G_2^{1-\sigma} = \frac{1}{\mu}\left[L_1\left(w_1 T\right)^{1-\sigma} + L_2 w_2^{1-\sigma}\right],$$

$$w_1^\sigma = Y_1 G_1^{\sigma-1} + Y_2 G_2^{\sigma-1} T^{1-\sigma},$$

$$w_2^\sigma = Y_1 G_1^{\sigma-1} T^{1-\sigma} + Y_2 G_2^{\sigma-1}.$$

where Y is income or demand, the superscript M is dropped because the focus is on manufacturing only. Differentiating the price indices and wage equations around the symmetric equilibrium and define a new variable:

$$Z \equiv \frac{1 - T^{1-\sigma}}{1 + T^{1-\sigma}},$$

an index of trade cost values between 0 and 1, FKV finds the home-market effect:

$$\left[\frac{\sigma}{Z} + Z\left(1-\sigma\right)\right]\frac{dw}{w} + Z\frac{dL}{L} = \frac{dY}{Y} \qquad (12.1)$$

FKV points out that if labor supply to manufacturing is perfectly elastic ($dw = 0$), then 'a one percent change in demand for manufactures (dY/Y) causes a $1/Z(>1)$ percent change in the employment, and hence production of manufactures, dL/L'.[1]

Following some of the normalization assumptions made by FKV, the authors of this chapter transfer equation (12.1) into a relationship between the change in output and the change in demand (see Appendix for details):

$$\left[\frac{\sigma}{Z} + Z\left(1-\sigma\right)\right]\frac{dw}{w} + Z\frac{dX}{X} = \frac{dY}{Y} \qquad (12.2)$$

where $X = nq^*$ is the total output of manufacturing goods at a location.

Multiplying by output X and then adding average output $\overline{X}$ on both sides of the equation, assuming dw/w equals zero, gives:

$$\overline{X} + dX = \overline{X} + \frac{1}{Z}\frac{dY}{Y} X \qquad (12.3)$$

Equation (12.3) says that the output is a function of the average output plus the change in output caused by the change in the idiosyncratic components of demand. This relationship is similar to the relationship identified in equation (4) in Davis and Wienstein (1999), except they use dY instead of dY/Y.

2.2. The Model

The hypothesis tested by this research is whether demand in a region can improve our understanding of production relative to the hypothesis that all production is determined by endowments. The analysis strategy is based on the framework developed by Helpman (1981), where endowments served to determine the broad sector structure of a country while monopolistic competition led to intra-sector specialization at the industry level. The empirical framework of this chapter will have four sectors covering 19 industries.

A typical empirical model of the classical comparative advantage theory is the square Heckscher–Ohlin model, which uses the endowments of a country to explain its output. Assume that there are R regions, N sectors with G_n industries in sector n and the number of industries equals the number of endowments. Assume that the inverse of the technology matrix mapping output into factors is Ω, the output of industry g is determined by endowments:

$$X_g^{nr} = \Omega_g^n E^r \tag{12.4}$$

where X_g^{nr} is industry g's output for region r and sector n, E^r is the vector of factor endowments in region r, and Ω_g^n is the corresponding row of matrix Ω.

This chapter will choose an alternative research approach from the above classical Heckscher–Ohlin model. The approach and two of the three models (equations (12.5) and (12.7)) tested in this chapter are taken from Davis and Weinstein (1996 and 1999).

On the sector level, we test the above hypotheses by estimating the following Heckscher–Ohlin model, in which endowments determine the structure of production by sector:

$$X^{nr} = \sum_{g=1}^{G_n} X_g^{nr} = \Omega^n E^r \tag{12.5}$$

Where X^{nr} is the vector of output for region r and sector n, E^r is the vector of factor endowments in region r, and Ω^n is an $N \times N$ matrix which mapping endowments into output for sector n. Note that the difference between equation (12.4) and (12.5) is that equation (12.4) is on the industry level while equation (12.5) is on the sector level.

On the industry level, we will test the hypotheses that the production is determined by economic geography. We will test two models, the empirical versions of FKV's theoretical model, equation (12.2) or Model I, and the model used by Davis and Weintein (1996 and 1999), similar to equation (12.3) or Model II.

In Model I, we use $\gamma_g^{nr} = X_g^{nr}/X^{nr}$ to measure industry g's production share in sector n for region r, and $\delta_g^{nr} = Y_g^{nr}/Y^{nr}$ to measure the portion of demand for industry g in sector n for region r, where X_g^{nr} represents output for industry g, sector n in region r; Y_g^{nr} is demand for good g, sector n in region r. Then $(\gamma_g^{nr} - \gamma_g^{nROC})/\gamma_g^{nROC}$ and $(\delta_g^{nr} - \delta_g^{nROC})/\delta_g^{nROC}$ present the percentage deviation of production of and demand for industry g of region r from the average of the rest of China in sector n, respectively. We then define the empirical version of Model I as the following:

$$\frac{\gamma_g^{nr} - \gamma_g^{nROC}}{\gamma_g^{nROC}} = a + b_1 \frac{\delta_g^{nr} - \delta_g^{nROC}}{\delta_g^{nROC}} + b_2 \frac{L^r - L^{ROC}}{L^{ROC}}$$

$$+ b_3 \frac{K^r - K^{ROC}}{K^{ROC}} + b_4 \frac{G_g^{nr} - G_g^{nROC}}{G_g^{nROC}} + \varepsilon_g^{nr} \qquad (12.6)$$

Where L represents labor input, K represents capital input. The term on the left is the relative deviation of output from the average across different regions and industries for the rest of China, which is a function of the relative deviation of demand from the sector average across different regions and industries, the second term on the right. To avoid the omitted variables bias, we also include the changes in labor and capital, which can be viewed as a Rybczynski effect of factor endowments (if a country accumulates a factor more rapidly than does the rest of the world, that country's production and exports will sift toward industries that more intensively use that factor).

To control the effect of government intervention factor, we introduce a government control index, G, which is the sales share of state-owned enterprises in total sales for each province and each 2-digit industry. The deviation of G from the average of the rest regions in China is used in equation (12.6). (See section 3 for the details of G's construction.)

We compare Model I with Davis and Weinstein's model, which is labeled as Model II in this chapter. The specification of Model II is taken exactly from Davis and Weinstein (1999). It assumes the base share of production of an industry in a region is the same as the average proportion of the industry in all other regions. $\gamma_g^{nROC} = X_g^{nROC}/X^{nROC}$ is used to measure industry g's production share in sector n for the rest of China. Above this base share of production, the output of industries will be adjusted by the impact of idiosyncratic components of demand. Then, $\delta_g^{nr} - \delta_g^{nROC}$, the demand deviation between region r and the rest of China, is used to measure idiosyncratic components of demand. If all regions have the same share of demand for an industry's product, this term will be zero for that industry. If an industry has a larger share of demand in a sector, this term will be positive. Then the element of economic geography is nested with the Heckscher-Ohlin model at the industries level:

$$X_g^{nr} = \alpha_g^n + \beta_1\gamma_g^{nROC}X^{nr} + \beta_2(\delta_g^{nr} - \delta_g^{nROC})X^{nr} + \Omega_g^n E^r + \beta_3 G + \varepsilon_g^{nr} \quad (12.7)$$

where X_g^{nr} is the industries' output for region r and industry g in sector n, γ_g^{nROC} is the share of output for sector n and industry g in the rest of China, δ_g^{nr} and δ_g^{nROC} are the shares of demand for industry g in region r and the rest of China, respectively, Ω_g^n is the corresponding row of Ω^n. Index G is also incorporated in equation (12.7) to capture the effect of government control. The second term on the right is the base level output of industry g for region r, which captures the tendency for each region to produce the same relative shares of each industry product as other regions. The third term measures the impacts of demand deviation for a region, and the forth term represents the impacts of endowments. Government control index G is also included in equation (12.7) to capture the effect of government control.

Coefficient b_1 in Model I (equation (12.6)) and β_2 in Model II (equation (12.7)) play a key role in hypothesis testing, since the economic geography framework predicts that the positive responsiveness of production to the changes in demand will be more than one-to-one. When b_1 or β_2 equals zero, we are in a world of frictionless comparative advantage in which transport costs do not matter. If b_1 or β_2 is between zero and one, we are in a world of comparative advantage in which transport costs affect the production location, but there are no scales economies. If b_1 or β_2 is greater than one, there are home-market effects that affect the location of production.

3. DATA

Using 1997 industrial outputs for 31 provinces, China's national input–output table, and provincial consumption and investment data from China State Statistical Bureau (1998), we create input–output tables and find direct

Table 12.4:   *Province Data Set, Percentage of the National Total, Sum of*
             19 industries

Province	% of Prod.	% of Demand	% of Fixed assets	% of Employ.	% of Sales, SOE
Beijing	2.63	2.47	5.05	1.04	0.8270
Tianjin	3.00	2.17	2.20	0.77	0.2316
Shanxi	1.44	1.56	1.70	2.33	0.6022
Inner Mongolia	0.90	1.16	1.31	1.65	0.2986
Jilin	1.87	1.90	1.68	1.94	0.3484
Heilongjiang	2.21	2.59	2.86	2.61	0.5185
Shanghai	6.95	5.49	7.35	1.21	0.4358
Fujian	3.10	3.35	3.17	2.53	0.7655
Jiangxi	1.50	1.76	1.43	3.26	0.4154
Hainan	0.28	0.42	0.93	0.52	0.1803
Chongqing	1.27	1.52	1.44	2.65	0.0689
Guizhou	0.83	0.94	0.89	3.03	0.8292
Yunnan	1.50	1.64	1.96	3.53	0.2647
Tibet	0.01	0.06	0.17	0.19	0.2328
Shaanxi	1.46	1.58	1.70	2.85	0.4568
Gansu	0.96	0.93	1.00	1.86	0.1010
Qinghai	0.19	0.24	0.36	0.37	0.2200
Ningxia	0.27	0.26	0.34	0.41	0.3333
Xinjiang	0.67	1.17	1.89	1.08	0.5237
Hebei	4.29	4.59	4.65	5.36	0.5597
Liaoning	5.06	4.48	4.63	3.24	0.1889
Jiangsu	11.93	10.14	8.42	5.88	0.0957
Zhejiang	6.14	5.95	6.47	4.24	0.2070
Anhui	3.75	3.38	2.43	5.22	0.1153
Shandong	8.68	8.33	7.07	7.39	0.7931
Henan	4.44	4.85	4.22	7.88	0.6405
Hubei	4.90	4.54	3.83	4.25	0.4116
Hunan	2.66	3.15	2.71	5.64	0.6405
Guangdong	12.35	10.93	11.64	5.94	0.2070
Guangxi	1.54	1.95	2.10	3.85	0.2875
Sichuan	3.22	3.89	4.41	7.25	0.2138
Mean	3.23	3.14	3.23	3.23	0.3876
Minimum	0.01	0.06	0.17	0.19	0.0689
Maximum	12.35	10.93	11.64	7.39	0.8292

and indirect demands for each of the 19 industries and 31 provinces. The output is total production in the industry, from the China State Statistical Bureau and Euromonitor/Soken (2000). Total demand for each area is derived by adding consumption, investment, and intermediate demand. Intermediate demand is derived by applying national input–output coefficient matrix to industrial output of each province. Using these data, we calculate the output, endowment and demand ratios required in equation (12.6) and equation (12.7).

3.1. Regions

Data from 31 provinces are originally from China State Statistical Bureau (1998) and China State Statistical Bureau and Euromonitor/Soken (2000). The regional data are either from China State Statistical Bureau and Euromonitor/Soken (2000) or calculated by the authors using urban and rural data weighted by the number of households. Table 12.4 shows the shares of production and demand for the provinces.

3.2. Industrial Categories

Data from 19 input–output industrial categories are used in the regression analysis; all of them are in manufacturing and utility sectors, while 26 industrial categories (including agriculture, construction, transport, trade, and services) are used when calculating intermediate and final demand (Table 12.5). When calculating demand, the 40×40 input–output table is aggregated into a 26×26 table, including 21 manufacturing-utility industries and five non-manufacturing-utility sectors (agriculture, construction, transport, trade, and services). The latter are grouped at the sector level. Two manufacturing industries are dropped in regression, because of missing data.

3.3. Final Demand

The data of urban and rural resident consumption in 1997 for 31 provinces are from China State Statistical Bureau (1998). Urban and rural consumption expenditure, which breaks household consumption into 41 categories for urban and eight for rural households, is converted into 26 input–output industrial categories by the author. Urban and rural consumption are aggregated into total consumption for each province weighted by the shares of the number of urban and rural households.

Table 12.5:   List of Input–Output (i–o) Industrial Categories*

Sector	Industry	Description
Non Man.	1–5	Agriculture, Coal mining and processing, Crude petroleum and natural gas products, Metal ore mining, Non-ferrous mineral mining
	6	Manufacture of food products and tobacco processing
	7	Textile goods
	8	Wearing apparel, leather, furs, down and related prod.
	9	Sawmills and furniture
	10	Paper, printing and record medium reproduction
	11	Petroleum processing and coking
	12	Chemicals
	13	Non-metal mineral products
	14	Metals melting and pressing
	15	Metal products
	16	Machinery and equipment
	17	Transport equipment
	18	Electric equipment and machinery
	19	Electronic and telecommunication equipment
	20	Instruments, meters, cultural and office machinery
	21	Maintenance and repair of machine and equipment
	22	Other manufacturing products
	23	Scrap and waste
	24	Electricity, steam and hot water production and supply
	25	Gas production and supply
	26	Water production and supply
Non Man.	27	Construction
Non Man.	28, 29, 32	Transport and warehousing, Post and telecom., Passenger transport
Non Man.	30, 31	Wholesale and retail trade, Eating and drinking places
Non Man.	33–40	Finance/insurance; Real estate, Social services; Health services, sports/social welfare; Education, culture and arts, radio, film and television; Scientific research; General technical services; Public admin. and other sectors

Notes: 19 of the industries, industries 6–20, 22 and 24–26 are used in the regression analysis. Industries 21 and 23 are dropped due to missing data. All 26 industrial categories listed in the above table (including agriculture, construction, transport, trade and services) are used when calculating intermediate and final demand, but not all of them are used in the regressions.

The data of total investments for the provinces in 1997 are from China State Statistical Bureau (1998). These data are disintegrated into 26 industries (of which data of 19 industries are used in the regression models) for each province, by using national fixed investment coefficients in the input–output table for these industries. Investment demand is one of the major components of aggregate demand. The proportion of product used for investment for a particular industry varies. For example, very small proportion (less than 1 percent in China in late 1990s) of the product in textile industry is used as investment goods.

The stock of fixed capital is calculated by using the perpetual inventory method[2] and investment data over the period from 1987 to 1996, assuming 5 percent annual depreciation and using the industrial mill price index to convert the data into 1997 price.

3.4.   Intermediate Demand

Total intermediate use from each industry and each province is calculated using the national direct input matrix and output value by industry and by province from China State Statistical Bureau and Euromonitor/Soken (2000). Region r's intermediate consumption vector is $INP' = AX'$, where A is direct input matrix and X' is total output vector of region r.

Total demand for each industry and each region is derived by adding intermediate demand, consumption and investment of that region.

3.5.   Index of Government Control

We create an index of government control to capture the effect of the non-market nature of the Chinese economy. We randomly draw a sample of 60 511 of firm level data from the Third National Industrial Survey, which includes data of total sales, ownership of the firm and the zip code of the firm. We calculate the share of total sales of the SOEs for 31 provinces and 19 industries, and use it as the index of government control. Table 12.6 presents the descriptive statistics of all independent variables, including the index of government control G.

4.   ECONOMETRIC ISSUES AND RESULTS

4.1.   Econometrics Issues

A problem with Model II (equation (12.7)) specified above is the fact that X^{rr} depends on X_g^{rr}, so that in the regression equation the independent

Table 12.6: Descriptive Statistics

Variable	Obs.	Mean	Std. Dev.	Min.	Max
X_g^{nr}, y 100 million	589	118	176	0	1 321
$(\delta_g^{nr} - \delta_g^{nROC})$	589	-2.60E^{-17}	0.047	−0.161	0.239
$\dfrac{\gamma_g^{nr} - \gamma^{nROC}}{\gamma^{nROC}}$	589	−0.025	0.676	−1.000	4.132
$\dfrac{\delta_g^{nr} - \delta^{nROC}}{\delta^{nROC}}$	589	0.006	0.221	−0.818	1.179
L, 10 000	31	2 053	1 409	120	5 017
K, y 100 million	31	4 142	3 442	222	14 946
G	589	0.441	0.014	0	1

variables are correlated with error terms. This violation of the Gaussian assumptions makes it impossible to isolate the impact of the independent variable on the dependent variable in the standard OLS regression. Following Davis and Weinstein (1999) we use an instrumental variable estimated from factor endowments to address the problem. The specification test results showed strong correlation between the instrumental variable and X^{nr}, while little correlation between the instrumental variable and the error terms.

Another potential problem is serial correlation or spatial autocorrelation, arising from the fact that regression is based on a relationship at the industries level, many of which are from the same sectors or from the same areas. It is highly probable that some of the common factors affecting different industries' output, such as interest rate, technology, local regulation and policies, are omitted from the individual equation. Their influences, along with the state of the economy, are all collected by the error terms. The resulted correlation between cross-sectional error terms violates the Gaussian assumption of no serial correlation. Under this situation, although the standard OLS estimators remain unbiased and consistent, they are not efficient (even asymptotically) any more. The Seemingly Unrelated Regression (SUR) method is then used to address the issue. In doing so, we assume two scenarios: (1) The output relations all have one common coefficient vector at industries level; (2) There is no coefficient restriction at all, each industry has its own coefficient.

The third problem is the heteroskedasticity, stemming from the cross-sectional nature of our data. It is possible that the industries output relationship as specified in the equation varies across sectors, as well as across geographical areas. One possible source of the varying effects is that in a larger geographic area the sector tends to be larger, the output of one industry is more likely to be affected by other factors such as scope of economy, urbanization level, infrastructure and facilities, and it might be less related to endowments and geographic economy. In other words, the variance may be larger in larger areas and smaller in smaller areas. We are then faced with the problem of heteroskedasticity. The normal procedure to fix this problem is to use Weighted Least Squares method (WLS), the same method used by previous studies as in Davis and Weinstein (1996, 1999). However, the problem with WLS in this context is, after specifying a variance function and estimating the transformed equation, it cannot address the serial correlation problem. Since the last two problems are all related to the structure of the variance–covariance matrix, we can address both by the method of Generalized Least Squares (GLS), as employed in the SUR model. If we really knew the exact form of the variance function, using WLS may be better than GLS. Under the situation of the unknown variance function and the joint presence of serial correlation, using GLS should be the better choice.

4.2. Results

Based on the theoretical framework, two levels of industrial division, industry level and sector level, are examined separately. With the assumption that endowments determine the broader sector structure of a country or region while monopolistic competition determines the specialization on the industries level, we conducted two groups of tests. In one version of their paper (Davis and Weinstein 1996), Davis and Weinstein considered sectors to be at the 3-digit level and goods (equivalent to industries in this chapter) at the 4-digit level. In another version (Davis and Weinstein 1999), when analyzing Japanese data, they chose 19 sectors (equivalent to industries in this chapter), which is at the 2-digit level. In this chapter, we define industries at the 2-digit level, because it is the most detailed data of production and demand by industry and by region available. We group industries into three sectors, non-durable, material-related, and durable, based on the traditional definition of industries. We think by doing this we can derive more meaningful policy implications.

4.2.1. Comparative advantage in the Heckscher–Ohlin specification
We first tested the above hypothesis at the sector level, by estimating the Heckscher–Ohlin model in which endowments are assumed to determine the structure of production by sector. Since we use relative change in

Table 12.7:   *Aggregate Production on Factor Endowments*

	Labor[a]	Capital	G	R^2
Heckscher–Ohlin Model				
Sector I	0.029**	0.036**	186.127**	0.598
Non-durable	(0.010)[c]	(0.004)	(45.542)	
Sector II	0.012	0.028**	162.180**	0.401
Material-related	(0.009)	(0.004)	(34.999)	
Sector III	−0.006	0.039**	31.546	0.531
Durable	(0.008)	(0.003)	(31.554)	
Sector IV	0.006	0.007**	427.508**	0.405
Utility	(0.005)	(0.002)	(72.535)	
Rybcznski Model[b]				
Sector I	0.237*	1.274**	0.138	0.658
Non-durable	(0.136)	(0.110)	(0.108)	
Sector II	0.139	0.939**	0.072	0.599
Material-related	(0.091)	(0.073)	(0.053)	
Sector III	−0.316*	1.748**	−0.082	0.060
Durable	(0.143)	(0.116)	(0.126)	
Sector IV	−0.181	1.282**	−0.044	0.539
Utility	(0.173)	(0.139)	(1.259)	

Notes:
[a] WLS regression.
[b] In Rybczski Models Labor and Capital are percentage changes to the industry average.
[c] Standard errors are below coefficients and * and ** indicate significance at 5 and 1 percent respectively.

variables in our economic geography models, we also estimate the Rybcznski model, in which relative changes in endowments are assumed to determine the structure of production by sector.

The results are reported in Table 12.7. The four sectors, non-durable, material-related, durable, and utility, are classified based on traditional criteria. The industrial composition in each sector is listed in Table 12.8. The results in Table 12.7 seem to support, to certain degree, the hypothesis that factor endowments determine the sector structure. The effect of the capital factor is significant at the 1 percent level in all four sectors in both models and the labor factor has negative signs in three of the eight cases and is not significant in five of the eight cases under investigation. The unlimited labor supply from the huge rural surplus labor and the inefficient use of labor in SOEs may explain the insignificance and the wrong signs of the labor factor. To capture the effect of government control, index *G* (share

Table 12.8:   *Sector Classification*

Sector	Industry	Description
I. Non-durable	6	Manufacture of food products and tobacco processing
	7	Textile goods
	8	Wearing apparel, leather, furs, down and related products
	10	Paper and products, printing and record medium reproduction
II. Material-related	9	Sawmills and furniture
	11	Petroleum processing and coking
	12	Chemicals
	13	Nonmetal mineral products
	14	Metals melting and pressing
	15	Metal products
III. Durable	16	Machinery and equipment
	17	Transport equipment
	18	Electric equipment and machinery
	19	Electronic and telecommunication equipment
	20	Instruments, meters, cultural and office machinery
	22	Other manufacturing products
IV. Utility	24	Electricity, steam and hot water production and supply
	25	Gas production and supply
	26	Water production and supply

Source: Industry codes and descriptions are from *China Statistical Yearbook*, 1999, pp. 422, 432.

of SOE in total sales) is also included. Three of four coefficients of G are positive and significant in the Heckscher–Ohlin model, but not significant in the Rybcznski model. This means that government control is significant in determining the level of output, but not significant concerning the change. The heteroskedasticity problem is fixed by using WLS in our estimation. So the total variance in aggregate production should not have borne any effects from the differing size in regions, but be the result of the variation in endowments or random factors. The variation explained by factor endowments for the four sectors are over 60 percent in two cases and over 50 percent in four other cases (with an average adjusted $R^2 = 0.54$).

Table 12.9:   Aggregate Production on Economic Geography

[a]	Model I-1[b]	Model I-2	Model I-3	Model I-4
$(\delta_g^{nr} - \delta_g^{nROC})/\delta_g^{nROC}$	1.088**	1.090**	1.107**	1.108**
	(0.039)[c]	(0.038)	(0.040)	(0.040)
$\dfrac{dL}{L*}$	-	−0.088**	-	−0.077**
		(0.008)		(0.008)
$\dfrac{dK}{K*}$	-	0.124**	-	0.106**
		(0.007)		(0.007)
$\dfrac{dG}{G*}$	-	-	0.021**	0.015**
			(0.005)	(0.004)
	Model II-1	Model II-2	Model II-3	Model II-4
$(\delta_g^{nr} - \delta_g^{nROC}) X^{nr}$	1.343**	1.331**	1.332**	1.317**
	(0.019)	(0.019)	(0.020)	(0.020)
$\gamma_g^{nROC} X^{nr}$	0.947**	0.933**	0.947**	0.920**
	(0.017)	(0.016)	(0.018)	(0.019)
L	-	−0.001*	-	−0.001*
		(0.001)		(0.0004)
K	-	0.002**	-	0.001**
		(0.0004)		(0.0001)
G	-	-	10.952**	11.888**
			(2.036)	(2.074)

Notes:
[a] There are 589 observations in each regression and each is a seemingly unrelated regression.
[b] Dependent variable is the percentage deviation in the share of industrial production in Model I and industries production in Model II.
[c] Standard deviation is below the coefficient in parentheses.

4.2.2.   Home-market effects

We then test for the home-market effects based on the hypotheses that the production is determined by economic geography on the industries level. According to the theoretical formulation in the previous sections, the home-market effect is indicated by a more than one-to-one relationship from the change in idiosyncratic demand to the change in total production relative to other areas. In Figure 12.1, the percentage deviation in the industry's share of demand in a sector for a region is on the horizontal axis, while the percentage deviation in the industry's share of production in the sector for the region is on the vertical axis. If home-market effects are present, the regression line derived from the data points should have a slope greater than one. As it turned out, the fitted line has a slope bigger than one (1.15).

We first test the hypothesis with a pure economic geography model, then incorporate labor and capital endowments in the economic geography model to see if the result is robust. We used both Model I (equation (12.6)) and Model II (equation (12.7)) or some of their variations and compared the results. The results of aggregate estimation using data of all industries are summarized in Table 12.9.

Strong home-market effects are indicated by the coefficients of idiosyncratic demand that are both significant and greater than one in both Model I and Model II. In Model I-1 (derived directly from FKV theory by the authors), the percentage deviation in the share of production is positively affected by the percentage deviation in the share of demand, with a coefficient of 1.088. In Model II-1 (Davis and Weinstein's model), for a particular region, in addition to the same general trend as in other regions in China ($\gamma_g^{nROC} X^{nr}$ term), its production of an industry is also affected by a unique demand of its own (($\delta_g^{nr} - \delta_g^{nROC}$)$X^{nr}$ term). Under the situation of increasing returns, when this demand is stronger than the rest of China, it causes its production to increase by a larger than proportionate amount (with a coefficient of 1.343), leading to aggregation of production in one

Figure 12.1:   *Idiosyncratic Demand vs. Production Deviation*

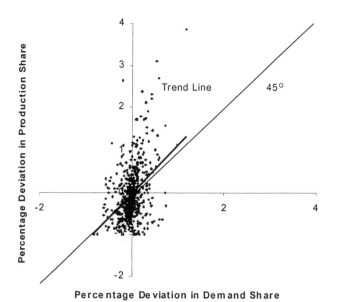

Table 12.10:   Disaggregated Estimation

| Industry (Code)[a] | Model I-2[b] | | | Model II-2 | | |
	Econ. Geo		Adj. R^2	Econ. Geo		Adj. R^2
Food (6)	Y	1.259** (0.097)	0.737	N	0.148 (0.192)	0.809
Textile (7)	Y	1.219** (0.113)	0.357	Y	3.272** (0.132)	0.888
Wearing apparel (8)	N	−0.416** (0.144)	0.536	N	−2.548** (0.197)	0.880
Sawmills/ furniture (9)	Y	3.550** (0.131)	0.809	Y	1.598** (0.112)	0.729
Paper (10)	N	0.066 (0.128)	0.101	N	0.167** (0.029)	0.880
Petroleum (11)	Y	3.009** (0.385)	0.116	Y	3.107** (0.596)	0.391
Chemicals (12)	Y	2.793** (0.151)	0.710	Y	3.039** (0.249)	0.841
Nonmetal mineral (13)	Y	1.612** (0.146)	0.282	N	−0.262** (0.062)	0.866
Metal melting (14)	Y	1.900** (0.086)	0.602	Y	2.892** (0.088)	0.935
Metal products (15)	N	0.777* (0.360)	0.651	N	−2.996** (0.401)	0.874
Machinery/ equip. (16)	Y	3.602** (0.316)	0.456	N	−0.426* (0.181)	0.874
Transport equip. (17)	Y	4.109** (0.244)	0.720	Y	3.665** (0.542)	0.689
Electric equip. (18)	Y	1.221** (0.441)	0.571	Y	2.031** (0.392)	0.926
Electron. & telecom. equip. (19)	Y	2.752** (0.092)	0.913	Y	2.749** (0.174)	0.969
Instruments (20)	N	−0.091 (0.512)	0.330	N	0.101 (0.431)	0.939
Other Manufacturing (22)	Y	1.494** (0.205)	0.373	Y	4.155** (0.471)	0.913
Electricity (24)	N	−0.150 (0.117)	0.091	N	−3.390** (0.474)	0.828
Gas (25)	N	0.154 (0.411)	0.107	N	0.296** (0.046)	0.684
Water (26)	N	−0.474* (0.230)	0.023	Y	1.128** (0.098)	0.816

Notes:
[a]   There are 31 observations for each industry.
[b]   Each is a seemingly unrelated regression where the dependent variables are percentage deviation in production in Model I and production in Model II. *L* and *K* are incorporated as independent variables. Standard errors are below coefficients in parentheses.

region and thus export of that industry from the region. This is how the home-market effects help shape the trade pattern.

Nesting the Heckscher–Ohlin and Rybczynski specifications in the economic geography models as in equations (12.6) and (12.7) (Model I-2 and II-2 in Table 12.9) did not change the above results much. As a matter of fact we got almost the same coefficients for the idiosyncratic demand variable in models with and without endowments.[3] Two reasons are responsible for the different values of the coefficients for idiosyncratic demand variables between the two models. First, Model II uses the absolute difference in demand $((\delta_g^{nr} - \delta_g^{nROC}))$, while Model I uses the relative difference in demand $((\delta_g^{nr} - \delta_g^{nROC})/\delta_g^{nROC})$. Second, the estimation in Model II is affected by the specific way the instrumental variable for X^{nr} is built.

Models I-3 and I-4 are versions of Model I-1 and I-2, respectively, and incorporated the change in the index of government control. Models II-3 and II-4 are versions of Model II-1 and II-2, respectively, and incorporated the level of the index of government control. The indices of government control are significant in all four cases, while coefficients for the idiosyncratic demand variables do not change much, with or without the government control indices.

Comparing the pure economic geography model and the model that nested the endowments, neither the Heckscher–Ohlin Hypothesis nor the Home-Market Hypothesis is rejected. It seems both explain the pattern of production well. To break down the home-market effects further, we did a disaggregated estimation for each industry type. The results are reported in Table 12.10. Looking for coefficients of idiosyncratic demand that are significantly greater than unity, Model I-2 in Table 12.10 shows that the home-market effects concentrate on 12 out of the 19 industries under examination. They are Food, Textile Goods, Sawmills and Furniture, Petroleum Processing, Chemicals, Nonmetal Mineral, Metals Melting and Pressing, Machinery, Transport Equipment, Electric Equipment, Electronic and Telecommunication Equipment, and Other Manufacturing Products. In the specification of Model II-2 we find nine industries with the home-market effect: Textile Goods, Sawmills and Furniture, Petroleum Processing, Chemicals, Metals Melting and Pressing, Transport Equipment, Electric Equipment, Electronic and Telecommunication Equipment, and Other Manufacturing Products. Public utilities sectors (sectors 24, 25, 26) are often state monopolies, thus are least likely to be candidates of the underlying market structure for economic geography. If public utilities sectors are not counted we can see nine of the 16 industries showed strong home-market effects estimated by both models.[4]

5. CONCLUSIONS

In this chapter, we derived a model for empirical testing directly from Fujita, Krugman and Venables (2000) and linked it with the empirical testing model in Davis and Weinstein (1996 and 1999). We use both models to test if production and trade patterns between different regions in China are shaped by home-market effects.

Our study on China's regional production and trade pattern uses China's production, demand and endowment data for 19 industrial sectors and 31 provinces. The results show the existence and importance of home-market effects in determining production and trade structure across regions in China. At the same time, we cannot reject the role of capital endowment as a significant factor in determining the production structure. Estimated by both Model I-2 and II-2, they tend to focus on at least nine industries: Textile Goods, Sawmills and Furniture, Petroleum Processing, Chemicals, Metal Melting, Transport Equipment, Electric Equipment, Electronic and Telecommunication Equipment, and Other Manufacturing Products. To

Table 12.11:   *Demand Concentration, Relative to the National Level*

Area/ Industry	Textile goods (7)	Sawmills/ furniture (9)	Petroleum process. (11)	Electric equip. (18)	Electronic/ Telecom. equip. (19)
North-East[b]	−0.29[a]	0.03	0.08	−0.05	−0.20
North-Central[c]	0.17	−0.03	0.02	−0.02	−0.04
East[d]	0.54	−0.01	−0.13	0.01	−0.01
South[e]	0.23	−0.05	−0.19	0.09	0.59
Central[f]	−0.07	0.07	0.07	−0.04	−0.25
South-West[g]	−0.40	0.03	0.00	0.00	0.01
North-West[h]	−0.09	−0.04	0.16	0.01	−0.03

Notes:
[a]   A positive value means the share of demand is above the national average in the sector.
[b]   North-East includes Liaoning, Jilin, and Heilongjiang.
[c]   North-Central includes Beijing, Tianjin, Hebei, Shandong, Shanxi, and Inner Mongolia.
[d]   East includes Shanghai, Jiangsu, Zhejiang, Anhui, Jiangxi, and Fujian.
[e]   South includes Guangdong, Guangxi, and Hainan.
[f]   Central includes Henan, Hubei, and Hunan.
[g]   South-West includes Chongqing, Sichuan, Guizhou, Yunnan, and Tibet.
[h]   North-West includes Shaaxi, Gansu, Qinghai, Ningxia, and Xinjiang.

some degree, the finding is comparable to Davis and Weinstein (1999), where they identified strong empirical support for home-market effects on regional trade patterns in Japan.

One policy implication can be derived from the results. It is likely to be difficult and costly to relocate industry from center (high demand) to peripheral (low demand) regions for the sectors where strong home-market effects are identified. These industries are concentrated in transportation equipment and electric equipment in the durable goods sector, textile in the non-durable goods sector, and petroleum and chemicals in the material-related sector. The location of these industries in the future may follow the distribution pattern of demand more than that of the endowments. That means these industries will be spatially concentrated in the areas with higher demand for their products. As shown in Table 12.11, some of these industries (e.g., textile goods) show a pattern of concentrating in the east coastal areas, probably driven by consumption demand. Other industries (e.g., petroleum) concentrate in the west interior areas, probably driven by intermediate demand of the existing factories. In other words, not all industries with home-market effects are concentrated in the east coastal area. Some of the material-related industries are located in the centre and the west. The location of those industries depends on the characteristics of the industry. The Chinese government should differentiate its regional industrial policy according to the intensity of the sector's home-market effect to achieve the maximum economic efficiency of resource allocation.

NOTES

1. FKV 2000, pp.46–58.
2. This method derives stocks of capital from aggregating investment over time subtracting depreciation.
3. The coefficients for the factor endowments in the nested economic geography model convey a mixed message. Capital is highly significant but labor has the wrong sign. This is consistent to some degree with our analyses of the factor endowments (Table 12.7). The theoretical implication could be interpreted as some evidence for the comparative advantage.
4. Among the nine industries that showed strong home-market effects by both models, four are the same as in the Davis and Weinstein (1999) study when they examine economic geography on a regional level using Japanese data. These four industries are textile, chemicals, electric equipment, and transport equipment.

REFERENCES

Batisse, Cecile (2002), 'Dynamic externalities and local growth: a panel data analysis applied to Chinese provinces', *China Economic Review*, **13**, 231–51.

Bao, Shuming, Gene Hsin Chang, Jeffrey D. Sachs and Wing Thye Woo (2002), 'Geographic factors and China's regional development under market reforms, 1978–1998', *China Economic Review*, **13**, 89–111.

Brun, J.F., J.L. Combes and M.F. Renard (2002), 'Are there spillover effects between coastal and noncoastal regions in China?', *China Economic Review*, **13**, 161–9.

Brülhart, Marius and Federico Trionfetti (2001), 'A test of trade theories when expenditure is home biased', *The Management Centre Research Papers 005*, Kings College, University of London.

China State Statistical Bureau (1997), *The Third National Industrial Survey CD*.

China State Statistical Bureau (1998) *China Statistical Yearbook 1998*, Beijing: Statistical Press.

China State Statistical Bureau and Euromonitor/Soken (2000), 'China marketing data and statistics', *Euromonitor International*, London, Chicago.

Davis, Donald R. and David E. Weinstein (1996), 'Does economic geography matter for international specialization', Working Paper no. 5706, NBER, Cambridge, MA.

Davis, Donald R. and David E. Weinstein (1999), 'Economic geography and regional production structure: an empirical investigation', *European Economic Review*, **43**, 379–407.

Dixit, Avinash K. and Joseph E. Stiglitz (1977), 'Monopolistic competition and optimum product diversity', *American Economic Review*, **67**(3), 297–308.

Feenstra, Robert C., James A. Markusen and Andrew K. Rose (1998), 'Understanding the home-market effect and the gravity equation: the role of differentiated goods', National Bureau of Economic Research Working Paper No. 6804.

Fujita, Masahisa, Paul Krugman and Anthony J. Venables (2000), *The Spatial Economy: Cities, Regions, and International Trade*, Cambridge, MA: MIT Press.

Grossman, G. and Elhanan Helpman (1991), *Innovation and Growth in the World Economy*, Cambridge, MA: MIT Press.

Head, Keith and John Ries (2001), 'Increasing returns versus national product differentiation as an explanation for the pattern of US–Canada trade', *American Economic Review*, **91**(4), 858–76.

Head, Keith, Thierry Mayer and John Ries (2002), 'On the pervasiveness of home-market effects', *Economica*, **69**(275), 371–90.

Helpman, Elhanan (1981) 'Imperfect competition and international trade: Evidence from fourteen industrial countries', in A. Michael Spence and Heather Hazard (eds), *International Competitiveness*, New York: Ballinger Publishing.

Helpman, Elhanan and Paul R. Krugman (1985), *Market Structure and Foreign Trade*, Cambridge, MA: MIT Press.

Justman, Moshe (1994), 'The effect of local demand on sector location', *Review of Economics and Statistics*, **76**(4), 742–53.

Krugman, Paul R. (1980), 'Scale economics, product differentiation, and the pattern of trade', *American Economic Review*, **70**(5), 950–59.

Krugman, Paul R. (1991), 'Increasing returns and economic geography', *Journal of Political Economy*, **99**(3), 483–99.

Linder, S.B. (1961), *An Essay on Trade and Transformation*, New York: Wiley.

Kundbäck, Jerker and Johan Torstensson (1997) 'Demand, comparative advantage and economic geography in international trade: Evidence from the OECD', *Weltwirtschaftliches Archiv*.

Trionfetti, Federico (2001), 'Using home-biased demand to test for trade theories', *Weltwirtschaftliches Archiv*, **137**, 404–26.
Weder, R. (1995), 'Linking absolute and comparative advantage to intra-sector trade theory', *Review of International Economics*, 3(3).

APPENDIX

The following is the derivation from the theory in FKV (2000) to the model used in this chapter.

We start from the price index (equation (4.34)) in FKV (2000):

$$G_r = \left[\sum_{s=1}^{R} n_s (p_s^M T_{sr}^M)^{(1-\sigma)} \right]^{\frac{1}{1-\sigma}} = \left[\frac{1}{\mu} \sum_{s=1}^{R} L_s^M (w_s^M T_{sr}^M)^{(1-\sigma)} \right]^{\frac{1}{1-\sigma}}$$

where n_s is the number of varieties (firms) at location s, p_s^M is price of variety produced at s, T_{sr}^M is the transport cost from location s to r, L_s^M is the number of manufacturing workers at location s, μ is the expenditure share of manufactured goods, M stands for manufacturing, and σ is the elasticity of substitution between varieties.

Define output of all manufacturing firms at s as $X_s^M = n_s q*$, where $q*$ is equilibrium output of any active firm, then the price index becomes:

$$G_r = \left[\frac{1}{q*} \sum_{s=1}^{R} X_s^M (p_s^M T_{sr}^M)^{(1-\sigma)} \right]^{\frac{1}{1-\sigma}}$$

Because $p_r^M = C^M w_r^M / \rho$ (FKV (4.20)),

$$G_r = \left[\frac{1}{q*} \sum_{s=1}^{R} X_s^M \left(\frac{C^M w_s^M}{\rho} T_{sr}^M \right)^{(1-\sigma)} \right]^{\frac{1}{1-\sigma}}$$

where C^M is the marginal input requirement, w_r^M is the wage rate for manufacturing workers at location r, ρ is the intensity of the preference for variety. Using FKV's normalizations assumptions $C^M = \rho$, $q* = \mu$ (FKV (4.29) and (4.33)), the price index becomes:

$$G_r = \left[\frac{1}{\mu} \sum_{s=1}^{R} X_s^M (w_s^M T_{sr}^M)^{(1-\sigma)} \right]^{\frac{1}{1-\sigma}}$$

The only difference between this equation and FKV's equation (4.34) (shown at the beginning of this section) is that FKV's L_s^M is replaced by X_s^M. Following FKV's steps, we can build a two location symmetric model, and derive the home-market effect like FKV's equation ((4.42) or equation (12.1) in this chapter) with dX/X (instead of dL/L) on the left-hand side:

$$\left[\frac{\sigma}{Z} + Z(1-\sigma) \right] \frac{dw}{w} + Z \frac{dX}{X} = \frac{dY}{Y}$$

Which is equation (12.2) in this chapter. (For details of the steps of FKV's derivation see Fujita, Krugman and Venables (2000) pp. 45–58 or section 'Theoretical Framework' in this chapter.)

Index